# A
# SERIOUS CALL
## to a
## Devout and Holy Life

# A
# SERIOUS CALL
## to a
# Devout and Holy Life

*Adapted to the State and Condition*
*of all Orders of Christians*

*By*

WILLIAM LAW, A.M.

*He that hath ears to hear, let him hear.* — St. Luke viii. 8
*And behold, I come quickly, and My reward is with Me.* — Rev. xxii. 12

INTRODUCTION BY G. W. BROMILEY

WILLIAM B. EERDMANS PUBLISHING COMPANY
GRAND RAPIDS, MICHIGAN

This paperback edition reprinted from the edition published in 1898 by Macmillan and Co. Limited in the English Theological Library, with preface and notes by J. H. Overton.

*Fourth printing, May 1977*

# INTRODUCTION

It is a singular privilege, and a source of no little pleasure, to write the foreword to a classic of Christian devotion like William Law's *Serious Call*. For, if this is a work which cannot be adorned by any comment, simply to introduce it is a delightful task, and association with it confers vicarious distinction.

Unlike many great writings, the *Serious Call* owes most of its force, not to the prominence of its author in other fields of endeavour, but almost solely to its intrinsic merit. If it still attracts readers, this is not because they are drawn to the book by the personality or achievement of the author. Here is a work which, by the sheer power of independent greatness, bears eloquent testimony to the influence of the written word and the efficacy of spiritual operation.

Law himself played no very conspicuous part in the affairs of his time. Born in 1686, he seemed destined for an academic and ecclesiastical career. He had become a Fellow of Emmanuel College, Cambridge, by 1711, but the accession of the Hanoverians brought him to a crisis of conscience in 1714. His High Church principles would not permit him to regard George I as the authentic ruler and he became a non-juror, refusing to take the oath of allegiance required of university teachers or parish ministers. The rest of his long life thus came to be passed in quiet obscurity, first, as tutor to the father of Gibbon, the historian, and then in retirement at King's Cliffe, where he devoted himself specifically to religious exercises and works of charity.

The quietness of his life should not lead us to the erroneous conclusion that Law made no impact except through the *Serious Call*. Debarred from the rostrum or pulpit by his non-juring principles, he sought expression for his thoughts and concerns in a whole series of writings. Some of these, like his *Letters to the Bishop of Bangor,* are polemical. An interesting treatise in 1726 deals with the *Absolute Unlawfulness of the Stage Entertainment.* His devotional writings are extensive, for in addition to the *Serious Call* there are important studies of *Christian Perfection, The Spirit of Love* and *The Spirit of Prayer.*

The *Serious Call* itself is no academic or rhetorical exercise. Demanding authentic Christianity, Law asked no more of his readers than he practiced himself. His day, which began at 5 a.m., was carefully planned to allow time for reading, writing, and works of charity, as well as prayer. Though not allowed to officiate at worship, he was scrupulous in attendance. He could hardly be described as an ascetic, for his financial circumstances were comfortable. But he was generous in almsgiving and austere in his personal manner of life. He fasted regularly, and his dress was plain. If the element of joy is not conspicuous in his life, there can be no mistaking the seriousness. The *Serious Call* could have the stamp of authenticity because Law took his own Christianity seriously. His very style has the force of discipline as well as eloquence.

Already in his own time the *Serious Call* was recognized to be an outstanding work. Johnson, the lexicographer, described it as "the finest piece of hortatory theology in any language." John Wesley, for all his initial reservations and later disagreements, was led by it to an "explicit resolve to be all devoted to God." When Dr. Trapp claimed that Methodism arose out of the *Serious Call* and the *Christian Perfection* — works which he had known at once would "certainly do mischief" — Wesley in his refutation could still allow that "Methodists carefully read these books and were greatly profited by them." In 1744 Wesley himself published extracts from the *Serious Call,* thereby adding to its extensive influence in religious circles.

The forces which shaped the author and his work were interesting and diverse. He learned much from the reading of medieval mystics like Tauler and a Kempis. This explains the mystical bent which was to bring him under the spell of Jacob Boehme, and finally to make him an apostle of the inner light. Yet his mysticism was tempered by the High Church tradition to which he was also heir. For all the differences, there is also a certain similarity between the *Serious Call* and Taylor's *Rules of Holy Living and Holy Dying*. The devotion of the *Serious Call* is individual, but it is set in the context of ecclesiastical order and finds a natural focus in worship and sacrament. One also suspects that the Puritan tradition, with its earnestness and practical piety, made no little contribution to the *Serious Call*. High Churchmen and Puritans differed in many things, but they were united in their promotion and practice of Christian dedication and discipline.

While it is important to speak of the influence of the *Serious Call,* and of the influences which shaped it, it is even more important that the work should finally be allowed to stand in its own right and to carry its message freely to the reader. What, then, is the secret of its power? Two points have been made already. It is extremely well written, and it is sustained by the inner integrity of the author. To this may be added that it is an intensely practical work, allowing of no evasion by theoretical detachment. On the other hand, it is no mere series of injunctions or examples. It moves on the high level of a personal relationship with God which brings all spheres of life within its compass. Law is not just giving moral advice; he is struggling for a profound and far-reaching decision, for what might now be described as an act of commitment. If it seems at times that the spirit of the book is too much that of the Law, the author is not unaware that achievement of the ideal of devotion is impossible apart from the Spirit and power of God and faith in Jesus Christ. The point is that his emphasis is on the sterner side of the Gospel, on faith as discipleship rather than repose, on discipleship itself as serious and wholehearted dedication. In

its summons to the disciplined and consecrated life the
*Serious Call* is expressing the solemn side of the Gospel
itself. This is perhaps the ultimate explanation of its
abiding validity and vitality.

We may fittingly conclude this preface with the testimony of a rural minister who in 1771 told how he
distributed copies of the *Serious Call* to all his parishioners, and then added: "My perseverance was now
rewarded with success; and I had the satisfaction of
beholding my people reclaimed from a life of folly and
impiety to a life of holiness and devotion." Through
the generations the *Serious Call* has continued to exercise a similar ministry, particularly in the lives of those
who call themselves Christians, but have not yet come
to grips with what this confession implies. This new
edition is published in the confidence that the *Serious
Call* will not merely be read as a historical document
but will still pursue its ministry in the lives of readers.

G. W. BROMILEY

Pasadena, California

# PREFACE

THE publication of the *Serious Call* in 1728 marked an epoch in the history of religion in England. It naturally took some little time for its influence to make itself generally felt; but there is little doubt that the great Evangelical Revival, which, roughly speaking, may be dated from about 1738, owed its first impetus to this book more than to any other. The fact is curious, for the book is certainly not, in the technical sense, an Evangelical book, and its author was very far indeed from identifying himself with either section of the Evangelical movement. A brief account, however, of the life of William Law, and of the state of religion in England at the time when the *Serious Call* appeared, will explain the difficulty.

William Law was born in 1686 at King's Cliffe in Northamptonshire, where his father was a grocer. His early religious training was that of the old-fashioned church type, from which he never really diverged, though he materially modified his views in later years; and it was, in the long run, among Churchmen of the old-fashioned type, rather than among Methodists or Evangelicals, that the *Serious Call* was most highly appreciated, and its influence most deeply felt. In 1705 he went as a sizar to Emmanuel College, Cambridge, and, having graduated in 1708, was elected a Fellow of the Society in 1711. In the same year he received Holy Orders; and for some time remained at the University, taking occasional duty in and about Cambridge, but chiefly engaged in private tuition. He made no secret of his Jacobite proclivities; but during the reign of Queen Anne the dynastic question was, to a great extent, in abeyance. The death of the Queen, however, in 1714, brought matters to a crisis; and William Law, declining to take the oaths of allegiance and abjuration, lost his Fellowship in consequence. He wrote a characteristically outspoken letter on the subject to his now widowed mother, giving his reasons for openly joining the ranks of the nonjurors, which were apparently satisfactory to his family. In 1717 he published his *Three Letters to the Bishop of Bangor*, a most brilliant and powerful defence of church principles against the latitudinarianism and erastianism of Bishop Hoadley. In 1726 appeared the first of his practical treatises, his *Christian Perfection*, which began the work which the *Serious Call* completed. About this time (it is impossible to ascertain the exact date) he became an inmate of the family of Mr. Edward Gibbon, grandfather of the historian, at Putney, being engaged as 'domestic tutor' to the second Edward Gibbon, the historian's father, but acting also as a sort of spiritual director to the whole family. His patron had strong Jacobite proclivities, which were intensified by the fact that he thought he had been shabbily treated by the Government, as a director of the ill-fated South Sea scheme; and it was not at all uncommon for nonjuring clergymen to act as tutors in such families. Law left a most favourable impression of integrity and ability in the Gibbon family, an impression which even affected the third Edward Gibbon, the historian, though the two men differed as widely as possible in their opinions. In 1727 Law accompanied his pupil as 'governor' to his old College, Emmanuel, Cambridge; and it was partly at Putney, partly at Cambridge, that the *Serious Call* was written.

To appreciate the significance of the work and to account for the effects which it produced, it is necessary to consider what was the state of religion in England at the time. Christianity was, in one sense, most triumphant; in another sense, quite the reverse. It had been, and was still being, defended with very great ability and success against assailants from various quarters. There really is no comparison at all between the works of the assailants and those of the defenders. The former would have lapsed into oblivion had not their memory been enshrined in the latter, many of which are 'possessions for ever.' Probably there has never been a time when there were such powerful advocates of Christianity, as the time when Butler and Waterland and Berkeley and Bentley and Sherlock (the younger) and Warburton and Leslie and Law himself were among their ranks. Objections to Christianity had been, and were being, more than adequately answered, and the objectors were fairly beaten out of the field. They were also, as a body, very unpopular. People were not only unconvinced by, but greatly exasperated against, the 'freethinkers,' for whom no name could be found hard enough. On the other hand, Christianity in general, and the Church of England in particular, were distinctly popular. "The Church in danger" was a popular cry which never failed to produce an effect in the early days of the eighteenth century. It was the fashion to attend church. It was the proper thing to do, and it was generally done,—a point most important to be remembered in connection with the *Serious Call.*

This was one side of the shield; but unfortunately there was another side. At the very time when the intellectual basis of Christianity was strongest, its moral influence was weakest; when attendance on public worship was, if one may use the expression, *de rigeur*, many so-called worshippers were living lives in glaring defiance of the laws of Christianity. Not that they were, as a rule, conscious hypocrites; their respect for religion and their dislike of its enemies were perfectly sincere; they simply followed the Horatian rule:

> "Video meliora proboque,
> Deteriora sequor."

It was a strangely illogical state of things; and the most logical man then living made war upon the inconsistency in the *Serious*

*Call.* The title was well chosen; the book is literally a 'call' to men 'to live more nearly as they prayed.' It is not, strictly speaking, a devotional book, and still less is it a manual of divinity. It is simply a 'call'—an appeal to 'all orders of Christians' to live the life that, by their very name of Christians, by their very attendance at public worship, they owned that they were bound to live.

This consideration will furnish an answer to some of the exceptions which have been taken to the book. For instance, it is an old complaint that there is too little of 'the Gospel' in the *Serious Call.* But to Law's logical mind it would have seemed out of place to dwell on doctrine—and the Gospel surely is doctrine—in a book the very gist of which was that men did not live up to the faith they had; in other words, that they did not want more knowledge, but more consistency in acting up to their knowledge. The keen intellect of Gibbon perceived this, and he declared that "a philosopher must allow that he [Law] exposes with equal sincerity and truth the strange contradiction which exists between the faith and practice of the Christian world."

A very acute and appreciative critic of Law in the present day (Mr. Leslie Stephen) thinks, as, indeed, others have thought, that "perhaps the logical character of Law's mind is rather too prominent in a writing which appeals to the emotions rather than to the intellect." But was the *Serious Call* intended to appeal to the emotions rather than to the intellect? That is not my own conception of its purpose. It was not intended to rouse men's feelings, but to convince their minds of the absurdity of believing one thing, and doing another. It said to them in effect, "You believe Christianity to be true, you dislike its opponents, you frequent its ordinances, and yet you live as if you disbelieved its truth, as if you sided with its opponents, as if you counted its ordinances as a thing of naught!"

Once more, it has been objected that the *Serious Call* made light of the duty of public worship. If it did, then the theory

of Law was strangely inconsistent with his practice ; for, unlike
many of the nonjurors, who held aloof from the services of the
National Church, he made a point of never missing a single
service, week-day or Sunday, in his own parish church at King's
Cliffe ; and one of the strictest rules which he himself drew
up for the charity schools which he and his disciple, Mrs.
Hutcheson, founded in that village, was that the children should
attend, not only every public service in the church, but also
every funeral, and join in singing the psalm. Now it was not
the wont of Law to say one thing and do another, least of all
in a matter so nearly touching the heart of religion. But the
fact is, that in the *Serious Call* he is addressing himself to
churchgoers, and what he desired to persuade them to do was,
not to neglect church, but to live, outside the church walls,
more in accordance with what they professed inside those walls.

All the objections, however, to the *Serious Call* sink into
nothing when compared with the chorus of testimony to the
value of the book, not merely as a composition—that would
have been a matter of little moment to the author—but as a
real help to 'devotion' in the wide sense in which Law used
the term, and as giving the first turning-point for good to very
many lives. The most notable instance is that of Dr. Johnson :
"I became," he says, "a sort of lax talker against religion, for
I did not think much against it ; and this lasted until I went
to Oxford, where it would not be suffered. When at Oxford, I
took up Law's *Serious Call*, expecting to find it a dull book
(as such books generally are), and perhaps to laugh at it. But
I found Law quite an overmatch for me ; and this was the first
occasion of my thinking in earnest of religion after I became
capable of rational enquiry."[1] The first Lord Lyttelton is said
to have taken up the *Serious Call* about bed-time, at a friend's
house, and to have been so fascinated with it that he read it

---

[1] See Boswell's *Life of Johnson*, ch. i. On another occasion Johnson
called it "the finest piece of hortatory theology in any language"; and on
another, "the best piece of paraenetic divinity."

quite through before he could go to sleep.   He expressed himself as "not a little astonished that one of the finest books
that ever were written had been penned by a crack-brained
enthusiast."[1]  Gibbon, the historian, among other expressions of
commendation of the *Serious Call*, declares that if " Mr. Law
finds a spark of piety in his reader's mind, he will soon kindle
it into a flame," intimating, of course, at the same time, that
the necessary spark is non-existent in himself.   It will be observed that in these cases there was, mingled with admiration,
a certain surprise that such a book should come from such a
man.    And it is not one of the least of Law's merits as a
writer that he did something to dispel the mischievous notion
that piety and weakness went hand in hand.   Intellectual power
was expected, and was found, in the controversial divinity of
the period ; but it seems to have been thought by many that
feebleness and dulness were only what were to be looked for
in practical and devotional works.

Among the leaders of the Evangelical Revival there was
scarcely one who was not more or less affected by the *Serious
Call*.   It was one of the three books which revived John
Wesley's religious impressions at Oxford ; and " for three years,"
he says, " I preached after the model of Mr. Law's practical
treatises."   It is true that after he came under the influence of
Peter Böhler he discarded Mr. Law as a guide ; but he never
lost his admiration of the *Serious Call*.   Only eighteen months
before his death he described it as " a treatise which will
hardly be excelled, if it be equalled, either for beauty of expression or for depth of thought";[2] and he made it a text book
for the highest class in his school at Kingswood.    Charles
Wesley declared that " the alteration in his views and feelings
were produced by reading the *Serious Call*."[3]   George Whitefield

[1] See Byrom's *Journal*, Vol. II., Part II., page 634.

[2] Sermon on a " Single Eye," No. cxviii. in Vol. III., p. 333, of *Wesley's
Sermons*.

[3] See Jackson's *Memoirs of the Rev. Charles Wesley*, p. 52

tells us: "Before I went to the University I met with Mr. Law's *Serious Call*, but had not money to purchase it. Soon after my coming up to Oxford, seeing a small edition of it in a friend's hand I soon purchased it. God worked powerfully upon my soul, as He has since upon many others, by that and his other excellent treatise upon *Christian Perfection*."[1] Henry Venn "read Law's *Serious Call* repeatedly, and tried to frame his life according to that model."[2] Thomas Scott "carelessly took it up as a book he had hitherto treated with contempt," but was so impressed with it that its perusal became the turning-point of his life.[3] John Newton, Thomas Adam, James Stillingfleet, and other noted Evangelicals express their obligations to the author of the *Serious Call*, though most of them add, at the same time, that they disagree with him, or, at any rate, consider his views inadequate. This was only natural. Law was never in full sympathy with the Evangelical movement; he set the ball a-rolling but he did not follow its course. Beyond an intensely earnest conviction of the truth and importance of the Christian religion, and an honest and consistent endeavour to lead a Christian life, he really had nothing in common with either Methodists or Evangelicals; both his high churchmanship and his mysticism were quite alien to their principles and their tone of thought.

This is not the place to follow Law into his mystic stage. Suffice it to say, that his strange attraction to Jacob Behmen did not in the least affect his adherence to the principles or the mode of life recommended in the *Serious Call*. He lived for thirty-three years after its publication—ten at Putney, as "the much-honoured friend and spiritual director of the whole family"[4]

---

[1] See *Life and Times of the Rev. George Whitefield*, by Robert Philip, p. 16.

[2] "Memoir of Henry Venn," prefixed to the *Complete Duty of Man*, published by the Religious Tract Society.

[3] See "Force of Truth," Part III., Scott's *Theological Works*, p. 18.

[4] See Gibbon's *Autobiography* (new edition, by John Murray), pp. 17, 18.

of Gibbon, twenty-three at his native King's Cliffe, in a house called the Hall Yard, still standing, where he strove to conform his own life and that of his two disciples, Mrs. Hutcheson and Miss Hester Gibbon, most literally to the standard of the *Serious Call*. He never became reconciled to the Hanoverian dynasty; his three characteristic traits are briefly and correctly summed up by the son of his pupil, who designates him as "Mr. William Law, a nonjuror, a saint, and a wit."[1] The last quality has not been touched upon in this sketch; but it will appear abundantly in the pages of the *Serious Call*.

Law was little known except by his pen; but those who did know him in his later years conceived an unbounded admiration for him, mingled with not a little awe, which his severe character, no less than his powerful and somewhat pungent intellect, was calculated to produce. He founded, and persuaded Mrs. Hutcheson to found, schools and alms-houses, at King's Cliffe; and his personal attention to these, especially to the schools, for, like many other great men, he loved to be with little children, constituted the chief outward employment of his life. It was the life of a recluse, but not of an ascetic; he was affable and on friendly terms with his richer neighbours; but he devoted his main care to the poor, who were relieved daily with lavish and rather too indiscriminate profusion at the Hall Yard. It would have been a remarkable life at any time; it was doubly remarkable in the middle of the eighteenth century, for it was the life of a saint—and saintship was rare at that period. It ended at Eastertide, 1761, very appropriately; for Law sang, almost with his last breath, the "Angels' Hymn."

J. H. O.

---

[1] Gibbon.

# CONTENTS.

# A SERIOUS CALL TO A DEVOUT
## AND HOLY LIFE.

## CHAPTER I.

*Concerning the nature and extent of Christian devotion.*

DEVOTION is neither private nor public prayer, but prayers whether private or public, are particular parts or instances of devotion. Devotion signifies a life given or devoted to God.[1]

He therefore is the devout man, who lives no longer to his own will, or the way and spirit of the world, but to the sole will of God, who considers God in everything, who serves God in everything, who makes all the parts of his common life, parts of piety, by doing everything in the name of God, and under such rules as are conformable to His glory.

We readily acknowledge, that God alone is to be the rule and measure of our prayers; that in them we are to look wholly unto Him, and act wholly for Him; that we are only to pray in such a manner, for such things, and such ends, as are suitable to His glory.

Now let anyone but find out the reason, why he is to be thus strictly pious in his prayers, and he will find the same as strong a reason, to be as strictly pious in all the other parts of his life. For there is not the least shadow of a reason, why we should make God the rule and measure of our prayers; why we should then look wholly unto Him, and pray according to His will; but what equally proves it necessary for us to look wholly unto God, and

---

[1] Law here brings back the word 'devotion' to its primary sense. 'Devotions' and 'Prayers' had become almost synonymous terms; but by the early Christian writers the Latin word 'devotio' was used in its proper sense to express 'a life given to God'; by degrees it came to be used for acts of devotion or prayers. The titles of such popular works as *Andrewes' Devotions, Cosin's Devotions, Spinckes' Devotions*, would naturally make a Christian of the eighteenth century limit it to its secondary sense.

make Him the rule and measure of all the other actions of our life.    For any ways of life, any employment of our talents, whether of our parts, our time, or money, that is not strictly according to the will of God, that is not for such ends as are suitable to His glory, are as great absurdities and failings, as prayers that are not according to the will of God.    For there is no other reason why our prayers should be according to the will of God, why they should have nothing in them, but what is wise, and holy, and heavenly, there is no other reason for this, but that our lives may be of the same nature, full of the same wisdom, holiness, and heavenly tempers, that we may live unto God in the same spirit that we pray unto Him.    Were it not our strict duty to live by reason,[2] to devote all the actions of our lives to God, were it not absolutely necessary to walk before Him in wisdom and holiness and all heavenly conversation, doing everything in His name, and for His glory, there would be no excellency or wisdom in the most heavenly prayers.    Nay, such prayers would be absurdities, they would be like prayers for wings, when it was no part of our duty to fly.

As sure, therefore, as there is any wisdom in praying for the Spirit of God, so sure is it, that we are to make that Spirit the rule of all our actions; as sure as it is our duty to look wholly unto God in our prayers, so sure is it, that it is our duty to live wholly unto God in our lives.    But we can no more be said to live unto God, unless we live unto Him in all the ordinary actions of our life, unless He be the rule and measure of all our ways, than we can be said to pray unto God, unless our prayers look wholly unto Him. So that unreasonable and absurd ways of life, whether in labour or diversion, whether they consume our time, or our money, are alike unreasonable and absurd prayers, and are as truly an offence unto God.

[2] All through the *Serious Call* Law uses the word 'reason' as equivalent to 'right reason'; that is, reason as opposed to folly, not reason as opposed to faith.    It is necessary to bear this in mind, otherwise there will seem to be a strange contradiction between the *Serious Call* and the very next work which Law published, *The Case of Reason* ; but the contradiction is only apparent, not real.    The '*Case of Reason*' was written in answer to Matthew Tindal, the chief of the Deists, who, in his *Christianity as Old as the Creation*, uses the term 'Reason' as opposed to 'Revelation,' and shows that the natural religion which 'reason' teaches renders revealed religion unnecessary.    But reason, in the sense in which Law means it in the *Serious Call*, so far from being opposed to revealed religion would lead men to it: Christian faith would be the highest exercise of reason.    It is the same with the words 'unreasonable' and 'absurd' in the next paragraph, and throughout the whole treatise.

'Tis for want of knowing, or at least considering this, that we see such a mixture of ridicule in the lives of many people. You see them strict as to some times and places of devotion, but when the service of the Church is over, they are but like those who seldom or never come there. In their way of life, their manner of spending their time and money, in their cares and fears, in their pleasures and indulgences, in their labour and diversions, they are like the rest of the world. This makes the loose part of the world generally make a jest of those who are devout, because they see their devotion goes no further than their prayers, and that when they are over, they live no more unto God, till the time of prayer returns again ; but live by the same humour and fancy, and in as full an enjoyment of all the follies of life as other people. This is the reason why they are the jest and scorn of careless and worldly people ; not because they are really devoted to God, but because they appear to have no other devotion but that of occasional prayers.

JULIUS [3] is very fearful of missing prayers ; all the parish supposes Julius to be sick, if he is not at Church. But if you were to ask him why he spends the rest of his time by humour and chance? why he is a companion of the silliest people in their most silly pleasures? why he is ready for every impertinent[4] entertainment and diversion? If you were to ask him why there is no amusement too trifling to please him? why he is busy at all balls and assemblies? why he gives himself up to an idle gossiping conversation? why he lives in foolish friendships and fondness for particular persons, that neither want nor deserve any particular kindness? why he allows himself in foolish hatreds and resentments against particular persons, without considering that he is to love everybody as himself? If you ask him why he never puts

---

[3] Julius is the first and slightest of a series of portraits by which Law points the lessons he would inculcate. Whether they were drawn from the life or purely imaginary will be discussed when we come to some portraits which have been identified with known people. Law had begun this mode of writing in his *Christian Perfection* ; but he carries it on much more elaborately and strikingly in the *Serious Call.* He did not of course originate it. It had been employed with great effect by Steele, Addison, and others in the *Tatler* and *Spectator*, and it was afterwards adopted by Johnson in the *Rambler* and *Idler*, and by Cowper in his ' Progress of Error ' and other poems ; in fact it was a very ordinary mode of writing in the eighteenth century. But though Addison may perhaps show a more graceful and delicate humour, no one employed it with more force and pungency than Law.

[4] Impertinent is used in its proper sense, *i.e.* not suitable to his condition and profession.

his conversation, his time, and fortune, under the rules of religion, Julius has no more to say for himself, than the most disorderly person. For the whole tenor of Scripture lies as directly against such a life, as against debauchery and intemperance : He that lives in such a course of idleness and folly, lives no more according to the religion of Jesus Christ, than he that lives in gluttony and intemperance.

If a man were to tell Julius that there was no occasion for so much constancy at prayers, and that he might, without any harm to himself, neglect the service of the Church, as the generality of people do, Julius would think such a one to be no Christian, and that he ought to avoid his company. But if a person only tells him, that he may live as the generality of the world does, that he may enjoy himself as others do, that he may spend his time and money as people of fashion do, that he may conform to the follies and frailties of the generality, and gratify his tempers and passions as most people do, Julius never suspects that man to want a Christian spirit, or that he is doing the devil's work.

And if Julius were to read all the New Testament from the beginning to the end, he would find his course of life condemned in every page of it.

And indeed there cannot anything be imagined more absurd in itself, than wise and sublime, and heavenly prayers added to a life of vanity and folly, where neither labour nor diversions, neither time nor money, are under the direction of the wisdom and heavenly tempers of our prayers. If we were to see a man pretending to act wholly with regard to God in everything that he did, that would neither spend time or money, or take any labour or diversion, but so far as he could act according to strict principles of reason and piety, and yet at the same time neglect all prayer, whether public or private, should we not be amazed at such a man, and wonder how he could have so much folly along with so much religion?

Yet this is as reasonable, as for any person to pretend to strictness in devotion, to be careful of observing times and places of prayer, and yet letting the rest of his life, his time, and labour, his talents and money, be disposed of without any regard to strict rules of piety and devotion. For it is as great an absurdity to suppose holy prayers, and divine petitions without an holiness of life suitable to them, as to suppose an holy and divine life without prayers.

Let anyone therefore think, how easily he could confute a man that pretended to great strictness of life without prayer, and the same arguments will as plainly confute another, that pretends to strictness of prayer, without carrying the same strictness into every other part of life.  For to be weak and foolish in spending our time and fortune, is no greater a mistake, than to be weak and foolish in relation to our prayers.  And to allow ourselves in any ways of life that neither are, nor can be offered to God, is the same irreligion, as to neglect our prayers, or use them in such a manner, as makes them an offering unworthy of God.

The short of the matter is this, either reason and religion prescribe rules and ends to all the ordinary actions of our life, or they do not: If they do, then it is as necessary to govern all our actions by those rules, as it is necessary to worship God.  For if religion teaches us anything concerning eating and drinking, or spending our time and money; if it teaches us how we are to use and contemn the world; if it tells us what tempers we are to have in common life, how we are to be disposed towards all people, how we are to behave towards the sick, the poor, the old and destitute; if it tells us whom we are to treat with a particular love, whom we are to regard with a particular esteem; if it tells us how we are to treat our enemies, and how we are to mortify and deny ourselves, he must be very weak, that can think these parts of religion are not to be observed with as much exactness, as any doctrines that relate to prayers.

It is very observable, that there is not one command in all the Gospel for public worship; and perhaps it is a duty that is least insisted upon in Scripture of any other.  The frequent attendance at it is never so much as mentioned in all the New Testament.[5]

---

[5] This is a passage which has been severely animadverted upon.  Charles Wesley, for instance, writes to John Byrom, "Do not you think that a palpable mistake in Mr. Law's *Serious Call*, that there is no command for public worship in Scripture?" (Byrom's *Journal*, vol. ii. part ii. p. 182). It certainly is a passage which is very liable to be misunderstood; and it is rather surprising that so self-collected a writer as Law, who was one of the last men to be carried away by his feelings into unguarded expressions, should have written it.  Perhaps he would have argued that it required some little straining of the words, "Where two or three are gathered together," etc., addressed to the inner circle of the Disciples, to construe them into a direct command for general public worship; and perhaps he would have regarded the description of the early Christians in the Acts of the Apostles (ii. 42) as applicable to private meetings and not as equivalent to general worship.  Another text, frequently adduced, Heb. x. 25, he might also apply to private religious meetings.  But I frankly own that these explanations are not satisfactory, and that I cannot altogether justify the passage.

Whereas that religion or devotion, which is to govern the ordinary actions of our life, is to be found in almost every verse of Scripture. Our blessed Saviour and His Apostles are wholly taken up in doctrines that relate to common life. They call us to renounce the world, and differ in every temper and way of life, from the spirit and way of the world: to renounce all its goods, to fear none of its evils, to reject its joys, and have no value for its happiness: to be as new born babes, that are born into a new state of things; to live as pilgrims in spiritual watching, in holy fear, and heavenly aspiring after another life: to take up our daily cross, to deny ourselves, to profess the blessedness of mourning, to seek the blessedness of poverty of spirit: to forsake the pride and vanity of riches, to take no thought for the morrow, to live in the profoundest state of humility, to rejoice in worldly sufferings: to reject the lust of the flesh, the lust of the eyes, and the pride of life; to bear injuries, to forgive and bless our enemies, and to love mankind as God loveth them: to give up our whole hearts and affections to God, and strive to enter through the strait gate into a life of eternal glory.

This is the common devotion which our blessed Saviour taught, in order to make it the common life of all Christians. Is it not therefore exceeding strange, that people should place so much piety in the attendance upon public worship, concerning which there is not one precept of our Lord's to be found, and yet neglect these common duties of our ordinary life, which are commanded in every page of the Gospel? I call these duties the devotion of our common life, because if they are to be practised, they must be made parts of our common life, they can have no place anywhere else.

If contempt of the world and heavenly affection, is a necessary temper of Christians, it is necessary that this temper appear in the whole course of their lives, in their manner of using the world, because it can have no place anywhere else.

If self-denial be a condition of salvation, all that would be saved must make it a part of their ordinary life. If humility be a Christian duty, then the common life of a Christian is to be a constant course of humility in all its kinds. If poverty of spirit be necessary, it must be the spirit and temper of every day of our lives. If we are to relieve the naked, the sick, and the prisoner, it must be the common charity of our lives, as far as we can render ourselves able to perform it. If we are to love our enemies, we must make our common life a visible exercise and demonstration of that love. If content and thankfulness, if the patient bearing of evil be duties to God, they are the duties of every day, and in every circumstance of our life. If we are to be wise and holy as the new-born sons of God, we can no otherwise be so, but by renouncing everything that is foolish and vain in every part of our common life. If we are to be in Christ new creatures, we must show that we are so, by having new ways of living in the world. If we are to follow Christ, it must be in our common way of spending every day.

Thus it is in all the virtues and holy tempers of Christianity, they are not ours unless they be the virtues and tempers of our ordinary life. So that Christianity is so far from leaving us to live in the common ways of life, conforming to the folly of customs, and gratifying the passions and tempers which the spirit of the world delights in, it is so far from indulging us in any of these things, that all its virtues which it makes necessary to salvation are only so many ways of living above, and contrary to the world in all the common actions of our life. If our common life is not a common course of humility, self-denial, renunciation of the world, poverty of spirit, and heavenly affection, we do not live the lives of Christians.

But yet though it is thus plain, that this, and this alone is Christianity, an uniform open and visible practice of all these virtues, yet it is as plain, that there is little or nothing of this to be found, even amongst the better sort of people. You see them often at Church, and pleased with fine preachers, but look into their lives, and you see them just the same sort of people as others are, that make no pretences to devotion. The difference that you find betwixt them is only the difference of their natural tempers. They have the same taste of the world,[6] the same worldly cares, and fears, and joys; they have the same turn of mind, equally vain in their desires: You see the same fondness for state and equipage, the same pride and vanity of dress, the same self-love and indulgence, the same foolish friendships, and groundless hatreds, the same levity of mind, and trifling spirit, the same fondness for diversions, the same idle dispositions, and vain ways of spending their time in visiting and conversation, as the rest of the world, that make no pretences to devotion.

[6] 'Taste *of*' is old-fashioned, but it is more strictly grammatical than the modern phrase 'taste for.'

I do not mean this comparison betwixt people seemingly good, and professed rakes, but betwixt people of sober lives. Let us take an instance in two modest women: let it be supposed, that one of them is careful of times of devotion, and observes them through a sense of duty, and that the other has no hearty concern about it, but is at Church seldom or often, just as it happens. Now it is a very easy thing to see this difference betwixt these persons. But when you have seen this, can you find any further difference betwixt them? Can you find that their common life is of a different kind? Are not the tempers, and customs, and manners of the one, of the same kind as of the other? Do they live as if they belonged to different worlds, had different views in their heads, and different rules and measures of all their actions? Have they not the same goods and evils, are they not pleased and displeased in the same manner, and for the same things? Do they not live in the same course of life? Does one seem to be of this world, looking at the things that are temporal, and the other to be of another world, looking wholly at the things that are eternal? Does the one live in pleasure, delighting herself in show or dress, and the other live in self-denial and mortification, renouncing everything that looks like vanity, either of person, dress, or carriage? Does the one follow public diversions, and trifle away her time in idle visits, and corrupt conversation, and does the other study all the arts of improving her time, living in prayer and watching, and such good works, as may make all her time turn to her advantage, and be placed to her account at the last day? Is the one careless of expense, and glad to be able to adorn herself with every costly ornament of dress, and does the other consider her fortune as a talent given her by God, which is to be improved religiously, and no more to be spent in vain and needless ornaments, than it is to be buried in the earth?

Where must you look, to find one person of religion differing in this manner, from another that has none? And yet if they do not differ in these things which are here related, can it with any sense be said, the one is a good Christian, and the other not?

Take another instance amongst the men. LEO has a great deal of good nature, has kept what they call good company, hates everything that is false and base, is very generous and brave to his friends, but has concerned himself so little with religion, that he hardly knows the difference betwixt a Jew and a Christian.

EUSEBIUS, on the other hand, has had early impressions of

religion, and buys books of devotion.    He can talk of all the
feasts and fasts of the Church, and knows the names of most men
that have been eminent for piety.    You never hear him swear, or
make a loose jest, and when he talks of religion, he talks of it as
of a matter of the last concern.

Here you see, that one person has religion enough, according to
the way of the world, to be reckoned a pious Christian, and the
other is so far from all appearance of religion, that he may fairly
be reckoned a heathen; and yet if you look into their common life,
if you examine their chief and ruling tempers in the greatest
articles of life, or the greatest doctrines of Christianity, you will
find the least difference imaginable.

Consider them with regard to the use of the world, because that
is what everybody can see.

Now to have right notions and tempers with relation to this
world is as essential to religion as to have right notions of God.
And it is as possible for a man to worship a crocodile, and yet
be a pious man, as to have his affections set upon this world,
and yet be a good Christian.

But now if you consider Leo and Eusebius in this respect, you
will find them exactly alike, seeking, using, and enjoying all that
can be got in this world in the same manner, and for the same
ends.    You will find that riches, prosperity, pleasures, indulgences,
state, equipage, and honour, are just as much the happiness of
Eusebius as they are of Leo.    And yet if Christianity has not
changed a man's mind and temper with relation to these things,
what can we say that it has done for him?

For if the doctrines of Christianity were practised, they would
make a man as different from other people as to all worldly
tempers, sensual pleasures, and the pride of life, as a wise man is
different from a natural; it would be as easy a thing to know
a Christian by his outward course of life as it is now difficult
to find anybody that lives it.    For it is notorious, that Christians
are now not only like other men in their frailties and infirmities;
this might be in some degree excusable, but the complaint is,
they are like heathens in all the main and chief articles of their
lives.    They enjoy the world, and live every day in the same
tempers, and the same designs, and the same indulgences, as they
do who know not God, nor of any happiness in another life.
Everybody who is capable of any reflection must have observed
that this is generally the state even of devout people, whether

men or women.   You may see them different from other people, so far as to times and places of prayer, but generally like the rest of the world in all the other parts of their lives.   That is, adding Christian devotion to a heathen life!   I have the authority of our blessed Saviour for this remark, where He says, "Take no thought, saying what shall we eat, or what shall we drink, or wherewithal shall we be clothed? for after all these things do the Gentiles seek." But if to be thus affected even with the necessary things of this life, shows that we are not yet of a Christian spirit, but are like the heathens, surely to enjoy the vanity and folly of the world as they did, to be like them in the main chief tempers of our lives, in self-love and indulgence, in sensual pleasures and diversions, in the vanity of dress, the love of show and greatness, or any other gaudy distinctions of fortune, is a much greater sign of a heathen temper.   And consequently, they who add devotion to such a life, must be said to pray as Christians, but live as heathens.

## CHAPTER II.

*An inquiry into the reason, why the generality of Christians fall so far short of the holiness and devotion of Christianity.*

It may now be reasonably inquired, how it comes to pass that the lives even of the better sort of people are thus strangely contrary to the principles of Christianity?

But before I give a direct answer to this, I desire it may also be inquired, how it comes to pass that swearing is so common a vice amongst Christians? It is indeed not yet so common amongst women as it is amongst men. But amongst men this sin is so common, that perhaps there are more than two in three that are guilty of it through the whole course of their lives, swearing more or less, just as it happens, some constantly, others only now and then as it were by chance.[1] Now, I ask how comes it, that two in three of the men are guilty of so gross and profane a sin as this is? There is neither ignorance, nor human infirmity to plead for it. It is against an express commandment, and the most plain doctrine of our blessed Saviour.

Do but now find the reason why the generality of men live in this notorious vice, and then you will have found the reason why the generality even of the better sort of people live so contrary to Christianity.

Now the reason of common swearing is this, it is because men have not so much as the intention to please God in all their

---

[1] It is a painful instance of the grossness of the age, that the almost universal prevalence of profane swearing could be adduced as an argument that even church-going people had "not so much as the intention to please God." But Law knew perfectly well what he was doing when he so employed it. Novels and plays are a fair index of the manners of contemporary society, and those of the eighteenth century fully bear out Law's assumption. For a different kind of evidence see the sermons of Law's friend and patron, Thomas Sherlock, afterwards Bishop of London, especially his two sermons on "Idle Words," Nos. iii. and iv. in Vol. III. of his *Sermons*.

CHAP. II. actions.[2]  For let a man but have so much piety as to intend
to please God in all the actions of his life, as the happiest and
best thing in the world, and then he will never swear more.
It will be as impossible for him to swear, whilst he feels this
intention within himself, as it is impossible for a man who intends
to please his prince to go up and abuse him to his face.

It seems but a small and necessary part of piety to have such
a sincere intention as this; and that he has no reason to look upon
himself as a disciple of Christ, who is not thus far advanced
in piety.  And yet it is purely for want of this degree of piety,
that you see such a mixture of sin and folly in the lives even
of the better sort of people.  It is for want of this intention,
that you see men that profess religion, yet live in swearing
and sensuality; that you see clergymen given to pride and covetousness, and worldly enjoyments.  It is for want of this intention,
that you see women who profess devotion, yet living in all the
folly and vanity of dress, wasting their time in idleness and
pleasures, and in all such instances of state and equipage as their
estates will reach.  For let but a woman feel her heart full of
this intention, and she will find it as impossible to patch or
paint, as to curse or swear; she will no more desire to shine at
balls and assemblies, or make a figure[3] amongst those who are
most finely dressed, than she will desire to dance upon a rope to
please spectators: she will know, that the one is as far from the
wisdom and excellency of the Christian spirit as the other.

It was this general intention that made the primitive Christians
such eminent instances of piety, that made the goodly fellowship of the saints, and all the glorious army of martyrs and con-
fessors.  And if you will here stop and ask yourself, why you
are not as pious as the primitive Christians were, your own heart
will tell you, that it is neither through ignorance, nor inability,
but purely because you never thoroughly intended it.  You
observe the same Sunday-worship that they did; and you are
strict in it, because it is your full intention to be so.  And when

[2] Chapters ii. and iii. are instances
of Law's directness of dealing with
people as well as of the clearness of
his logic.  "What is the use," he asks
in effect, "of pleading human frailty
as rendering the life of devotion
difficult, when they obviously have no
intention of leading such a life?  Let
them first show that they really intend to lead such a life, and then, if
they break down, they may fairly
plead human frailty, but not till
then."

[3] 'Figure' here and elsewhere in the
Serious Call means 'a distinguished
appearance,' a sense in which it is
frequently used by Addison and the
best writers of the 18th century.

you as fully intend to be like them in their ordinary common life, when you intend to please God in all your actions, you will find it as possible as to be strictly exact in the service of the Church. And when you have this intention to please God in all your actions, as the happiest and best thing in the world, you will find in you as great an aversion to everything that is vain and impertinent in common life, whether of business or pleasure, as you now have to anything that is profane. You will be as fearful of living in any foolish way, either of spending your time, or your fortune, as you are now fearful of neglecting the public worship.

Now who that wants this general sincere intention can be reckoned a Christian? And yet if it was amongst Christians it would change the whole face of the world; true piety, and exemplary holiness, would be as common and visible as buying and selling, or any trade in life.

Let a clergyman but be thus pious, and he will converse as if he had been brought up by an Apostle; he will no more think and talk of noble preferment than of noble eating, or a glorious chariot. He will no more complain of the frowns of the world, or a small cure, or the want of a patron, than he will complain of the want of a laced coat, or a running horse. Let him but intend to please God, in all his actions, as the happiest and best thing in the world, and then he will know, that there is nothing noble in a clergyman, but a burning zeal for the salvation of souls; nor anything poor in his profession, but idleness and a worldly spirit.

Again, let a tradesman have this intention, and it will make him a saint in his shop; his every-day business will be a course of wise and reasonable actions made holy to God, by being done in obedience to His will and pleasure. He will buy and sell, and labour and travel, because by so doing he can do some good to himself and others. But then, as nothing can please God but what is wise, and reasonable, and holy, so he will neither buy nor sell, nor labour in any other manner, nor to any other end, but such as may be shown to be wise, and reasonable, and holy. He will therefore consider, not what arts, or methods, or application will soonest make him richer and greater than his brethren, or remove him from a shop to a life of state and pleasure; but he will consider what arts, what methods, what application can make worldly business most acceptable to God, and make a life of trade a life of holiness, devotion, and piety. This will be the temper and spirit of every tradesman; he cannot stop short of these degrees of piety, whenever it is his intention to please God in all his actions, as the best and happiest thing in the world.

And on the other hand, whoever is not of this spirit and temper in his trade and profession, and does not carry it on only so far as is best subservient to a wise, and holy, and heavenly life, it is certain that he has not this intention; and yet without it, who can be shown to be a follower of Jesus Christ?

Again, let the gentleman of birth and fortune but have this intention, and you will see how it will carry him from every appearance of evil to every instance of piety and goodness. He cannot live by chance, or as humour and fancy carry him, because he knows that nothing can please God but a wise and regular course of life.   He cannot live in idleness and indulgence, in sports and gaming, in pleasures and intemperance, in vain expenses and high living, because these things cannot be turned into means of piety and holiness, or made so many parts of a wise and religious life.

As he thus removes from all appearance of evil, so he hastens and aspires after every instance of goodness.  He does not ask what is allowable and pardonable, but what is commendable and praiseworthy.  He does not ask, whether God will forgive the folly of our lives, the madness of our pleasures, the vanity of our expenses, the richness of our equipage, and the careless consumption of our time; but he asks, whether God is pleased with these things, or whether these are the appointed ways of gaining His favour?  He does not inquire, whether it be pardonable to hoard up money, to adorn ourselves with diamonds, and gild our chariots, whilst the widow and the orphan, the sick and the prisoner, want to be relieved; but he asks, whether God has required these things at our hands, whether we shall be called to account at the last day for the neglect of them; because it is not his intent to live in such ways as, for aught we know, God may perhaps pardon; but to be diligent in such ways, as we know that God will infallibly reward.

He will not therefore look at the lives of Christians, to learn how he ought to spend his estate, but he will look into the Scriptures, and make every doctrine, parable, precept, or instruction, that relates to rich men, a law to himself in the use of his estate.

He will have nothing to do with costly apparel, because the rich man in the Gospel was "clothed with purple and fine linen."

He denies himself the pleasures and indulgences which his estate could procure, because our blessed Saviour saith, "Woe unto you that are rich, for ye have received your consolation." He will have but one rule for charity, and that will be, to spend all that he can that way, because the Judge of quick and dead hath said, that all that is so given is given to Him.

He will have no hospitable table for the rich and wealthy to come and feast with him, in good eating and drinking; because our blessed Lord saith, "When thou makest a dinner, call not thy friends, nor thy brethren, neither thy kinsmen, nor thy rich neighbours, lest they also bid thee again, and a recompense be made thee. But when thou makest a feast, call the poor, the maimed, the lame, the blind, and thou shalt be blessed. For they cannot recompense thee; for thou shalt be recompensed at the resurrection of the just" (Luke xiv. 12, 13, 14).

He will waste no money in gilded roofs, or costly furniture: He will not be carried from pleasure to pleasure, in expensive state and equipage, because an inspired Apostle hath said, that "all that is in the world, the lust of the flesh, the lust of the eyes, and the pride of life, is not of the Father, but is of the world."

Let not anyone look upon this as an imaginary description of charity, that looks fine in the notion, but cannot be put in practice. For it is so far from being an imaginary impracticable form of life, that it has been practised by great numbers of Christians in former ages, who were glad to turn their whole estates into a constant course of charity. And it is so far from being impossible now, that if we can find any Christians that sincerely intend to please God in all their actions, as the best and happiest thing in the world, whether they be young or old, single or married, men or women, if they have but this intention, it will be impossible for them to do otherwise. This one principle will infallibly carry them to the height of charity, and they will find themselves unable to stop short of it.

For how is it possible for a man that intends to please God in the use of his money, and intends it because he judges it to be his greatest happiness, how is it possible for such a one in such a state of mind to bury his money in needless, impertinent finery, in covering himself or his horses with gold, whilst there are any works of piety and charity to be done with it, or any ways of spending it well?

This is as strictly impossible, as for a man who intends to please

CHAP. II. God in his words, to go into company on purpose to swear and lie. For as all waste and unreasonable expense is done designedly, and with deliberation, so no one can be guilty of it, whose constant intention is to please God in the use of his money.

I have chosen to explain this matter by appealing to this intention, because it makes the case so plain, and because everyone who has a mind may see it in the clearest light, and feel it in the strongest manner, only by looking into his own heart. For it is as easy for every person to know, whether he intends to please God in all his actions; as for any servant to know, whether this be his intention towards his master. Everyone also can as easily tell how he lays out his money, and whether he considers how to please God in it, as he can tell where his estate is, and whether it be in money or land. So that there is no plea left for ignorance or frailty; as to this matter, everybody is in the light, and everybody has power. And no one can fail, but he who is not so much a Christian, as to intend to please God in the use of his estate.

You see two persons, one is regular in public and private prayer, the other is not. Now the reason of this difference is not this, that one has strength and power to observe prayer, and the other has not; but the reason is this, that one intends to please God in the duties of devotion, and the other has no intention about it. Now the case is the same, in the right or wrong use of our time and money. You see one person throwing away his time in sleep and idleness, in visiting and diversions, and his money in the most vain and unreasonable expenses. You see another careful of every day, dividing his hours by rules of reason and religion, and spending all his money in works of charity; now the difference is not owing to this, that one has strength and power to do thus, and the other has not; but it is owing to this, that one intends to please God in the right use of all his time, and all his money, and the other has no intention about it.

Here therefore let us judge ourselves sincerely, let us not vainly content ourselves with the common disorders of our lives, the vanity of our expenses, the folly of our diversions, the pride of our habits, the idleness of our lives, and the wasting of our time, fancying that these are such imperfections as we fall into through the unavoidable weakness and frailty of our natures; but let us be assured, that these disorders of our common life are owing to this, that we have not so much Christianity, as to intend to please God in all the actions of our life, as the best and happiest thing in the world. So that we must not look upon ourselves in a state of common and pardonable imperfection, but in such a state as wants the first and most fundamental principle of Christianity, viz., an intention to please God in all our actions.

And if anyone were to ask himself, how it comes to pass, that there are any degrees of sobriety which he neglects, any practices of humility which he wants, any method of charity which he does not follow, any rules of redeeming time which he does not observe, his own heart will tell him, that it is because he never intended to be so exact in those duties. For whenever we fully intend it, it is as possible to conform to all this regularity of life as it is possible for a man to observe times of prayer.

So that the fault does not lie here, that we desire to be good and perfect, but through the weakness of our nature fall short of it ; but it is, because we have not piety enough to intend to be as good as we can, or to please God in all the actions of our life. This we see is plainly the case of him who spends his time in sports, when he should be at Church ; it is not his want of power, but his want of intention, or desire to be there.

And the case is plainly the same in every other folly of human life. She that spends her time and money in the unreasonable ways and fashions of the world, does not do so because she wants power to be wise and religious in the management of her time and money, but because she has no intention or desire of being so. When she feels this intention, she will find it as possible to act up to it as to be strictly sober and chaste, because it is her care and desire to be so.

This doctrine does not suppose that we have no need of divine grace, or that it is in our own power to make ourselves perfect. It only supposes that through the want of a sincere intention of pleasing God in all our actions, we fall into such irregularities of life as by the ordinary means of grace we should have power to avoid.

And that we have not that perfection, which our present state of grace makes us capable of, because we do not so much as intend to have it.

It only teaches us, that the reason why you see no real mortification, or self-denial, no eminent charity, no profound humility, no heavenly affection, no true contempt of the world, no Christian meekness, no sincere zeal, no eminent piety in the common lives of Christians, is this, because they do not so much as intend to be exact and exemplary in these virtues.

# CHAPTER III.

*Of the great danger and folly of not intending to be as eminent and exemplary as we can, in the practice of all Christian virtues.*

ALTHOUGH the goodness of God, and His rich mercies in Christ Jesus, are a sufficient assurance to us, that He will be merciful to our unavoidable weaknesses and infirmities, that is, to such failings as are the effects of ignorance or surprise; yet we have no reason to expect the same mercy towards those sins which we have lived in, through a want of intention to avoid them.

For instance, the case of a common swearer, who dies in that guilt, seems to have no title to the divine mercy, for this reason, because he can no more plead any weakness, or infirmity in his excuse, than the man that hid his talent in the earth could plead his want of strength to keep it out of the earth.

But now, if this be right reasoning in the case of a common swearer, that his sin is not to be reckoned a pardonable frailty, because he has no weakness to plead in its excuse, why then do we not carry this way of reasoning to its true extent? Why do not we as much condemn every other error of life that has no more weakness to plead in its excuse than common swearing?

For if this be so bad a thing because it might be avoided, if we did but sincerely intend it, must not then all other erroneous ways of life be very guilty, if we live in them, not through weakness and inability, but because we never sincerely intended to avoid them?

For instance, you perhaps have made no progress in the most important Christian virtues, you have scarce gone half way in humility and charity; now if your failure in these duties is purely owing to your want of intention of performing them in any true degree, have you not then as little to plead for yourself, and are you not as much without all excuse as the common swearer?

18

Why, therefore, do you not press these things home upon your conscience? Why do you not think it as dangerous for you to live in such defects, as are in your power to amend, as it is dangerous for a common swearer to live in the breach of that duty, which it is in his power to observe? Is not negligence, and a want of a sincere intention, as blameable in one case as in another?

You, it may be, are as far from Christian perfection as the common swearer is from keeping the third Commandment; are you not therefore as much condemned by the doctrines of the Gospel as the swearer is by the third Commandment?

You perhaps will say, that all people fall short of the perfection of the Gospel, and therefore you are content with your failings. But this is saying nothing to the purpose. For the question is not whether Gospel perfection can be fully attained, but whether you come as near it as a sincere intention and careful diligence can carry you. Whether you are not in a much lower state than you might be, if you sincerely intended, and carefully laboured to advance yourself in all Christian virtues.

If you are as forward in the Christian life as your best endeavours can make you, then you may justly hope, that your imperfections will not be laid to your charge; but if your defects in piety, humility, and charity are owing to your negligence, and want of sincere intention, to be as eminent as you can in these virtues, then you leave yourself as much without excuse as he that lives in the sin of swearing, through the want of a sincere intention to depart from it.

The salvation of our souls is set forth in Scripture as a thing of difficulty, that requires all our diligence, that is to be worked out with fear and trembling.

We are told, that "strait is the gate, and narrow is the way, that leadeth unto life, and few there be that find it; that many are called, but few are chosen." And that many will miss of their salvation, who seem to have taken some pains to obtain it: as in these words, "Strive to enter in at the strait gate, for many I say unto you will seek to enter in, and shall not be able."

Here our blessed Lord commands us to strive to enter in, because many will fail, who only seek to enter. By which we are plainly taught, that religion is a state of labour and striving,

CHAP. III. and that many will fail of their salvation; not because they took no pains or care about it, but because they did not take pains and care enough; they only sought, but did not strive to enter in.

Every Christian therefore should as well examine his life by these doctrines as by the Commandments. For these doctrines are as plain marks of our condition as the Commandments are plain marks of our duty.

For if salvation is only given to those who strive for it, then it is as reasonable for me to consider, whether my course of life be a course of striving to obtain it as to consider, whether I am keeping any of the Commandments.

If my religion is only a formal compliance with those modes of worship that are in fashion where I live; if it costs me no pains or trouble; if it lays me under no rules and restraints; if I have no careful thoughts and sober reflections about it, is it not great weakness to think that I am "striving to enter in at the strait gate"?

If I am seeking everything that can delight my senses, and regale my appetites; spending my time and fortune in pleasures, in diversions, and worldly enjoyments, a stranger to watchings, fastings, prayers, and mortifications, how can it be said that I am "working out my salvation with fear and trembling"?

If there is nothing in my life and conversation that shows me to be different from the Jews and heathens; if I use the world, and worldly enjoyments, as the generality of people now do, and in all ages have done, why should I think that I am amongst those few, who are walking in the narrow way to heaven?

And yet if the way is narrow, if none can walk in it but those that strive, is it not as necessary for me to consider, whether the way I am in be narrow enough, or the labour I take be a sufficient striving, as to consider whether I sufficiently observe the second or third Commandment?

The sum of this matter is this: From the above-mentioned and many other passages of Scripture, it seems plain, that our salvation depends upon the sincerity and perfection of our endeavours to obtain it.

Weak and imperfect men shall, notwithstanding their frailties and defects, be received as having pleased God, if they have done their utmost to please Him.

The rewards of charity, piety, and humility will be given to those whose lives have been a careful labour to exercise these CHAP. III. virtues in as high a degree as they could.

We cannot offer to God the service of angels; we cannot obey Him as man in a state of perfection could; but fallen men can do their best, and this is the perfection that is required of us; it is only the perfection of our best endeavours, a careful labour to be as perfect as we can.

But if we stop short of this, for aught we know, we stop short of the mercy of God, and leave ourselves nothing to plead from the terms of the Gospel. For God has there made no promises of mercy to the slothful and negligent. His mercy is only offered to our frail and imperfect, but best endeavours to practise all manner of righteousness.

As the law to angels is angelical righteousness, as the law to perfect beings is strict perfection, so the law to our imperfect nature is, the best obedience that our frail nature is able to perform.

The measure of our love to God seems in justice to be the measure of our love of every virtue. We are to love and practise it "with all our heart, with all our soul, with all our mind, and with all our strength." And when we cease to live with this regard to virtue, we live below our nature, and instead of being able to plead our infirmities we stand chargeable with negligence.

It is for this reason that we are exhorted to work out our salvation with fear and trembling; because unless our heart and passions are eagerly bent upon the work of our salvation; unless holy fears animate our endeavours, and keep our consciences strict and tender about every part of our duty, constantly examining how we live, and how fit we are to die, we shall in all probability fall into a state of negligence, and sit down in such a course of life as will never carry us to the rewards of heaven.

And he that considers that a just God can only make such allowances as are suitable to His justice, that our works are all to be examined by fire, will find that fear and trembling are proper tempers for those that are drawing near so great a trial.

And indeed there is no probability that anyone should do all the duty that is expected from him, or make that progress in piety, which the holiness and justice of God requires of him, but he that is constantly afraid of falling short of it.

Now this is not intended to possess people's minds with a scrupulous anxiety and discontent in the service of God, but to fill them with a just fear of living in sloth and idleness, and in the neglect of such virtues, as they will want at the day of Judgment.

It is to excite them to an earnest examination of their lives, to such zeal, and care, and concern after Christian perfection, as they use in any matter that has gained their heart and affections.

It is only desiring them to be so apprehensive of their state, so humble in the opinion of themselves, so earnest after higher degrees of piety, and so fearful of falling short of happiness, as the great Apostle St. Paul was when he thus wrote to the Philippians.

"Not as though I had already attained, either were already perfect;—but this one thing I do, forgetting those things which are behind, and reaching forth unto those things which are before, I press toward the mark for the prize of the high calling of God in Christ Jesus." And then he adds, "Let us therefore, as many as are perfect, be thus minded."

But now, if the Apostle thought it necessary for those, who were in his state of perfection, to be thus minded, that is, thus labouring, pressing and aspiring after some degrees of holiness, to which they were not then arrived, surely it is much more necessary for us, who are born in the dregs of time, and labouring under great imperfections, to be thus minded, that is, thus earnest and striving after such degrees of a holy and divine life as we have not yet attained.

The best way for anyone to know how much he ought to aspire after holiness is to consider, not how much will make his present life easy, but to ask himself, how much he thinks will make him easy at the hour of death.

Now any man that dares be so serious as to put this question to himself, will be forced to answer, that at death everyone will wish that he had been as perfect as human nature can be.

Is not this therefore sufficient to put us not only upon wishing, but labouring after all that perfection, which we shall then lament the want of? Is it not excessive folly, to be content with such a course of piety as we already know cannot content us, at a time when we shall so want it as to have nothing else to comfort us? How can we carry a severer condemnation against ourselves than to believe that at the hour of death we shall want the virtues of the saints, and wish that we had been amongst the first servants of God, and yet take no methods of arriving at their height of piety whilst we are alive?

Though this is an absurdity that we can easily pass over at CHAP. III. present, whilst the health of our bodies, the passions of our minds, the noise, and hurry, and pleasures, and business of the world, lead us on with eyes that see not, and ears that hear not; yet at death, it will set itself before us in a dreadful magnitude, it will haunt us like a dismal ghost, and our conscience will never let us take our eyes from it.

We see in worldly matters, what a torment self-condemnation is, and how hardly a man is able to forgive himself, when he has brought himself into any calamity, or disgrace, purely by his own folly. The affliction is made doubly tormenting, because he is forced to charge it all upon himself, as his own act and deed, against the nature and reason of things, and contrary to the advice of all his friends.

Now by this we may in some degree guess, how terrible the pain of that self-condemnation will be, when a man shall find himself in the miseries of death, under the severity of a self-condemning conscience, charging all his distress upon his own folly and madness, against the sense and reason of his own mind, against all the doctrines and precepts of religion, and contrary to all the instructions, calls, and warnings, both of God and man.

PENITENS was a busy, notable tradesman, and very prosperous in his dealings, but died in the thirty-fifth year of his age.

A little before his death, when the doctors had given him over, some of his neighbours came one evening to see him, at which time he spake thus to them:

"I see," says he, "my friends, the tender concern you have for me by the grief that appears in your countenances, and I know the thoughts that you now have about me. You think how melancholy a case it is, to see so young a man, and in such flourishing business, delivered up to death. And perhaps, had I visited any of you in my condition, I should have had the same thoughts of you.

"But now, my friends, my thoughts are no more like your thoughts than my condition is like yours.

"It is no trouble to me now to think, that I am to die young, or before I have raised an estate.

"These things are now sunk into such mere nothings, that I have no name little enough to call them by. For if in a few days, or hours, I am to leave this carcase to be buried in the

CHAP. III. earth, and to find myself either for ever happy in the favour of God, or eternally separated from all light and peace, can any words sufficiently express the littleness of everything else?

"Is there any dream like the dream of life, which amuses us with the neglect and disregard of these things? Is there any folly like the folly of our manly state, which is too wise and busy to be at leisure for these reflections?

"When we consider death as a misery, we only think of it as a miserable separation from the enjoyments of this life. We seldom mourn over an old man that dies rich, but we lament the young that are taken away in the progress of their fortune. You yourselves look upon me with pity, not that I am going unprepared to meet the Judge of quick and dead, but that I am to leave a prosperous trade in the flower of my life.

"This is the wisdom of our manly thoughts. And yet what folly of the silliest children is so great as this?

"For what is there miserable, or dreadful in death, but the consequences of it? When a man is dead, what does anything signify to him, but the state he is then in?

"Our poor friend Lepidus died, you know, as he was dressing himself for a feast; do you think it is now part of his trouble, that he did not live till that entertainment was over? Feast, and business, and pleasures, and enjoyments, seem great things to us, whilst we think of nothing else, but as soon as we add death to them, they all sink into an equal littleness; and the soul that is separated from the body no more laments the loss of business than the losing of a feast.

"If I am going into the joys of God, could there be any reason to grieve that this happened to me before I was forty years of age? Could it be a sad thing to go to heaven before I had made a few more bargains, or stood a little longer behind a counter?

"And if I am to go amongst lost spirits, could there be any reason to be content that this did not happen to me till I was old, and full of riches?

"If good angels were ready to receive my soul, could it be any grief to me that I was dying upon a poor bed in a garret?

"And if God has delivered me up to evil spirits, to be dragged by them to places of torments, could it be any comfort to me that they found me upon a bed of state?

"When you are as near death as I am, you will know that CHAP. III. all the different states of life, whether of youth or age, riches or poverty, greatness or meanness, signify no more to you than whether you die in a poor, or stately apartment.

"The greatness of those things which follow death makes all that goes before it sink into nothing.

"Now that judgment is the next thing that I look for, and everlasting happiness, or misery is come so near me, all the enjoyments and prosperities of life seem as vain and insignificant, and to have no more to do with my happiness, than the clothes that I wore before I could speak.

"But, my friends, how am I surprised that I have not always had these thoughts? for what is there in the terrors of death, in the vanities of life, or the necessities of piety, but what I might have as easily and fully seen in any part of my life?

"What a strange thing is it, that a little health, or the poor business of a shop, should keep us so senseless of these great things that are coming so fast upon us!

"Just as you came into my chamber, I was thinking with myself, what numbers of souls there are now in the world, in my condition at this very time, surprised with a summons to the other world; some taken from their shops and farms, others from their sports and pleasures, these at suits of law, those at gaming-tables, some on the road, others at their own fire-sides, and all seized at an hour when they thought nothing of it; frighted at the approach of death, confounded at the vanity of all their labours, designs, and projects, astonished at the folly of their past lives, and not knowing which way to turn their thoughts to find any comfort. Their consciences flying in their faces, bringing all their sins to their remembrance, tormenting them with deepest convictions of their own folly, presenting them with the sight of the angry Judge, the worm that never dies, the fire that is never quenched, the gates of hell, the powers of darkness, and the bitter pains of eternal death.

"Oh, my friends! bless God that you are not of this number, that you have time and strength to employ yourselves in such works of piety as may bring you peace at the last.

"And take this along with you, that there is nothing but a life of great piety, or a death of great stupidity, that can keep off these apprehensions.

"Had I now a thousand worlds, I would give them all for

one year more, that I might present unto God one year of such devotion and good works as I never before so much as intended.

"You perhaps, when you consider that I have lived free from scandal and debauchery, and in the communion of the Church, wonder to see me so full of remorse and self-condemnation at the approach of death.

"But, alas! what a poor thing is it, to have lived only free from murder, theft, and adultery, which is all that I can say of myself.

"You know indeed, that I have never been reckoned a sot, but you are at the same time witnesses, and have been frequent companions, of my intemperance, sensuality, and great indulgence. And if I am now going to a Judgment, where nothing will be rewarded but good works, I may well be concerned, that though I am no sot, yet I have no Christian sobriety to plead for me.

"It is true, I have lived in the communion of the Church, and generally frequented its worship and service on Sundays, when I was neither too idle, or not otherwise disposed of by my business and pleasures. But then, my conformity to the public worship has been rather a thing of course than any real intention of doing that which the service of the Church supposes; had it not been so, I had been oftener at Church, more devout when there, and more fearful of ever neglecting it.

"But the thing that now surprises me above all wonders is this, that I never had so much as a general intention of living up to the piety of the Gospel. This never so much as entered into my head, or my heart. I never once in my life considered, whether I were living as the laws of religion direct, or whether my way of life was such as would procure me the mercy of God at this hour.

"And can it be thought, that I have kept the Gospel terms of salvation, without ever so much as intending in any serious and deliberate manner, either to know them, or keep them? Can it be thought, that I have pleased God with such a life as He requires, though I have lived without ever considering what He requires, or how much I have performed? How easy a thing would salvation be, if it could fall into my careless hands, who have never had so much serious thought about it, as about any one common bargain that I have made?

"In the business of life I have used prudence and reflection. CHAP. III. I have done everything by rules and methods. I have been glad to converse with men of experience and judgment, to find out the reasons why some fail and others succeed in any business. I have taken no step in trade but with great care and caution, considering every advantage or danger that attended it. I have always had my eye upon the main end of business, and have studied all the ways and means of being a gainer by all that I undertook.

"But what is the reason that I have brought none of these tempers to religion? What is the reason that I, who have so often talked of the necessity of rules and methods, and diligence in worldly business, have all this while never once thought of any rules, or methods, or managements, to carry me on in a life of piety?

"Do you think anything can astonish and confound a dying man like this? What pain do you think a man must feel, when his conscience lays all this folly to his charge, when it shall show him how regular, exact, and wise he has been in small matters, which are passed away like a dream, and how stupid and senseless he has lived, without any reflection, without any rules, in things of such eternal moment as no heart can sufficiently conceive them!

"Had I only my frailties and imperfections to lament, at this time, I should lie here humbly trusting in the mercies of God. But, alas! how can I call a general disregard, and a thorough neglect of all religious improvement, a frailty or imperfection; when it was as much in my power to have been exact, and careful, and diligent in a course of piety as in the business of my trade.

"I could have called in as many helps, have practised as many rules, and been taught as many certain methods of holy living, as of thriving in my shop, had I but so intended and desired it.

"Oh, my friends! a careless life, unconcerned and unattentive to the duties of religion, is so without all excuse, so unworthy of the mercy of God, such a shame to the sense and reason of our minds, that I can hardly conceive a greater punishment than for a man to be thrown into the state that I am in, to reflect upon it."

Penitens was here going on, but had his mouth stopped by

CHAP. III. a convulsion, which never suffered him to speak any more. He lay convulsed about twelve hours, and then gave up the ghost.[1]

Now if every reader would imagine this Penitens to have been some particular acquaintance or relation of his, and fancy that he saw and heard all that is here described, that he stood by his bedside when his poor friend lay in such distress and agony, lamenting the folly of his past life, it would, in all probability, teach him such wisdom as never entered into his heart before. If to this, he should consider how often he himself might have been surprised in the same state of negligence, and made an example to the rest of the world, this double reflection, both upon the distress of his friend, and the goodness of that God, Who had preserved him from it, would in all likelihood soften his heart into holy tempers, and make him turn the remainder of his life into a regular course of piety.

This therefore being so useful a meditation, I shall here leave the reader, as I hope, seriously engaged in it.

[1] The portrait of 'Penitens' is the first of the passages in the *Serious Call* which may have led Gibbon to write, surely with enormous exaggeration, " Hell-fire and damnation are darted from every page of the book " (Gibbon's *Autobiography*, new edition, edited by John Murray, 1896, pp. 26, 27). Soon after the publication of the *Serious Call*, Law's mysticism led him to modify greatly, indeed to alter, his views on eschatology.

# CHAPTER IV.

*We can please God in no state, or employment of life, but by intending and devoting it all to His honour and glory.*

HAVING in the first Chapter stated the general nature of devotion, and shown, that it implies not any form of prayer, but a certain form of life, that is offered to God not at any particular times, or places, but everywhere and in everything, I shall now descend to some particulars, and show how we are to devote our labour and employment, our time and fortunes unto God.

As a good Christian should consider every place as holy, because God is there, so he should look upon every part of his life as a matter of holiness, because it is to be offered unto God.

The profession of a clergyman is a holy profession, because it is a ministration in holy things, an attendance at the Altar. But worldly business is to be made holy unto the Lord, by being done as a service to Him, and in conformity to His divine will.

For as all men, and all things in the world, as truly belong unto God as any places, things, or persons that are devoted to divine service, so all things are to be used, and all persons are to act in their several states and employments for the glory of God.

Men of worldly business, therefore, must not look upon themselves as at liberty to live to themselves, to sacrifice to their own humours and tempers, because their employment is of a worldly nature. But they must consider, that as the world and all worldly professions, as truly belong to God, as persons and things that are devoted to the Altar, so it is as much the duty of men in worldly business to live wholly unto God as it is the duty of those who are devoted to divine service.

As the whole world is God's, so the whole world is to act

for God. As all men have the same relation to God, as all men have all their powers and faculties from God, so all men are obliged to act for God, with all their powers and faculties.

As all things are God's, so all things are to be used and regarded as the things of God. For men to abuse things on earth, and live to themselves, is the same rebellion against God as for angels to abuse things in heaven; because God is just the same Lord of all on earth as He is the Lord of all in heaven.

Things may, and must differ in their use, but yet they are all to be used according to the will of God.

Men may, and must differ in their employments, but yet they must all act for the same ends, as dutiful servants of God, in the right and pious performance of their several callings.

Clergymen must live wholly unto God in one particular way, that is, in the exercise of holy offices, in the ministration of prayers and sacraments, and a zealous distribution of spiritual goods.

But men of other employments are in their particular ways as much obliged to act as the servants of God, and live wholly unto Him in their several callings.

This is the only difference between clergymen and people of other callings.

When it can be shown, that men might be vain, covetous, sensual, worldly minded, or proud in the exercise of their worldly business, then it will be allowable for clergymen to indulge the same tempers in their sacred profession. For though these tempers are most odious and most criminal in clergymen, who, besides their baptismal vow, have a second time devoted themselves to God, to be His servants, not in the common offices of human life, but in the spiritual service of the most holy, sacred things, and who are therefore to keep themselves as separate and different from the common life of other men, as a Church or an Altar is to be kept separate from houses and tables of common use; yet as all Christians are by their baptism devoted to God, and made professors of holiness, so are they all in their several callings to live as holy and heavenly persons; doing everything in their common life only in such a manner as it may be received by God as a service done to Him. For things spiritual and temporal, sacred and common, must, like men and angels, like heaven and earth, all conspire in the glory of God.

As there is but one God and Father of us all, Whose glory CHAP. IV. gives light and life to everything that lives ; Whose presence fills all places, Whose power supports all beings, Whose providence ruleth all events ; so everything that lives, whether in heaven or earth, whether they be thrones or principalities, men or angels, they must all with one spirit live wholly to the praise and glory of this one God and Father of them all. Angels as angels, in their heavenly ministrations, but men as men, women as women, bishops as bishops, priests as priests, and deacons as deacons ; some with things spiritual, and some with things temporal, offering to God the daily sacrifice of a reasonable life, wise actions, purity of heart, and heavenly affections.

This is the common business of all persons in this world. It is not left to any women in the world to trifle away their time in the follies and impertinences[1] of a fashionable life, nor to any men to resign themselves up to worldly cares and concerns : it is not left to the rich to gratify their passions in the indulgences and pride of life, nor to the poor to vex and torment their hearts with the poverty of their state ; but men and women, rich and poor, must, with bishops and priests, walk before God in the same wise and holy spirit, in the same denial of all vain tempers, and in the same discipline and care of souls ; not only because they have all the same rational nature, and are servants of the same God, but because they all want the same holiness to make them fit for the same happiness, to which they are all called. It is therefore absolutely necessary for all Christians, whether men or women, to consider themselves, as persons that are devoted to holiness ; and so order their common ways of life, by such rules of reason and piety, as may turn it into continual service unto Almighty God.

Now to make our labour or employment an acceptable service unto God, we must carry it on with the same spirit and temper, that is required in giving of alms, or any work of piety. For, if "whether we eat or drink, or whatsoever we do, we must do all to the glory of God" (1 Cor. x. 31); if "we are to use this world as if we used it not"; if we are to "present our bodies a living sacrifice, holy, acceptable to God" (Rom. xii. 1); if "we are to live by faith, and not by sight," and to "have our conversation in heaven," then it is necessary, that the common

---

[1] 'Impertinences,' that is, employ-ments unsuitable to their profession ; "what has no relation to the matter in hand" (Johnson)

CHAP. IV. way of our life in every state be made to glorify God by such tempers as make our prayers and adorations acceptable to Him. For if we are worldly, or earthly-minded in our employments, if they are carried on with vain desires, and covetous tempers, only to satisfy ourselves, we can no more be said to live to the glory of God than gluttons and drunkards can be said to eat and drink to the glory of God.

As the glory of God is one and the same thing, so whatever we do suitably to it must be done with one and the same spirit. That same state and temper of mind, which makes our alms and devotions acceptable, must also make our labour, or employment, a proper offering unto God. If a man labours to be rich, and pursues his business that he may raise himself to a state of figure and glory in the world, he is no longer serving God in his employment; he is acting under other masters, and has no more title to a reward from God than he that gives alms that he may be seen, or prays that he may be heard of men. For vain and earthly desires are no more allowable in our employ-ments than in our alms and devotions. For these tempers of worldly pride, and vain glory, are not only evil, when they mix with our good works, but they have the same evil nature, and make us odious to God, when they enter into the common business of our employment. If it were allowable to indulge covetous or vain passions in our worldly employments, it would then be allowable to be vain-glorious in our devotions. But as our alms and devotions are not an acceptable service, but when they proceed from a heart truly devoted to God, so our common employment cannot be reckoned a service to Him, but when it is performed with the same temper and piety of heart.

Most of the employments of life are in their own nature lawful; and all those that are so may be made a substantial part of our duty to God, if we engage in them only so far, and for such ends, as are suitable to beings that are to live above the world, all the time that they live in the world. This is the only measure of our application to any worldly business; let it be what it will, where it will, it must have no more of our hands, our hearts, or our time, than is consistent with an hearty, daily, careful preparation of ourselves for another life. For as all Christians, as such, have renounced this world, to prepare themselves by daily devotion, and universal holiness, for an eternal state of quite another nature, they must look upon

worldly employments, as upon worldly wants, and bodily infirmi- CHAP. IV.
ties; things not to be desired, but only to be endured and
suffered, till death and the resurrection has carried us to an
eternal state of real happiness.

Now he that does not look at the things of this life in this
degree of littleness cannot be said either to feel or believe
the greatest truths of Christianity. For if he thinks anything
great or important in human business, can he be said to feel
or believe those Scriptures which represent this life, and the
greatest things of life, as bubbles, vapours, dreams, and shadows?

If he thinks figure and show, and worldly glory, to be any
proper happiness of a Christian, how can he be said to feel or
believe this doctrine, "Blessed are ye when men shall hate you,
and when they shall separate you from their company, and shall
reproach you, and cast out your name as evil for the Son of
Man's sake"? For surely, if there was any real happiness in
figure and show, and worldly glory; if these things deserved
our thoughts and care, it could not be matter of the highest
joy, when we are torn from them by persecutions and sufferings.
If, therefore, a man will so live as to show that he feels and
believes the most fundamental doctrines of Christianity, he must
live above the world; this is the temper that must enable him to
do the business of life, and yet live wholly unto God, and to go
through some worldly employment with a heavenly mind. And it
is as necessary that people live in their employments with this
temper as it is necessary that their employment itself be lawful.

The husbandman that tilleth the ground is employed in an
honest business, that is necessary in life and very capable of
being made an acceptable service unto God. But if he labours
and toils, not to serve any reasonable ends of life, but in order
to have his plough made of silver, and to have his horses
harnessed in gold, the honesty of his employment is lost as to
him, and his labour becomes his folly.

A tradesman may justly think that it is agreeable to the will
of God for him to sell such things as are innocent and useful
in life, such as help both himself and others to a reasonable
support, and enable them to assist those that want to be assisted.
But if instead of this, he trades only with regard to himself,
without any other rule than that of his own temper, if it be
his chief end in it to grow rich, that he may live in figure and
indulgence. and be able to retire from business to idleness and

luxury, his trade, as to him, loses all its innocency, and is so far from being an acceptable service to God, that it is only a more plausible course of covetousness, self-love, and ambition. For such a one turns the necessities of employment into pride and covetousness, just as the sot and epicure turn the necessities of eating and drinking into gluttony and drunkenness. Now he that is up early and late, that sweats and labours for these ends, that he may be sometime or other rich, and live in pleasure and indulgence, lives no more to the glory of God, than he that plays and games for the same ends. For though there is a great difference between trading and gaming, yet most of that difference is lost, when men once trade with the same desires and tempers, and for the same ends, that others game. Charity and fine dressing are things very different; but if men give alms, for the same reasons that others dress fine, only to be seen and admired, charity is then but like the vanity of fine clothes. In like manner, if the same motives make some people painful[2] and industrious in their trades, which make others constant at gaming, such pains are but like the pains of gaming.

CALIDUS has traded above thirty years in the greatest city of the kingdom; he has been so many years constantly increasing his trade, and his fortune.[3] Every hour of the day is with him an hour of business; and though he eats and drinks very heartily, yet every meal seems to be in a hurry, and he would say grace if he had time. Calidus ends every·day at the tavern, but has not leisure to be there till near nine o'clock. He is always forced to drink a good hearty glass, to drive thoughts of business out of his head, and make his spirits drowsy enough for sleep. He does business all the time that he is rising, and has settled several matters before he can get to his counting-room. His prayers are a short ejaculation or two, which he never misses in stormy, tempestuous weather, because he has always something or other at sea. Calidus will tell you, with great pleasure, that he has been in this hurry for so many years, and that it must have killed him long ago, but that it has been a rule with him

---

[2] 'Painful' means what we should call 'painstaking.' 'A painful preacher' in this sense was a very common expression among the Puritans in the seventeenth century.

[3] When the *Serious Call* was written the greed for gain had recently led to innumerable dishonest projects, of which the South Sea Bubble, which burst in 1722, was the most notorious. Commercial dishonesty was one of the crying evils of the time. This should be borne in mind in reading the whole of this chapter

to get out of the town every Saturday, and make the Sunday a CHAP. IV. day of quiet and good refreshment in the country.

He is now so rich, that he would leave off his business, and amuse his old age with building and furnishing a fine house in the country, but that he is afraid he should grow melancholy, if he were to quit his business. He will tell you with great gravity, that it is a dangerous thing for a man that has been used to get money, ever to leave it off. If thoughts of religion happen at any time to steal into his head, Calidus contents himself with thinking that he never was a friend to heretics and infidels, that he has always been civil to the minister of his parish, and very often given something to the charity schools.[4]

Now this way of life is at such a distance from all the doctrines and discipline of Christianity, that no one can live in it through ignorance or frailty. Calidus can no more imagine that "he is born again of the Spirit"; that he is "in Christ a new creature"; that he lives "here as a stranger and pilgrim, setting his affections upon things above, and laying up treasures in heaven" (St. John iii. 5; 2 Cor. v. 17; Col. iii. 1),—he can no more imagine this than he can think that he has been all his life an Apostle, working miracles, and preaching the Gospel.

It must also be owned that the generality of trading people, especially in great towns, are too much like Calidus. You see them all the week buried in business, unable to think of anything else; and then spending the Sunday in idleness and refreshment, in wandering into the country, in such visits and jovial meetings, as make it often the worst day of the week.

Now they do not live thus because they cannot support themselves with less care and application to business; but they live thus because they want to grow rich in their trades, and to maintain their families in some such figure and degree of finery as a reasonable Christian life has no occasion for. Take away but this temper, and then people of all trades will

---

[4] 'Charity Schools.' These institutions were founded in great abundance in the later part of the seventeenth and earlier part or the eighteenth centuries, and they were kept up better than most church organizations in the dead time of the Georges. They were often very lavish in their benefactions; not only educating and clothing, in more or less quaint garbs, the children who were fortunate enough to be admitted to them, but apprenticing them to a useful trade when their schooldays were over. There were charity schools at King's Cliffe, founded by Mr. Law himself and his disciple, Mrs. Hutcheson.

find themselves at leisure to live every day like Christians, to be careful of every duty of the Gospel, to live in a visible course of religion, and be every day strict observers both of private and public prayer.[5]

Now the only way to do this is for people to consider their trade as something that they are obliged to devote to the glory of God, something that they are to do only in such a manner as that they may make it a duty to Him. Nothing can be right in business that is not under these rules.—The Apostle commands servants, "to be obedient to their masters, in single-ness of heart, as unto Christ. Not with eye-service as men-pleasers, but as the servants of Christ, doing the will of God from the heart. With good will doing service as unto the Lord, and not to men" (Eph. vi. 5 ; Col. iii. 22, 23).

This passage sufficiently shows, that all Christians are to live wholly unto God in every state and condition, doing the work of their common calling, in such a manner, and for such ends, as to make it a part of their devotion or service to God. For certainly if poor slaves are not to comply with their business as men-pleasers, if they are to look wholly unto God in all their actions, and serve in singleness of heart, as unto the Lord, surely men of other employments and conditions must be as much obliged to go through their business with the same singleness of heart; not as pleasing the vanity of their own minds, not as gratifying their own selfish, worldly passions, but as the servants of God in all that they have to do. For surely no one will say, that a slave is to devote his state of life unto God, and make the will of God the sole rule and end of his service, but that a tradesman need not act with the same spirit of devotion in his business. For this is as absurd, as to make it necessary for one man to be more just, or faithful than another.

It is therefore absolutely certain, that no Christian is to enter any further into business, nor for any other ends, than such as he can in singleness of heart offer unto God as a reasonable service. For the Son of God has redeemed us for this only end, that we should, by a life of reason and piety, live to the glory of God; this is the only rule and measure for every

---

[5] The assumption that people might be 'every day strict observers both of private and public prayer' implies that in towns at any rate daily service was the rule, not the exception. This very soon ceased to be the case, but in the early days of the eighteenth century it certainly was so.

order and state of life.    Without this rule, the most lawful CHAP. IV.
employment becomes a sinful state of life.

Take away this from the life of a clergyman, and his holy
profession serves only to expose him to a greater damnation.
Take away this from tradesmen, and shops are but so many
houses of greediness and filthy lucre.    Take away this from
gentlemen, and the course of their life becomes a course of
sensuality, pride, and wantonness.    Take away this rule from
our tables, and all falls into gluttony and drunkenness.    Take
away this measure from our dress and habits, and all is turned
into such paint, and glitter, and ridiculous ornaments, as are
a real shame to the wearer.    Take away this from the use of
our fortunes, and you will find people sparing in nothing but
charity.    Take away this from our diversions, and you will find
no sports too silly, nor any entertainments too vain and corrupt
to be the pleasure of Christians.

If therefore we desire to live unto God, it is necessary to
bring our whole life under this law, to make His glory the
sole rule and measure of our acting in every employment of
life.    For there is no other true devotion, but this of living
devoted to God in the common business of our lives.

So that men must not content themselves with the lawfulness
of their employments, but must consider whether they use
them, as they are to use everything, as strangers and pilgrims,
that are baptized into the resurrection of Jesus Christ, that
are to follow Him in a wise and heavenly course of life, in
the mortification of all worldly desires, and in purifying and
preparing their souls for the blessed enjoyment of God (Coloss.
iii. 1; 1 Pet. i. 15, 16; Eph. v. 26, 27).

For to be vain, or proud, or covetous, or ambitious in the
common course of our business, is as contrary to these holy
tempers of Christianity as cheating and dishonesty.

If a glutton were to say in excuse of his gluttony, that he
only eats such things as it is lawful to eat, he would make as
good an excuse for himself as the greedy, covetous, ambitious
tradesman that should say, he only deals in lawful business.
For as a Christian is not only required to be honest, but to
be of a Christian spirit, and make his life an exercise of humility,
repentance, and heavenly affection, so all tempers that are contrary to these are as contrary to Christianity as cheating is
contrary to honesty.

So that the matter plainly comes to this, all irregular tempers in trade and business are but like irregular tempers in eating and drinking.

Proud views, and vain desires, in our worldly employments, are as truly vices and corruptions as hypocrisy in prayer, or vanity in alms. And there can be no reason given, why vanity in our alms should make us odious to God, but what will prove any other kind of pride to be equally odious. He that labours and toils in a calling, that he may make a figure in the world, and draw the eyes of people upon the splendour of his condition, is as far from the pious humility of a Christian as he that gives alms that he may be seen of men. For the reason, why pride and vanity in our prayers and alms renders them an unacceptable service to God, is not because there is anything particular in prayers and alms that cannot allow of pride, but because pride is in no respect, nor in anything made for man ; it destroys the piety of our prayers and alms, because it destroys the piety of everything that it touches, and renders every action that it governs incapable of being offered unto God.

So that if we could so divide ourselves as to be humble in some respects and proud in others, such humility would be of no service to us, because God requires us as truly to be humble in all our actions and designs as to be true and honest in all our actions and designs.

And as a man is not honest and true, because he is so to a great many people, or upon several occasions, but because truth and honesty is the measure of all his dealings with every-body ; so the case is the same in humility, or any other temper ; it must be the general ruling habit of our minds, and extend itself to all our actions and designs before it can be imputed to us.

We indeed sometimes talk, as if a man might be humble in some things, and proud in others; humble in his dress, but proud of his learning ; humble in his person, but proud in his views and designs. But though this may pass in common discourse, where few things are said according to strict truth, it cannot be allowed when we examine into the nature of our actions.

It is very possible for a man that lives by cheating to be very punctual in paying for what he buys; but then everyone is assured that he does not do so out of any principle of true honesty.

In like manner, it is very possible for a man that is proud CHAP. IV. of his estate, ambitious in his views, or vain of his learning, to disregard his dress, and person, in such a manner as a truly humble man would do; but to suppose that he does so out of a true principle of religious humility is full as absurd as to suppose that a cheat pays for what he buys, out of a principle of religious honesty.

As therefore all kinds of dishonesty destroy our pretences to an honest principle of mind, so all kinds of pride destroy our pretences to an humble spirit.

No one wonders that those prayers, and alms, which proceed from pride and ostentation, are odious to God; but yet it is as easy to show that pride is as pardonable there as anywhere else.

If we could suppose that God rejects pride in our prayers and alms, but bears with pride in our dress, our persons, or estates, it would be the same thing as to suppose that God condemns falsehood in some actions, but allows it in others. For pride in one thing differs from pride in another thing as the robbing of one man differs from the robbing of another.

Again, if pride and ostentation is so odious that it destroys the merit and worth of the most reasonable actions, surely it must be equally odious in those actions which are only founded in the weakness and infirmity of our nature. As thus, alms are commanded by God, as excellent in themselves, as true instances of a divine temper, but clothes are only allowed to cover our shame; surely therefore it must at least be as odious a degree of pride to be vain in our clothes as to be vain in our alms.

Again, we are commanded to pray without ceasing, as a means of rendering our souls more exalted and divine, but we are forbidden to lay up treasures upon earth; and can we think that it is not as bad to be vain of those treasures, which we are forbidden to lay up, as to be vain of those prayers, which we are commanded to make?

Women are required to have their heads covered (1 Cor. xi. 13), and to adorn themselves with shamefacedness (1 Tim. ii. 9); if therefore they are vain in those things, which are expressly forbidden, if they patch and paint that part, which can only be adorned by shamefacedness, surely they have as much to repent of for such a pride, as they have, whose pride is the motive to their prayers and charity. This must be granted, unless we will say, that it is more pardonable to glory in our shame than to glory in our virtue.

All these instances are only to show us the great necessity of such a regular and uniform piety as extends itself to all the actions of our common life.

That we must eat and drink, and dress and discourse, according to the sobriety of the Christian spirit, engage in no employments but such as we can truly devote unto God, nor pursue them any further than so far as conduces to the reasonable ends of a holy devout life.

That we must be honest, not only on particular occasions, and in such instances as are applauded in the world, easy to be performed, and free from danger, or loss, but from such a living principle of justice as makes us love truth and integrity in all its instances, follow it through all dangers, and against all opposition; as knowing that the more we pay for any truth, the better is our bargain, and that then our integrity becomes a pearl, when we have parted with all to keep it.

That we must be humble, not only in such instances as are expected in the world, or suitable to our tempers, or confined to particular occasions, but in such an humility of spirit as renders us meek and lowly in the whole course of our lives, as shows itself in our dress, our person, our conversation, our enjoyment of the world, the tranquillity of our minds, patience under injuries, submission to superiors, and condescensions to those that are below us, and in all the outward actions of our lives.

That we must devote, not only times and places to prayer, but be everywhere in the spirit of devotion, with hearts always set towards heaven, looking up to God in all our actions, and doing everything as His servants, living in the world as in a holy temple of God, and always worshipping Him, though not with our lips, yet with the thankfulness of our hearts, the holiness of our actions, and the pious and charitable use of all His gifts. That we must not only send up petitions and thoughts, now and then to heaven, but must go through all our worldly business with an heavenly spirit, as members of Christ's mystical body, that with new hearts and new minds are to turn an earthly life into a preparation for a life of greatness and glory in the kingdom of heaven.

Now the only way to arrive at this piety of spirit is to bring all your actions to the same rule as your devotions and alms. CHAP. IV. You very well know what it is that makes the piety of your alms or devotions; now the same rules, the same regard to God, must render everything else that you do a fit and acceptable service unto God.

Enough, I hope, has been said, to show you the necessity of thus introducing religion into all the actions of your common life, and of living and acting with the same regard to God in all that you do as in your prayers and alms.

Eating is one of the lowest actions of our lives, it is common to us with mere animals, yet we see that the piety of all ages of the world has turned this ordinary action of an animal life into a piety to God, by making every meal to begin and end with devotion.

We see yet some remains of this custom in most Christian families; some such little formality as shows you that people used to call upon God at the beginning and end of their meals. But, indeed, it is now generally so performed as to look more like a mockery upon devotion than any solemn application of the mind unto God. In one house you may perhaps see the head of the family just pulling off his hat; in another half getting up from his seat; another shall, it may be, proceed so far as to make as if he had said something; but, however, these little attempts are the remains of some devotion that was formerly used at such times, and are proofs that religion has formerly belonged to this part of common life.

But to such a pass are we now come, that though the custom is yet preserved, yet we can hardly bear with him that seems to perform it with any degree of seriousness, and look upon it as a sign of a fanatical temper if a man has not done it as soon as he begins.

I would not be thought to plead for the necessity of long prayers at these times; but this much I think may be said, that if prayer is proper at these times, we ought to oblige ourselves to use such a form of words as should show that we solemnly appeal to God for such graces and blessings as are then proper to the occasion. Otherwise the mock ceremony, instead of blessing our victuals, does but accustom us to trifle with devotion, and give us a habit of being unaffected with our prayers.

If every head of a family was, at the return of every meal, to oblige himself to make a solemn adoration of God, in such a decent manner as becomes a devout mind, it would be very likely to teach him, that swearing, sensuality, gluttony, and loose discourse were very improper at those meals, which were to begin and end with devotion.

And in these days of general corruption, this part of devotion is fallen into a mock ceremony, it must be imputed to this cause, that sensuality and intemperance have got too great a power over us to suffer us to add any devotion to our meals. But thus much must be said, that when we are as pious as Jews and heathens of all ages have been, we shall think it proper to pray at the beginning and end of our meals.[6]

I have appealed to this pious custom of all ages of the world as a proof of the reasonableness of the doctrine of this and the foregoing chapters; that is, as a proof that religion is to be the rule and measure of all the actions of ordinary life. For surely, if we are not to eat, but under such rules of devotion, it must plainly appear, that whatever else we do must, in its proper way, be done with the same regard to the glory of God, and agreeably to the principles of a devout and pious mind.

[6] Though Law professed, especially in his later years, the greatest contempt for 'human learning,' he betrays his possession of it by a thousand little touches. Here is one. That the Greeks and Romans, 'heathens' though they were, 'said grace' before their meals is shown with characteristic wealth of learned illustration by Bishop Christopher Wordsworth. See his *Life*, 1st edition, pp. 440-1 n.

# CHAPTER V.

*Persons that are free from the necessity of labour and employments, are to consider themselves as devoted to God in a higher degree.*

GREAT part of the world are free from the necessities of labour and employments, and have their time and fortunes in their own disposal.[1]

But as no one is to live in his employment according to his own humour, or for such ends as please his own fancy, but is to do all his business in such a manner as to make it a service unto God ; so those who have no particular employment are so far from being left at greater liberty to live to themselves, to pursue their own humours, and spend their time and fortunes as they please, that they are under greater obligations of living wholly unto God in all their actions.

The freedom of their state lays them under a greater necessity of always choosing, and doing the best things.

They are those of whom much will be required, because much is given unto them.

A slave can only live unto God in one particular way, that is, by religious patience and submission in his state of slavery.

But all ways of holy living, all instances, and all kinds of virtue,

---

[1] There would be many more to whom this description would apply in the eighteenth century than there are now, owing to the great numbers of lesser gentry, who did not belong either to the county families, or to the professions or trades. This class has now almost died out. When it flourished it would be more 'free from the necessities of labour' than any other class. The lesser gentry had not the responsibilities and the public duties of the class above them, nor the need of working for their daily bread like the classes below them. They were, as a rule, coarse and illiterate, and too often vicious—a natural consequence of idleness. Tony Lumpkin, in Goldsmith's delightful comedy, *She Stoops to Conquer*, is a caricature, but not an exaggerated caricature of the class. His prospective income, however, was much larger than the average of his kind. 'It don't take much larning,' pleaded Mrs. Hardcastle, his mother, 'to spend £1500 a year,' still less from three to six hundred, between which sums the income of the lesser gentry usually ranged.

CHAP. V. lie open to those, who are masters of themselves, their time and their fortune.

It is as much the duty therefore, of such persons, to make a wise use of their liberty, to devote themselves to all kinds of virtue, to aspire after everything that is holy and pious, to endeavour to be eminent in all good works, and to please God in the highest and most perfect manner; it is as much their duty to be thus wise in the conduct of themselves, and thus extensive in their endeavours after holiness, as it is the duty of a slave to be resigned unto God in his state of slavery.

You are no labourer, or tradesman, you are neither merchant, nor soldier; consider yourself therefore, as placed in a state in some degree like that of good angels, who are sent into the world as ministering spirits, for the general good of mankind, to assist, protect, and minister for them who shall be heirs of salvation.

For the more you are free from the common necessities of men, the more you are to imitate the higher perfections of angels.

Had you, SERENA, been obliged, by the necessities of life, to wash clothes for your maintenance, or to wait upon some mistress, that demanded all your labour, it would then be your duty to serve and glorify God, by such humility, obedience, and faithfulness as might adorn that state of life.

It would then be recommended to your care, to improve that one talent to its greatest height. That when the time came, that mankind were to be rewarded for their labours by the great Judge of quick and dead, you might be received with a "Well done, good and faithful servant, enter thou into the joy of thy Lord" (Matt. xxv. 21).

But as God has given you five talents, as He has placed you above the necessities of life, as He has left you in the hands of yourself, in the happy liberty of choosing the most exalted ways of virtue; as He has enriched you with many gifts of fortune, and left you nothing to do, but to make the best use of variety of blessings, to make the most of a short life, to study your own perfection, the honour of God, and the good of your neighbour; so it is now your duty to imitate the greatest servants of God, to inquire how the most eminent saints have lived, to study all the arts and methods of perfection, and to set no bounds to your love and gratitude to the CHAP. V bountiful author of so many blessings.

It is now your duty to turn your five talents into five more, and to consider how your time, and leisure, and health, and fortune, may be made so many happy means of purifying your own soul, improving your fellow-creatures in the ways of virtue, and of carrying you at last to the greatest heights of eternal glory.

As you have no mistress to serve, so let your own soul be the object of your daily care and attendance. Be sorry for its impurities, its spots and imperfections, and study all the holy arts of restoring it to its natural and primitive purity.

Delight in its service, and beg of God to adorn it with every grace and perfection.

Nourish it with good works, give it peace in solitude, get it strength in prayer, make it wise with reading, enlighten it by meditation, make it tender with love, sweeten it with humility, humble it with penance,[2] enliven it with Psalms and Hymns, and comfort it with frequent reflections upon future glory. Keep it in the presence of God, and teach it to imitate those guardian angels, which though they attend on human affairs, and the lowest of mankind, yet "always behold the face of our Father which is in heaven" (Matt. xviii. 10).

This, Serena, is your profession. For as sure as God is one God, so sure it is, that He has but one command to all mankind, whether they be bond or free, rich or poor; and that is, to act up to the excellency of that nature which He has given them, to live by reason, to walk in the light of religion, to use everything as wisdom directs, to glorify God in all His gifts, and dedicate every condition of life to His service.

This is the one common command of God to all mankind. If you have an employment, you are to be thus reasonable, and pious, and holy, in the exercise of it; if you have time and a fortune in your own power, you are obliged to be thus reasonable, and holy, and pious, in the use of all your time, and all your fortune.

---

[2] 'Humble it with penance.' This expression would offend the popular Protestantism of the eighteenth century; but in this, as in many other respects, Law was not a representative man. Though he had not the faintest inclination to join the Church of Rome, he admired her devotional writers, and regretted the loss of some rites which were then popularly, though erroneously, regarded as distinctively Roman. Among these penance would be one, and by 'humbling the soul with penance' he meant by some distinct act of penance, not by penitence generally.

CHAP. V.    The right religious use of everything and every talent is the indispensable duty of every being that is capable of knowing right and wrong.

For the reason why we are to do anything as unto God, and with regard to our duty and relation to Him, is the same reason why we are to do everything as unto God, and with regard to our duty and relation to Him.

That which is a reason for our being wise and holy in the discharge of all our business is the same reason for our being wise and holy in the use of all our money.

As we have always the same natures, and are everywhere the servants of the same God, as every place is equally full of His presence, and everything is equally His gift, so we must always act according to the reason of our nature; we must do everything as the servants of God; we must live in every place as in His presence; we must use everything as that ought to be used which belongs to God.

Either this piety and wisdom and devotion is to go through every way of life, and to extend to the use of everything, or it is to go through no part of life.

If we might forget ourselves, or forget God, if we might disregard our reason, and live by humour and fancy, in anything, or at any time, or in any place, it would be as lawful to do the same in everything, at every time, and every place.

If therefore some people fancy, that they must be grave and solemn at church, but may be silly and frantic at home; that they must live by some rule on the Sunday, but may spend other days by chance; that they must have some times of prayer, but may waste the rest of their time as they please; that they must give some money in charity, but may squander away the rest as they have a mind; such people have not enough considered the nature of religion, or the true reasons of piety. For he that upon principles of reason can tell, why it is good to be wise and heavenly-minded at church, can tell that it is always desirable to have the same tempers in all other places. He that truly knows why he should spend any time well, knows that it is never allowable to throw any time away. He that rightly understands the reasonableness and excellency of charity will know that it can never be excusable to waste any of our money in pride and folly, or in any needless expenses.

For every argument that shows the wisdom and excellency

of charity, proves the wisdom of spending all our fortune well. CHAP. V.
Every argument that proves the wisdom and reasonableness of
having times of prayer, shows the wisdom and reasonableness of
losing none of our time.

If anyone could show, that we need not always act as in
the divine presence, that we need not consider and use everything as the gift of God, that we need not always live by reason,
and make religion the rule of all our actions, the same arguments would show, that we need never act as in the presence
of God, nor make religion and reason the measure of any of our
actions.   If therefore we are to live unto God at any time, or in
any place, we are to live unto Him at all times, and in all places.
If we are to use anything as the gift of God, we are to use
everything as His gift.   If we are to do anything by strict rules
of reason and piety, we are to do everything in the same
manner.   Because reason, and wisdom, and piety are as much
the best things at all times, and in all places, as they are
the best things at any time, or in any place.

If it is our glory and happiness to have a rational nature,
that is endued with wisdom and reason, that is capable of
imitating the Divine nature, then it must be our glory and
happiness to improve our reason and wisdom, to act up to the
excellency of our rational nature, and to imitate God in all our
actions to the utmost of our power.   They therefore who con-
fine religion to times and places, and some little rules of retirement, who think that it is being too strict and rigid to
introduce religion into common life, and make it give laws to all
their actions and ways of living, they who think thus, not only
mistake, but they mistake the whole nature of religion.   For
surely they mistake the whole nature of religion who can think
any part of their life is made more easy for being free from
it.   They may well be said to mistake the whole nature of
wisdom, who do not think it desirable to be always wise.   He
has not learnt the nature of piety, who thinks it too much to
be pious in all his actions.   He does not sufficiently understand
what reason is, who does not earnestly desire to live in everything according to it.

If we had a religion that consisted in absurd superstitions,
that had no regard to the perfection of our nature, people
might well be glad to have some part of their life excused from
it.   But as the religion of the Gospel is only the refinement

and exaltation of our best faculties, as it only requires a life of the highest reason, as it only requires us to use this world as in reason it ought to be used, to live in such tempers as are the glory of intelligent beings, to walk in such wisdom as exalts our nature, and to practise such piety as will raise us to God; who can think it grievous to live always in the spirit of such a religion, to have every part of his life full of it, but he that would think it much more grievous to be as the angels of God in heaven?

Further, as God is one and the same being, always acting like Himself, and suitably to His own nature, so it is the duty of every being that He has created, to live according to the nature that He has given it, and always to act like itself.

It is therefore an immutable law of God, that all rational beings should act reasonably in all their actions; not at this time, or in that place, or upon this occasion, or in the use of some particular thing, but at all times, in all places, on all occasions, and in the use of all things. This is a law that is as unchangeable as God, and can no more cease to be than God can cease to be a God of wisdom and order.

When therefore any being that is endued with reason, does an unreasonable thing at any time, or in any place, or in the use of anything, it sins against the great law of its nature, abuses itself, and sins against God, the author of that nature.

They therefore who plead for indulgences and vanities, for any foolish fashions, customs, and humours of the world, for the misuse of our time, or money, plead for a rebellion against our nature, for a rebellion against God, Who has given us reason for no other end, than to make it the rule and measure of all our ways of life.

When therefore you are guilty of any folly or extravagance, or indulge any vain temper, do not consider it as a small matter, because it may seem so, if compared to some other sins; but consider it, as it is acting contrary to your nature, and then you will see that there is nothing small that is unreasonable. Because all unreasonable ways are contrary to the nature of all rational beings, whether men, or angels. Neither of which can be any longer agreeable to God, than so far as they act according to the reason and excellence of their nature.

The infirmities of human life make such food and raiment necessary for us as angels do not want; but then it is no more allowable for us to turn these necessities into follies, and indulge ourselves in the luxury of food, or the vanities of dress, CHAP. V. than it is allowable for angels to act below the dignity of their proper state. For a reasonable life and a wise use of our proper condition is as much the duty of all men, as it is the duty of all angels and intelligent beings. These are not speculative flights, or imaginary notions, but are plain and undeniable laws, that are founded in the nature of rational beings, who as such are obliged to live by reason, and glorify God by a continual right use of their several talents and faculties. So that though men are not angels, yet they may know for what ends, and by what rules, men are to live and act, by considering the state and perfection of angels. Our blessed Saviour has plainly turned our thoughts this way by making this petition a constant part of all our prayers, "Thy will be done on earth, as it is in heaven." A plain proof, that the obedience of men is to imitate the obedience of angels, and that rational beings on earth are to live unto God as rational beings in Heaven live unto Him.

When therefore you would represent to your mind how Christians ought to live unto God, and in what degrees of wisdom and holiness they ought to use the things of this life, you must not look at the world, but you must look up to God and the society of angels, and think what wisdom and holiness is fit to prepare you for such a state of glory. You must look to all the highest precepts of the Gospel, you must examine yourself by the spirit of Christ, you must think how the wisest men in the world have lived, you must think how departed souls would live, if they were again to act the short part of human life; you must think what degrees of wisdom and holiness you will wish for, when you are leaving the world.

Now all this is not over-straining the matter, or proposing to ourselves any needless perfection. It is but barely complying with the Apostle's advice, where he says, "Finally, brethren, whatsoever things are true, whatsoever things are just, whatsoever things are pure, whatsoever things are of good report; if there be any virtue, and if there be any praise, think on these things" (Phil. iv. 8). For no one can come near the doctrine of this passage but he that proposes to himself to do everything in this life as the servant of God, to live by reason in everything that he does, and to make the wisdom and holiness of the Gospel the rule and measure of his desiring, and using, every gift of God.

# CHAPTER VI.

*Containing the great obligations, and the advantages of making a wise and religious use of our estates and fortunes.*

As the holiness of Christianity consecrates all states and employments of life unto God, as it requires us to aspire after an universal obedience, doing and using everything as the servants of God, so are we more especially obliged to observe this religious exactness in the use of our estates and fortunes.[1]

The reason of this would appear very plain, if we were only to consider, that our estates are as much the gift of God as our eyes, or our hands, and are no more to be buried, or thrown away at pleasure than we are to put out our eyes, or throw away our limbs as we please.

But besides this consideration, there are several other great and important reasons, why we should be religiously exact in the use of our estates.

First, Because the manner of using our money, or spending our estate, enters so far into the business of every day, and makes so great a part of our common life, that our common life must be much of the same nature as our common way of spending our estate. If reason and religion govern us in this, then reason and religion hath got great hold of us; but if hum-

---

[1] The rules which Law lays down in this and the three following chapters on the Christian use of money he thoroughly carried out at King's Cliffe ; devoting the greater part of his own fortune, and persuading Mrs. Hutcheson and Miss Hester Gibbon, who placed themselves under his spiritual direction, to devote the greater part of theirs, to works of piety and charity. The result was not encouraging. King's Cliffe became a resort of beggars and impostors, who flocked thither to become re- cipients of the indiscriminate bounty which flowed in a daily stream from the Hall yard. The more respectable inhabitants, not unnaturally, protested against a system which caused the place to be invaded by such unwelcome intruders, and tended in many ways to pauperize and demoralize it. Mr. Piemont, the rector, preached constantly, it would appear, against it ; and the pious, but not very judicious, benefactors threatened to withdraw, but did not carry out their threat.

our, pride, and fancy, are the measures of our spending our estate, then humour, pride, and fancy, will have the direction of the greatest part of our life.

Secondly, Another great reason for devoting all our estate to right uses is this, because it is capable of being used to the most excellent purposes, and is so great a means of doing good. If we waste it, we do not waste a trifle that signifies little, but we waste that which might be made as eyes to the blind, as a husband to the widow, as a father to the orphan: we waste that which not only enables us to minister worldly comforts to those that are in distress, but that which might purchase for ourselves everlasting treasures in heaven. So that if we part with our money in foolish ways, we part with a great power of comforting our fellow-creatures, and of making ourselves for ever blessed.

If there be nothing so glorious as doing good, if there is nothing that makes us so like to God, then nothing can be so glorious in the use of our money as to use it all in works of love and goodness, making ourselves friends, and fathers, and benefactors, to all our fellow-creatures, imitating the divine love, and turning all our power into acts of generosity, care, and kindness, to such as are in need of it.

If a man had eyes, and hands, and feet, that he could give to those that wanted them; if he should either lock them up in a chest, or please himself with some needless, or ridiculous use of them, instead of giving them to his brethren that were blind and lame, should we not justly reckon him an inhuman wretch? If he should rather choose to amuse himself with furnishing his house with those things than to entitle himself to an eternal reward by giving them to those that wanted eyes and hands, might we not justly reckon him mad?

Now money has very much the nature of eyes and feet; if we either lock it up in chests, or waste it in needless and ridiculous expenses upon ourselves, whilst the poor and the distressed want it for their necessary uses: if we consume it in the ridiculous ornaments of apparel, whilst others are starving in nakedness, we are not far from the cruelty of him, that chooses rather to adorn his house with the hands and eyes than to give them to those that want them. If we choose to indulge ourselves in such expensive enjoyments as have no real use in them, such as satisfy no real want, rather than to entitle ourselves to an eternal reward, by disposing of our money well, we are guilty of his madness, that rather chooses to lock up eyes and hands than to make himself for ever blessed by giving them to those that want them.

For after we have satisfied our own sober and reasonable wants, all the rest of our money is but like spare eyes, or hands; it is something that we cannot keep to ourselves without being foolish in the use of it, something that can only be used well by giving it to those that want it.

Thirdly, If we waste our money, we are not only guilty of wasting a talent which God has given us, we are not only guilty of making that useless which is so powerful a means of doing good, but we do ourselves this further harm, that we turn this useful talent into a powerful means of corrupting ourselves; because so far as it is spent wrong, so far it is spent in the support of some wrong temper, in gratifying some vain and unreasonable desires, in conforming to those fashions and pride of the world, which, as Christians and reasonable men, we are obliged to renounce.

As wit and fine parts cannot be trifled away, and only lost, but will lead those that have them into greater follies, if they are not strictly devoted to piety: so money, if it is not used strictly according to reason and religion, cannot only be trifled away, but it will betray people into greater follies, and make them live a more silly and extravagant life than they could have done without it. If, therefore, you do not spend your money in doing good to others, you must spend it to the hurt of yourself. You will act like a man that should refuse to give that as a cordial to a sick friend, though he could not drink it himself without inflaming his blood. For this is the case of superfluous money; if you give it to those that want it, it is a cordial; if you spend it upon yourself in something that you do not want, it only inflames and disorders your mind, and makes you worse than you would be without it.

Consider again the fore-mentioned comparison; if the man that would not make a right use of spare eyes and hands, should, by continually trying to use them himself, spoil his own eyes and hands, we might justly accuse him of still greater madness.

Now this is truly the case of riches spent upon ourselves in vain and needless expenses; in trying to use them where they have no real use, nor we any real want, we only use them to CHAP. VI. our great hurt, in creating unreasonable desires, in nourishing ill tempers, in indulging our passions, and supporting a worldly, vain turn of mind.  For high eating and drinking, fine clothes, and fine houses, state, and equipage, gay pleasures, and diversions, do all of them naturally hurt and disorder our hearts; they are the food and nourishment of all the folly and weakness of our nature, and are certain means to make us vain and worldly in our tempers.  They are all of them the support of something that ought not to be supported; they are contrary to that sobriety and piety of heart which relishes divine things; they are like so many weights upon our minds that make us less able and less inclined to raise up our thoughts and affections to the things that are above.

So that money thus spent is not merely wasted, or lost, but it is spent to bad purposes, and miserable effects, to the corruption and disorder of our hearts, and to the making us less able to live up to the sublime doctrines of the Gospel.  It is but like keeping money from the poor to buy poison for ourselves.

For so much as is spent in the vanity of dress may be reckoned so much laid out to fix vanity in our minds.  So much as is laid out for idleness and indulgence may be reckoned so much given to render our hearts dull and sensual.  So much as is spent in state and equipage may be reckoned so much spent to dazzle your own eyes, and render you the idol of your own imagination.  And so in everything, when you go from reasonable wants, you only support some unreasonable temper, some turn of mind, which every good Christian is called upon to renounce.

So that on all accounts, whether we consider our fortune as a talent, and trust from God, or the great good that it enables us to do, or the great harm that it does to ourselves, if idly spent; on all these great accounts it appears, that it is absolutely necessary to make reason and religion the strict rule of using all our fortune.

Every exhortation in Scripture to be wise and reasonable, satisfying only such wants as God would have satisfied; every exhortation to be spiritual and heavenly, pressing after a glorious change of our nature; every exhortation to love our neighbour as ourselves, to love all mankind as God has loved them, is a command to be strictly religious in the use of our money.  For

CHAP. VI. none of these tempers can be complied with, unless we be wise and reasonable, spiritual and heavenly, exercising a brotherly love, a godlike charity in the use of all our fortune. These tempers, and this use of our worldly goods, is so much the doctrine of all the New Testament, that you cannot read a chapter without being taught something of it. I shall only produce one remarkable passage of Scripture, which is sufficient to justify all that I have said concerning this religious use of our fortune.

"When the Son of man shall come in His glory, and all the holy angels with Him, then shall He sit upon the throne of His glory. And before Him shall be gathered all nations; and He shall separate them one from another, as a shepherd divideth the sheep from the goats; and He shall set the sheep on His right hand, but the goats on the left. Then shall the King say unto them on His right hand, Come, ye blessed of My Father, inherit the kingdom prepared for you from the foundation of the world. For I was an hungered, and ye gave Me meat: I was thirsty, and ye gave Me drink; I was a stranger, and ye took Me in; naked, and ye clothed Me; I was sick, and ye visited Me; I was in prison, and ye came unto Me. Then shall He say unto them on the left hand, Depart from Me, ye cursed, into everlasting fire, prepared for the devil and his angels; for I was an hungered, and ye gave Me no meat; I was thirsty, and ye gave Me no drink; I was a stranger, and ye took Me not in; naked, and ye clothed Me not; sick, and in prison, and ye visited Me not. These shall go away into everlasting punishment, but the righteous into life eternal."

I have quoted this passage at length, because, if one looks at the way of the world, one would hardly think that Christians had ever read this part of Scripture. For what is there in the lives of Christians that looks as if their salvation depended upon these good works? And yet the necessity of them is here asserted in the highest manner, and pressed upon us by a lively description of the glory and terrors of the day of judgment.

Some people, even of those who may be reckoned virtuous Christians, look upon this text only as a general recommendation of occasional works of charity; whereas it shows the necessity not only of occasional charities now and then, but the necessity of such an entire charitable life as is a continual exercise of all such works of charity as we are able to perform.

You own that you have no title to salvation if you have CHAP. VI. neglected these good works; because such persons as have neglected them are at the last day to be placed on the left hand, and banished with a "Depart, ye cursed." There is, therefore, no salvation but in the performance of these good works. Who is it, therefore, that may be said to have performed these good works? Is it he that has sometimes assisted a prisoner, or relieved the poor or sick? This would be as absurd as to say that he had performed the duties of devotion who had sometime said his prayers. Is it, therefore, he that has several times done these works of charity? This can no more be said than he can be said to be the truly just man who had done acts of justice several times. What is the rule, therefore, or measure of performing these good works? How shall a man trust that he performs them as he ought?

Now the rule is very plain and easy, and such as is common to every other virtue or good temper as well as to charity. Who is the humble, or meek, or devout, or just, or faithful man? Is it he that has several times done acts of humility meekness, devotion, justice, or fidelity? No; but it is he that lives in the habitual exercise of these virtues. In like manner, he only can be said to have performed these works of charity who lives in the habitual exercise of them to the utmost of his power. He only has performed the duty of divine love who loves God with all his heart, and with all his mind, and with all his strength. And he only has performed the duty of these good works who has done them with all his heart, and with all his mind, and with all his strength; for there is no other measure of our doing good than our power of doing it.

The Apostle St. Peter puts this question to our blessed Saviour, "Lord, how oft shall my brother sin against me, and I forgive him? till seven times? Jesus saith unto him, I say not unto thee, Until seven times, but, Until seventy times seven" (St. Matt. xviii. 21, 22). Not as if after this number of offences a man might cease to forgive; but the expression of seventy times seven is to show us that we are not to bind our forgiveness by any number of offences, but are to continue forgiving the most repeated offences against us. Thus, our Saviour saith in another place, "If he trespass against thee seven times in a day, and seven times in a day turn again to thee, saying, I repent, thou shalt forgive him" (St. Luke xvii. 4). If, therefore, a man ceases to forgive his brother because he has forgiven him often already; if he excuses himself from forgiving this man because he has forgiven several others; such a one breaks this law of Christ concerning the forgiving one's brother.

Now the rule of forgiving is also the rule of giving; you are not to give or do good to seven, but to seventy times seven; you are not to cease from giving because you have given often to the same person or to other persons, but must look upon yourself as much obliged to continue relieving those that continue in want as you were obliged to relieve them once or twice. Had it not been in your power you had been excused from relieving any person once; but if it is in your power to relieve people often, it is as much your duty to do it often as it is the duty of others to do it but seldom, because they are but seldom able. He that is not ready to forgive every brother as often as he wants to be forgiven does not forgive like a disciple of Christ; and he that is not ready to give to every brother that wants to have something given him does not give like a disciple of Christ; for it is as necessary to give to seventy times seven, to live in the continual exercise of all good works to the utmost of our power, as it is necessary to forgive until seventy times seven, and live in the habitual exercise of this forgiving temper towards all that want it.

And the reason of all this is very plain, because there is the same goodness, the same excellency, and the same necessity of being thus charitable at one time as at another. It is as much the best use of our money to be always doing good with it as it is the best use of it at any particular time; so that that which is a reason for a charitable action is as good a reason for a charitable life. That which is a reason for forgiving one offence is the same reason for forgiving all offences. For such charity has nothing to recommend it to-day but what will be the same recommendation of it to-morrow; and you cannot neglect it at one time without being guilty of the same sin as if you neglected it at another time.

As sure, therefore, as these works of charity are necessary to salvation, so sure is it that we are to do them to the utmost of our power; not to-day or to-morrow, but through the whole course of our life. If, therefore, it be our duty at any time to deny ourselves any needless expenses, to be moderate and frugal, that we may have to give to those that want, it is as much our duty to do so at all times, that we may be further CHAP. VI. able to do more good. For if it is at any time a sin to prefer needless vain expense to works of charity, it is so at all times; because charity as much excels all needless and vain expenses at one time as at another. So that if it is ever necessary to our salvation to take care of these works of charity, and to see that we make ourselves in some degree capable of doing them, it is as necessary to our salvation to take care to make ourselves as capable as we can be of performing them in all the parts of our life.

Either, therefore, you must so far renounce your Christianity as to say, that you need never perform any of these good works; or you must own that you are to perform them all your life in as high a degree as you are able. There is no middle way to be taken, any more than there is a middle way betwixt pride and humility, or temperance and intemperance. If you do not strive to fulfil all charitable works, if you neglect any of them that are in your power, and deny assistance to those that want what you can give, let it be when it will or where it will, you number yourself amongst those that want Christian charity; because it is as much your duty to do good with all that you have, and to live in the continual exercise of good works, as it is your duty to be temperate in all that you eat and drink.

Hence also appears the necessity of renouncing all those foolish and unreasonable expenses which the pride and folly of mankind have made so common and fashionable in the world. For if it is necessary to do good works as far as you are able, it must be as necessary to renounce those needless ways of spending money, which render you unable to do works of charity.

You must, therefore, no more conform to these ways of the world than you must conform to the vices of the world; you must no more spend with those that idly waste their money as their own humour leads them than you must drink with the drunken, or indulge yourself with the epicure; because a course of such expenses is no more consistent with a life of charity than excess in drinking is consistent with a life of sobriety. When, therefore, any one tells you of the lawfulness of expensive apparel, or the innocency of pleasing yourself with costly satisfactions, only imagine that the same person was to tell you that you need not do works of charity, that Christ does not require you to do good unto your poor brethren as unto Him, and then you will see the wickedness of such advice; for to tell you that you may live in such expenses as make it impossible for you to live in the exercise of good works, is the same thing as telling you that you need not have any care about such good works themselves.

# CHAPTER VII.[1]

*How the imprudent use of an estate corrupts all the tempers of the
mind, and fills the heart with poor and ridiculous passions
through the whole course of life; represented in the character of
Flavia.*

IT has already been observed, that a prudent and religious care is
to be used in the manner of spending our money or estate,
because the manner of spending our estates makes so great a part
of our common life, and is so much the business of every day,
that, according as we are wise or imprudent in this respect, the
whole course of our lives will be rendered either very wise or very
full of folly.

Persons that are well affected to religion, that receive instructions

[1] In this and the following chapter
we have the famous portraits of
Flavia and Miranda, immortalized
by Gibbon, the historian, who says
of them ("Memoir of My Life and
Writings," *Misc. Works*, edited by
Lord Sheffield, i. 15): "Under the
names of Flavia and Miranda, he
(Law) has admirably described my
two aunts, the heathen and the
Christian sister"; and in his various
autobiographies, lately published by
Mr. John Murray, he repeats the
remark in various forms. It is a
bold thing to measure swords with
the great historian, especially in
matters concerning his own family;
but really we must take account of
facts and dates, and the known characters of all concerned, before accepting
too literally Gibbon's interpretation.
Now the portraits of Flavia and
Miranda were drawn not later (probably earlier) than 1727, at which time
Law had only recently become an
inmate of Mr. Gibbon's family. Gibbon, the historian, was not born.
It was singularly unlike Law to betray
the confidences of private life, and
especially the private life of a family
to which he was much indebted.
There is nothing in the sketches
themselves to identify them with any
individual whatever. Flavia and
Miranda are simply typical instances
of the self-indulgent worldling and
the self-denying Christian respectively.
As far as one can ascertain, the two
Misses Gibbon, Catherine and Hester,
were not in a position, when the *Serious
Call* was written, to exercise the virtues attributed to Miranda, or to
neglect them as Flavia did. That
Gibbon may in after years have observed the resemblance of his aunt
Hester to Miranda is highly probable;
but might not the reason be, not that
Miss Gibbon had unconsciously sat for
the portrait of Miranda, but that she had
herself consciously taken Miranda as
the model for her own conduct, which
she would naturally do as the devoted
disciple of Mr. Law? I am glad to see
that Mr. Leslie Stephen takes the same
view (see art. on 'Law, William,' in
*The Dictionary of National Biography*).

59

CHAP. VII. of piety with pleasure and satisfaction, often wonder how it comes to pass that they make no greater progress in that religion which they so much admire.

Now the reason of it is this: it is because religion lives only in their head, but something else has possession of their hearts; and therefore they continue from year to year mere admirers and praisers of piety, without ever coming up to the reality and perfection of its precepts.

If it be asked why religion does not get possession of their hearts, the reason is this: It is not because they live in gross sins or debaucheries, for their regard to religion preserves them from such disorders.

But it is because their hearts are constantly employed, perverted, and kept in a wrong state, by the indiscreet use of such things as are lawful to be used.

The use and enjoyment of their estates is lawful, and, therefore, it never comes into their heads to imagine any great danger from that quarter. They never reflect that there is a vain and imprudent use of their estates, which, though it does not destroy like gross sins, yet so disorders the heart, and supports it in such sensuality and dulness, such pride and vanity, as makes it incapable of receiving the life and spirit of piety.

For our souls may receive an infinite hurt, and be rendered incapable of all virtues, merely by the use of innocent and lawful things.

What is more innocent than rest and retirement? And yet what more dangerous than sloth and idleness? What is more lawful than eating and drinking? And yet what more destructive of all virtue, what more fruitful of all vice, than sensuality and indulgence?

How lawful and praise-worthy is the care of a family! And yet how certainly are many people rendered incapable of all virtue by a worldly and solicitous temper?

Now it is for want of religious exactness in the use of these innocent and lawful things that religion cannot get possession of our hearts. And it is in the right and prudent management of ourselves as to these things that all the arts of holy living chiefly consist.

Gross sins are plainly seen, and easily avoided by persons that profess religion. But the indiscreet and dangerous use of innocent and lawful things, as it does not shock and offend our consciences so it is difficult to make people at all sensible of CHAP. VII. the danger of it.

A gentleman that expends all his estate in sports, and a woman that lays out all her fortune upon herself, can hardly be persuaded that the spirit of religion cannot subsist in such a way of life.

These persons, as has been observed, may live free from debaucheries; they may be friends of religion so far as to praise and speak well of it, and admire it in their imaginations; but it cannot govern their hearts, and be the spirit of their actions, till they change their way of life, and let religion give laws to the use and spending of their estates.

For a woman that loves dress, that thinks no expense too great to bestow upon the adorning of her person, cannot stop there.   For that temper draws a thousand other follies along with it, and will render the whole course of her life, her business, her conversation, her hopes, her fears, her taste, her pleasures, and diversions, all suitable to it.

Flavia and Miranda are two maiden sisters that have each of them two hundred pounds a year.   They buried their parents twenty years ago, and have since that time spent their estate as they pleased.[2]

FLAVIA has been the wonder of all her friends for her excellent management in making so surprising a figure in so moderate a fortune.   Several ladies that have twice her fortune are not able to be always so genteel, and so constant at all places of pleasure and expense.   She has every thing that is in the fashion, and is in every place where there is any diversion.   Flavia is very orthodox, she talks warmly against heretics and schismatics, is generally at Church, and often at the sacrament.   She once commended a sermon that was against the pride and vanity of dress, and thought it was very just against Lucinda, whom she takes to be a great deal finer than she need to be.   If any one asks Flavia to do something in charity, if she likes the person who makes the proposal, or happens to be in a right temper, she will toss him half-a-crown or a crown, and tell him, if he knew what a long milliner's bill she had just received, he would think it a great deal for her to give.   A quarter of a year

---

[2] This does not at all correspond with the circumstances of the Misses Gibbon.   They had not ' buried their parents twenty years ago.'   When the *Serious Call* was written, old Mr. Gibbon was living and very vigorous; he lived on for ten years longer.

after this she hears a sermon upon the necessity of charity; she thinks the man preaches well, that it is a very proper subject, that people want much to be put in mind of it; but she applies nothing to herself, because she remembers that she gave a crown some time ago when she could so ill spare it.

As for poor people themselves, she will admit of no complaints from them; she is very positive they are all cheats and liars, and will say anything to get relief, and, therefore, it must be a sin to encourage them in their evil ways.

You would think Flavia had the tenderest conscience in the world, if you were to see how scrupulous and apprehensive she is of the guilt and danger of giving amiss.

She buys all books of wit and humour, and has made an expensive collection of all our English poets: for, she says, one cannot have a true taste of any of them without being very conversant with them all.

She will sometimes read a book of piety, if it is a short one, if it is much commended for style and language, and she can tell where to borrow it.

Flavia is very idle, and yet very fond of fine work; this makes her often sit working in bed until noon, and be told many a long story before she is up; so that I need not tell you that her morning devotions are not always rightly performed.

Flavia would be a miracle of piety if she were but half so careful of her soul as she is of her body. The rising of a pimple in her face, the sting of a gnat, will make her keep her room two or three days, and she thinks they are very rash people that do not take care of things in time. This makes her so over-careful of her health, that she never thinks she is well enough, and so over-indulgent that she never can be really well. So that it costs her a great deal in sleeping-draughts and waking-draughts, in spirits for the head, in drops for the nerves, in cordials for the stomach, and in saffron for her tea.

If you visit Flavia on the Sunday, you will always meet good company, you will know what is doing in the world, you will hear the last lampoon, be told who wrote it, and who is meant by every name that is in it. You will hear what plays were acted that week, which is the finest song in the opera, who was intolerable at the last assembly, and what games are most in fashion. Flavia thinks they are atheists that play at cards on the Sunday, but she will tell you the nicety of all the games, what cards she held, how she played them, and the history of all that happened at CHAP. VII. play, as soon as she comes from Church. If you would know who is rude and ill-natured, who is vain and foppish, who lives too high, and who is in debt; if you would know what is the quarrel at a certain house, or who and who are in love; if you would know how late Belinda comes home at night, what clothes she has bought, how she loves compliments, and what a long story she told at such a place; if you would know how cross Lucius is to his wife, what ill-natured things he says to her when nobody hears him; if you would know how they hate one another in their hearts, though they appear so kind in public; you must visit Flavia on the Sunday. But still she has so great a regard for the holiness of the Sunday that she has turned a poor old widow out of her house, as a profane wretch, for having been found once mending her clothes on the Sunday night.

Thus lives Flavia; and if she lives ten years longer, she will have spent about fifteen hundred and sixty Sundays after this manner. She will have worn about two hundred different suits of clothes. Out of this thirty years of her life, fifteen of them will have been disposed of in bed; and of the remaining fifteen, about fourteen of them will have been consumed in eating, drinking, dressing, visiting, conversation, reading and hearing plays and romances, at operas, assemblies, balls, and diversions. For you may reckon all the time that she is up thus spent, except about an hour and a half that is disposed of at Church, most Sundays in the year. With great management, and under mighty rules of economy, she will have spent sixty hundred pounds upon herself, bating only some shillings, crowns, or half-crowns, that have gone from her in accidental charities.

I shall not take upon me to say, that it is impossible for Flavia to be saved; but thus much must be said, that she has no grounds from Scripture to think she is in the way of salvation. For her whole life is in direct opposition to all those tempers and practices which the Gospel has made necessary to salvation.

If you were to hear her say that she had lived all her life like Anna the prophetess, "who departed not from the temple, but served God with fastings and prayers, night and day," you would look upon her as very extravagant; and yet this would be no greater an extravagance than for her to say, that she had been "striving to enter in at the strait gate," or making any one doctrine of the Gospel a rule of her life.

She may as well say that she lived with our Saviour when He was upon earth as that she has lived in imitation of Him, or made it any part of her care to live in such tempers as He required of all those that would be His disciples. She may as truly say that she has every day washed the saints' feet as that she has lived in Christian humility and poverty of spirit; and as reasonably think that she has taught a charity school[3] as that she has lived in works of charity. She has as much reason to think that she has been a sentinel in an army as that she has lived in watching and self-denial. And it may as fairly be said that she lived by the labour of her hands as that she had "given all diligence to make her calling and election sure."

And here it is to be well observed that the poor, vain turn of mind, the irreligion, the folly and vanity of this whole life of Flavia, is all owing to the manner of using her estate. It is this that has formed her spirit, that has given life to every idle temper, that has supported every trifling passion, and kept her from all thoughts of a prudent, useful, and devout life.

When her parents died she had no thought about her two hundred pounds a year, but that she had so much money to do what she would with, to spend upon herself, and purchase the pleasures and gratifications of all her passions.

And it is this setting out, this false judgment, and indiscreet use of her fortune, that has filled her whole life with the same indiscretion, and kept her from thinking of what is right, and wise, and pious, in everything else.

If you have seen her delighted in plays and romances, in scandal and backbiting, easily flattered, and soon affronted; if you have seen her devoted to pleasures and diversions, a slave to every passion in its turn, nice in everything that concerned her body and dress, careless of everything that might benefit her soul, always wanting some new entertainment, and ready for every happy invention in show or dress, it was because she had purchased all these tempers with the yearly revenue of her fortune.

She might have been humble, serious, devout, a lover of good books, an admirer of prayer and retirement, careful of her time, diligent in good works, full of charity and the love of God, but

[3] Charity schools, founded during the Church Revival at the close of the seventeenth and the early years of the eighteenth centuries, were one of the few organizations which did not droop, at any rate to the same extent as others did, in the dead times of the first two Georges.

that the imprudent use of her estate forced all the contrary tem- pers upon her.

And it was no wonder that she should turn her time, her mind, her health, her strength to the same uses that she turned her fortune. It is owing to her being wrong in so great an article of life that you can see nothing wise, or reasonable, or pious in any other part of it.

Now though the irregular trifling spirit of this character belongs, I hope, but to few people, yet many may here learn some instruction from it, and perhaps see something of their own spirit in it.

For as Flavia seems to be undone by the unreasonable use of her fortune, so the lowness of most people's virtue, the imperfections of their piety, and the disorders of their passions, is generally owing to their imprudent use and enjoyment of lawful and innocent things.

More people are kept from a true sense and state of religion by a regular kind of sensuality and indulgence than by gross drunkenness. More men live regardless of the great duties of piety through too great a concern for worldly goods than through direct injustice.

This man would perhaps be devout if he were not so great a virtuoso. Another is deaf to all the motives to piety by indulging an idle, slothful temper.

Could you cure this man of his great curiosity and inquisitive temper, or that of his false satisfaction and thirst after learning, you need do no more to make them both become men of great piety.

If this woman would make fewer visits, or that not be always talking, they would neither of them find it half so hard to be affected with religion.

For all these things are only little when they are compared to great sins: and though they are little in that respect yet they are great as they are impediments and hindrances of a pious spirit.

For as consideration is the only eye of the soul, as the truths of religion can be seen by nothing else, so whatever raises a levity of mind, a trifling spirit, renders the soul incapable of seeing, apprehending, and relishing the doctrines of piety.

Would we, therefore, make a real progress in religion, we must not only abhor gross and notorious sins, but we must regulate the innocent and lawful parts of our behaviour, and put the most common and allowed actions of life under the rules of discretion and piety.

# CHAPTER VIII.

*How the wise and pious use of an estate naturally carrieth us to great perfection in all the virtues of the Christian life; represented in the character of Miranda.*

ANY one pious regularity of any one part of our life is of great advantage, not only on its own account, but as it uses us to live by rule, and think of the government of ourselves.

A man of business that has brought one part of his affairs under certain rules is in a fair way to take the same care of the rest.

So he that has brought any one part of his life under the rules of religion may thence be taught to extend the same order and regularity into other parts of his life.

If any one is so wise as to think his time too precious to be disposed of by chance, and left to be devoured by anything that happens in his way; if he lays himself under a necessity of observing how every day goes through his hands, and obliges himself to a certain order of time in his business, his retirements, and devotions; it is hardly to be imagined how soon such a conduct would reform, improve, and perfect the whole course of his life.

He that once thus knows the value, and reaps the advantage, of a well-ordered time, will not be long a stranger to the value of anything else that is of any real concern to him.

A rule that relates even to the smallest part of our life is of great benefit to us, merely as it is a rule.

For, as the proverb saith, " He that has begun well, has half done," so he that has begun to live by rule has gone a great way towards the perfection of his life.

By rule must here be constantly understood, a religious rule, observed upon a principle of duty to God.

For if a man should oblige himself to be moderate in his meals, only in regard to his stomach; or abstain from drinking, only to CH. VIII. avoid the headache; or be moderate in his sleep, through fear of a lethargy; he might be exact in these rules without being at all the better man for them.

But when he is moderate and regular in any of these things out of a sense of Christian sobriety and self-denial, that he may offer unto God a more reasonable and holy life, then it is that the smallest rule of this kind is naturally the beginning of great piety.

For the smallest rule in these matters is of great benefit, as it teaches us some part of the government of ourselves, as it keeps up a tenderness of mind, as it presents God often to our thoughts, and brings a sense of religion into the ordinary actions of our common life.

If a man whenever he was in company where any one swore, talked lewdly, or spoke evil of his neighbour, should make it a rule to himself either gently to reprove him, or if that was not proper, then to leave the company as decently as he could; he would find that this little rule, like a little leaven hid in a great quantity of meal, would spread and extend itself through the whole form of his life.

If another should oblige himself to abstain on the Lord's Day from many innocent and lawful things, as travelling, visiting, common conversation, and discoursing upon worldly matters, as trade, news, and the like; if he should devote the day, besides the public worship, to greater retirement, reading, devotion, instruction, and works of charity; though it may seem but a small thing, or a needless nicety, to require a man to abstain from such things as may be done without sin, yet whoever would try the benefit of so little a rule would perhaps thereby find such a change made in his spirit, and such a taste of piety raised in his mind, as he was an entire stranger to before.

It would be easy to show, in many other instances, how little and small matters are the first steps and natural beginnings of great perfection.

But the two things which of all others most want to be under a strict rule, and which are the greatest blessings both to ourselves and others, when they are rightly used, are our time and our money. These talents are continual means and opportunities of doing good.

He that is piously strict and exact in the wise management of either of these cannot be long ignorant of the right use of the

CH. VIII. other; and he that is happy in the religious care and disposal of them both is already ascended several steps upon the ladder of Christian perfection.

MIRANDA (the sister of Flavia) is a sober, reasonable Christian; as soon as she was mistress of her time and fortune, it was her first thought how she might best fulfil everything that God required of her in the use of them, and how she might make the best and happiest use of this short life. She depends upon the truth of what our blessed Lord hath said, That there is but one thing needful, and therefore makes her whole life but one continual labour after it. She has but one reason for doing or not doing, for liking or not liking, anything, and that is the will of God. She is not so weak as to pretend to add what is called the fine lady to the true Christian. Miranda thinks too well to be taken with the sound of such silly words; she has renounced the world to follow Christ in the exercise of humility, charity, devotion, abstinence, and heavenly affections; and that is Miranda's fine breeding.

Whilst she was under her mother, she was forced to be genteel, to live in ceremony, to sit up late at nights, to be in the folly of every fashion, and always visiting on Sundays; to go patched and loaded with a burden of finery to the holy sacrament; to be in every polite conversation; to hear profaneness at the playhouse, and wanton songs and love intrigues at the opera; to dance at public places that fops and rakes might admire the fineness of her shape, and the beauty of her motions. The remembrance of this way of life makes her exceedingly careful to atone for it by a contrary behaviour.

Miranda does not divide her duty between God, her neighbour, and herself; but she considers all as due to God, and so does everything in His name, and for His sake. This makes her consider her fortune as the gift of God, that is to be used as everything is that belongs to God, for the wise and reasonable ends of a Christian and holy life. Her fortune, therefore, is divided betwixt herself and several other poor people, and she has only her part of relief from it. She thinks it the same folly to indulge herself in needless vain expenses as to give to other people to spend in the same way. Therefore she will not give a poor man money to go see a puppet-show, neither will she allow herself any to spend in the same manner; thinking it very proper to be as wise herself as she expects poor men should be. For is it a folly and a crime in a poor man, says Miranda, to waste what is given him in foolish trifles, whilst he wants meat, drink, and clothes? And is it less folly, or a less crime, in me to spend that money in silly diversions, which might be so much better spent in imitation of the divine goodness, in works of kindness and charity towards my fellow-creatures, and fellow-Christians? If a poor man's own necessities are a reason why he should not waste any of his money idly, surely the necessities of the poor, the excellency of charity, which is received as done to Christ Himself, is a much greater reason why no one should ever waste any of his money. For if he does so, he does not only do like the poor man, only waste that which he wants himself, but he wastes that which is wanted for the most noble use, and which Christ Himself is ready to receive at his hands. And if we are angry at a poor man, and look upon him as a wretch, when he throws away that which should buy his own bread, how must we appear in the sight of God if we make a wanton idle use of that which should buy bread and clothes for the hungry and naked brethren, who are as near and dear to God as we are, and fellow-heirs of the same state of future glory? This is the spirit of Miranda, and thus she uses the gifts of God; she is only one of a certain number of poor people that are relieved out of her fortune, and she only differs from them in the blessedness of giving.

Excepting her victuals, she never spent ten pounds a year upon herself. If you were to see her you would wonder what poor body it was that was so surprisingly neat and clean. She has but one rule that she observes in her dress, to be always clean and in the cheapest things. Everything about her resembles the purity of her soul, and she is always clean without, because she is always pure within.

Every morning sees her early at her prayers; she rejoices in the beginning of every day, because it begins all her pious rules of holy living, and brings the fresh pleasure of repeating them. She seems to be as a guardian angel to those that dwell about her, with her watchings and prayers blessing the place where she dwells, and making intercession with God for those that are asleep.

Her devotions have had some intervals, and God has heard several of her private prayers, before the light is suffered to enter into her sister's room. Miranda does not know what it is to have a dull half-day; the return of her hours of prayer, and her religious

CH. VIII. exercises, come too often to let any considerable part of time lie heavy upon her hands.

When you see her at work, you see the same wisdom that governs all her other actions; she is either doing something that is necessary for herself, or necessary for others who want to be assisted. There is scarce a poor family in the neighbourhood but wears something or other that has had the labour of her hands. Her wise and pious mind neither wants the amusement, nor can bear with the folly of idle and impertinent work. She can admit of no such folly as this in the day, because she is to answer for all her actions at night. When there is no wisdom to be observed in the employment of her hands, when there is no useful or charitable work to be done, Miranda will work no more. At her table she lives strictly by this rule of holy Scripture, "Whether ye eat or drink, or whatsoever ye do, do all to the glory of God." This makes her begin and end every meal, as she begins and ends every day, with acts of devotion: she eats and drinks only for the sake of living, and with so regular an abstinence, that every meal is an exercise of self-denial, and she humbles her body every time that she is forced to feed it. If Miranda were to run a race for her life, she would submit to a diet that was proper for it. But as the race which is set before her is a race of holiness, purity, and heavenly affection, which she is to finish in a corrupt, disordered body of earthly passions, so her every-day diet has only this one end, to make her body fitter for this spiritual race. She does not weigh her meat in a pair of scales, but she weighs it in a much better balance; so much as gives a proper strength to her body, and renders it able and willing to obey the soul, to join in psalms and prayers, and lift up eyes and hands towards heaven with greater readiness, so much is Miranda's meal. So that Miranda will never have her eyes swell with fatness, or pant under a heavy load of flesh, until she has changed her religion.

The holy Scriptures, especially of the New Testament, are her daily study; these she reads with a watchful attention, constantly casting an eye upon herself, and trying herself by every doctrine that is there. When she has the New Testament in her hand, she supposes herself at the feet of our Saviour and His Apostles, and makes everything that she learns of them so many laws of her life. She receives their sacred words with as much attention and reverence as if she saw their persons, and knew that they were just come from heaven on purpose to teach her the way that leads to it.

She thinks that the trying herself every day by the doctrines of Scripture is the only possible way to be ready for her trial at the last day. She is sometimes afraid that she lays out too much money in books, because she cannot forbear buying all practical books of any note, especially such as enter into the heart of religion, and describe the inward holiness of the Christian life. But of all human writings, the lives of pious persons and eminent saints are her greatest delight. In these she searches as for hidden treasure, hoping to find some secret of holy living, some uncommon degree of piety, which she may make her own. By this means Miranda has her head and heart stored with all the principles of wisdom and holiness; she is so full of the one main business of life, that she finds it difficult to converse upon any other subject; and if you are in her company when she thinks proper to talk, you must be made wiser and better whether you will or no.

To relate her charity would be to relate the history of every day for twenty years; for so long has all her fortune been spent that way. She has set up near twenty poor tradesmen that had failed in their business, and saved as many from failing. She has educated several poor children that were picked up in the streets, and put them in a way of an honest employment. As soon as any labourer is confined at home with sickness, she sends him, till he recovers, twice the value of his wages, that he may have one part to give to his family as usual, and the other to provide things convenient for his sickness.

If a family seems too large to be supported by the labour of those that can work in it, she pays their rent, and gives them something yearly towards their clothing. By this means there are many poor families that live in a comfortable manner, and are from year to year blessing her in their prayers.

If there is any poor man or woman that is more than ordinarily wicked and reprobate, Miranda has her eye upon them; she watches their time of need and adversity; and if she can discover that they are in any great straits or affliction, she gives them speedy relief. She has this care for this sort of people, because she once saved a very profligate person from being carried to prison, who immediately became a true penitent.

There is nothing in the character of Miranda more to be admired than this temper. For this tenderness of affection towards the most abandoned sinners is the highest instance of a divine and Godlike soul.

Miranda once passed by a house where the man and his wife were cursing and swearing at one another in a most dreadful manner, and three children crying about them; this sight so much affected her compassionate mind that she went the next day and bought[1] the three children, that they might not be ruined by living with such wicked parents; they now live with Miranda, are blessed with her care and prayers, and all the good works which she can do for them. They hear her talk, they see her live, they join with her in psalms and prayers. The eldest of them has already converted his parents from their wicked life, and shows a turn of mind so remarkably pious that Miranda intends him for holy orders; that being thus saved himself he may be zealous in the salvation of souls, and do to other miserable objects as she has done to him.

Miranda is a constant relief to poor people in their misfortunes and accidents; there are sometimes little misfortunes that happen to them which, of themselves, they could never be able to overcome. The death of a cow, or a horse, or some little robbery, would keep them in distress all their lives. She does not suffer them to grieve under such accidents as these. She immediately gives them the full value of their loss, and makes use of it as a means of raising their minds towards God.

She has a great tenderness for old people that are grown past their labour. The parish allowance to such people is very seldom a comfortable maintenance. For this reason they are the constant objects of her care; she adds so much to their allowance as somewhat exceeds the wages they got when they were young.

---

[1] When labourers' wages averaged six shillings a week, it was not unnatural that poor parents should be willing to part with their superfluous children for a consideration; and as charitable organisations were far less numerous than they are now, rich people often exercised their charity by adopting and supporting such children. We have many instances of this. One of the most notable is that of Thomas Hearne, the famous antiquary, who was the son of poor parents, but was practically adopted by the excellent Mr. Cherry, of Shottisbrook, who took him into his house, and, in conjunction with Mr. Dodwell, superintended his education, and finally sent him to Oxford.

A curious comment on the custom to which Law refers is found in the fact that when Hannah More set up her schools at Cheddar and the neighbourhood, some parents were afraid to let their children attend, lest Miss More should acquire legal control over them, and sell them as slaves.

This she does to comfort the infirmities of their age, that, being free from trouble and distress, they may serve God in peace and tranquillity of mind. She has generally a large number of this kind, who, by her charities and exhortations to holiness, spend their last days in great piety and devotion.

Miranda never wants compassion, even to common beggars,[2] especially toward those that are old or sick, or full of sores, that want eyes or limbs; she hears their complaints with tenderness, gives them some proof of her kindness, and never rejects them with hard or reproachful language for fear of adding affliction to her fellow-creatures.

If a poor traveller tells her that he has neither strength, nor food, nor money left, she never bids him go to the place from whence he came, or tells him that she cannot relieve him, because he may be a cheat, or she does not know him; but she relieves him for that reason, because he is a stranger and unknown to her. For it is the most noble part of charity to be kind and tender to those whom we never saw before, and perhaps never may see again in this life. "I was a stranger, and ye took me in," saith our blessed Saviour; but who can perform this duty that will not relieve persons that are unknown to him?

Miranda considers that Lazarus was a common beggar, that he was the care of angels, and carried into Abraham's bosom. She considers that our blessed Saviour and His Apostles were kind to beggars; that they spoke comfortably to them, healed their diseases, and restored eyes and limbs to the lame and blind; that Peter said to the beggar that wanted an alms from him, "Silver and gold have I none, but such as I have give I thee; in the name of Jesus Christ of Nazareth, rise up and walk." Miranda, therefore, never treats beggars with disregard and aversion, but she imitates the kindness of our Saviour and His Apostles towards them; and though she cannot, like them, work miracles for their relief, yet she relieves them with that power that she hath; and may say, with the Apostle, "Such as I have give I thee, in the name of Jesus Christ."

It may be, says Miranda, that I may often give to those that do not deserve it, or that will make an ill use of my alms. But what then? Is not this the very method of divine goodness?

[2] It was the carrying out of this principle literally that brought so many beggars to King's Cliffe, and led to the consequences related in the note to ch. vi.

CH. VIII. Does not God make "His sun to rise on the evil and on the good?" Is not this the very goodness that is recommended to us in Scripture, that, by imitating of it, we may be children of our Father which is in heaven, "Who sendeth rain on the just and on the unjust"? And shall I withhold a little money or food from my fellow-creature for fear he should not be good enough to receive it of me? Do I beg of God to deal with me, not according to my merit, but according to His own great goodness; and shall I be so absurd as to withhold my charity from a poor brother because he may perhaps not deserve it? Shall I use a measure towards him, which I pray God never to use towards me? Besides, where has the Scripture made merit the rule or measure of charity? On the contrary, the Scripture saith, "If thy enemy hunger, feed him; if he thirst, give him drink."

Now this plainly teaches us that the merit of persons is to be no rule of our charity, but that we are to do acts of kindness to those that least of all deserve it. For if I am to love and do good to my worst enemies; if I am to be charitable to them, notwithstanding all their spite and malice, surely merit is no measure of charity. If I am not to withhold my charity from such bad people, and who are at the same time my enemies, surely I am not to deny alms to poor beggars, whom I neither know to be bad people, nor any way my enemies.

You will perhaps say that, by this means, I encourage people to be beggars.[3] But the same thoughtless objection may be made against all kinds of charities, for they may encourage people to depend upon them. The same may be said against forgiving our enemies, for it may encourage people to do us hurt. The same may be said even against the goodness of God, that, by pouring His blessing on the evil and on the good, on the just and on the unjust, evil and unjust men are encouraged in their wicked ways. The same may be said against clothing the naked, or giving medicines to the sick, for that may encourage people to neglect themselves, and be careless of their health. But when the love of God dwelleth in you, when it has enlarged your heart, and filled you with bowels of mercy and compassion, you will make no more such objections as these.

When you are at any time turning away the poor, the old, the sick and helpless traveller, the lame or the blind, ask yourself this question, Do I sincerely wish these poor creatures may be as

[3] Law anticipates the events which afterwards occurred at King's Cliffe.

happy as Lazarus, that was carried by angels into Abraham's CH. VIII. bosom? Do I sincerely desire that God would make them fellow-heirs with me in eternal glory? Now if you search into your soul, you will find that there are none of these motions there, that you are wishing nothing of this. For it is impossible for any one heartily to wish a poor creature so great a happiness and yet not have a heart to give him a small alms. For this reason, says Miranda, as far as I can I give to all, because I pray to God to forgive all; and I cannot refuse an alms to those whom I pray God to bless, whom I wish to be partakers of eternal glory, but am glad to show some degree of love to such as I hope will be the objects of the infinite love of God. And if, as our Saviour has assured us, "It be more blessed to give than to receive," we ought to look upon those that ask our alms as so many friends and benefactors, that come to do us a greater good than they can receive, that come to exalt our virtue, to be witnesses of our charity, to be monuments of our love, to be our advocates with God, to be to us in Christ's stead, to appear for us at the day of judgment, and to help us to a blessedness greater than our alms can bestow on them.

This is the spirit, and this is the life of the devout Miranda; and if she lives ten years longer, she will have spent fifty hundred pounds in charity, for that which she allows herself may be fairly reckoned amongst her alms.

When she dies she must shine amongst Apostles, and saints, and martyrs; she must stand amongst the first servants of God, and be glorious amongst those that have fought the good fight, and finished their course with joy.[4]

---

[4] Perhaps this portrait of Miranda was the one which Law drew most of all *con amore*. Though essentially a man's man, whose writings were, and are, perhaps, more appreciated by men than women, he had the highest opinion of woman's intellectual capacity, and of their immense influence over society; and Miranda was his ideal woman, of whom Miss Hester Gibbon was at best a very imperfect copy.

# CHAPTER IX.

*Containing some reflections upon the life of Miranda, and showing how it may, and ought to, be imitated by all her sex.*

Now this life of Miranda, which I heartily recommend to the imitation of her sex, however contrary it may seem to the way and fashion of the world, is yet suitable to the true spirit, and founded upon the plainest doctrines of Christianity.

To live as she does is as truly suitable to the Gospel of Christ as to be baptized, or receive the sacrament.

Her spirit is that which animated the saints of former ages; and it is because they lived as she does that we now celebrate their memories, and praise God for their examples.

There is nothing that is whimsical, trifling, or unreasonable in her character, but everything there described is a right and proper instance of a solid and real piety.

It is as easy to show that it is whimsical to go to Church, or to say one's prayers, as that it is whimsical to observe any of these rules of life. For all Miranda's rules of living unto God, of spending her time and fortune, of eating, working, dressing, and conversing, are as substantial parts of a reasonable and holy life as devotion and prayer.

For there is nothing to be said for the wisdom of sobriety, the wisdom of devotion, the wisdom of charity, or the wisdom of humility, but what is as good an argument for the wise and reasonable use of apparel.

Neither can anything be said against the folly of luxury, the folly of sensuality, the folly of extravagance, the folly of prodigality, the folly of ambition, of idleness or indulgence, but what must be said against the folly of dress; for religion is as deeply concerned in the one as in the other.

If you may be vain in one thing you may be vain in everything; for one kind of vanity only differs from another as one kind of intemperance differs from another.

If you spend your fortune in the needless vain finery of dress, CHAP. IX you cannot condemn prodigality, or extravagance, or luxury, without condemning yourself.

If you fancy that it is your only folly, and that, therefore, there can be no great matter in it, you are like those that think they are only guilty of the folly of covetousness, or the folly of ambition. Now though some people may live so plausible a life as to appear chargeable with no other fault than that of covetousness or ambition, yet the case is not as it appears, for covetousness or ambition cannot subsist in a heart that is in other respects rightly devoted to God.

In like manner, though some people may spend most that they have in needless expensive ornaments of dress, and yet seem to be in every other respect truly pious, yet it is certainly false; for it is as impossible for a mind that is in a true state of religion to be vain in the use of clothes as to be vain in the use of alms or devotions. Now to convince you of this from your own reflections, let us suppose that some eminent saint, as, for instance, that the holy Virgin Mary was sent into the world to be again in a state of trial for a few years, and that you were going to her to be edified by her great piety. Would you expect to find her dressed out and adorned in fine and expensive clothes? No. You would know in your own mind that it was as impossible as to find her learning to dance. Do but add saint, or holy, to any person, either man or woman, and your own mind tells you immediately that such a character cannot admit of the vanity of fine apparel. A saint genteelly dressed is as great nonsense as an Apostle in an embroidered suit; everyone's own natural sense convinces him of the inconsistency of these things.[1]

Now what is the reason that, when you think of a saint or eminent servant of God, you cannot admit of the vanity of apparel? Is it not because it is inconsistent with such a right state of heart, such true and exalted piety? And is not this, therefore, a demonstration that, where such vanity is admitted, there a right state of heart, true and exalted piety, must needs be wanted? For as certainly as the holy Virgin Mary could not indulge herself, or conform to the vanity of the world in dress

---

[1] The early Methodists, who took many of their rules of living from the Wesleys through the *Serious Call*, were very particular about the neatness and plainness of their dress. Indeed, many of their females had a peculiar dress of their own, not unlike that of the Quakers, as many of our older readers will no doubt remember.

and figure, so certain is it that none can indulge themselves in this vanity but those who want her piety of heart; and, consequently, it must be owned, that all needless and expensive finery of dress is the effect of a disordered heart that is not governed by the true spirit of religion.

Covetousness is not a crime because there is any harm in gold or silver, but because it supposes a foolish and unreasonable state of mind that is fallen from its true good, and sunk into such a poor and wretched satisfaction.

In like manner the expensive finery of dress is not a crime because there is anything good or evil in clothes, but because the expensive ornaments of clothing shows a foolish and unreasonable state of heart that is fallen from right notions of human nature, that abuses the end of clothing, and turns the necessities of life into so many instances of pride and folly.

All the world agree in condemning remarkable fops. Now what is the reason of it? Is it because there is anything sinful in their particular dress or affected manners? No; but it is because all people know that it shows the state of a man's mind, and that it is impossible for so ridiculous an outside to have anything wise, or reasonable, or good within. And, indeed, to suppose a fop of great piety is as much nonsense as to suppose a coward of great courage. So that all the world agree in owning that the use and manner of clothes is a mark of the state of a man's mind, and consequently that it is a thing highly essential to religion. But then it should be well considered that as it is not only the sot that is guilty of intemperance, but every one that transgresses the right and religious measures of eating and drinking; so it should be considered that it is not only the fop that is guilty of the vanity and abuse of dress, but everyone that departs from the reasonable and religious ends of clothing.

As, therefore, every argument against sottishness is as good an argument against all kinds of intemperance, so every argument against the vanity of fops is as good an argument against all vanity and abuse of dress. For they are all of the same kind, and only differ as one degree of intemperance may differ from another. She that only paints a little may as justly accuse another because she paints a great deal, as she that uses but a common finery of dress accuse another that is excessive in her finery.

For as, in the matter of temperance, there is no rule but the sobriety that is according to the doctrines and spirit of our religion; so, in the matter of apparel, there is no rule to be CHAP. IX. observed but such a right use of clothes as is strictly according to the doctrines and spirit of our religion. To pretend to make the way of the world our measure in these things is as weak and absurd as to make the way of the world the measure of our sobriety, abstinence, or humility. It is a pretence that is exceedingly absurd in the mouths of Christians, who are to be so far from conforming to the fashions of this life, that to have overcome the world is made an essential mark of Christianity.

This, therefore, is the way that you are to judge of the crime of vain apparel. You are to consider it as an offence against the proper use of clothes, as covetousness is an offence against the proper use of money; you are to consider it as an indulgence of proud and unreasonable tempers, as an offence against the humility and sobriety of the Christian spirit; you are to consider it as an offence against all those doctrines that require you to do all to the glory of God, that require you to make a right use of your talents; you are to consider it as an offence against all those texts of Scripture that command you to love your neighbour as yourself, to feed the hungry, to clothe the naked, and do all works of charity that you are able; so that you must not deceive yourself with saying, Where can be the harm of clothes? for the covetous man might as well say, Where can be the harm of gold or silver? but you must consider that it is a great deal of harm to want that wise, and reasonable, and humble state of heart, which is according to the spirit of religion, and which no one can have in the manner that he ought to have it, who indulges himself either in the vanity of dress or the desire of riches.

There is, therefore, nothing right in the use of clothes, or in the use of anything else in the world, but the plainness and simplicity of the Gospel. Every other use of things (however polite and fashionable in the world) distracts and disorders the heart, and is inconsistent with that inward state of piety, that purity of heart, that wisdom of mind, and regularity of affection, which Christianity requireth.

If you would be a good Christian there is but one way; you must live wholly unto God; and if you would live wholly unto God, you must live according to the wisdom that comes from God; you must act according to right judgments of the nature and value of things; you must live in the exercise of holy and

CHAP. IX. heavenly affections, and use all the gifts of God to His praise and glory.

Some persons, perhaps, who admire the purity and perfection of this life of Miranda, may say, How can it be proposed as a common example?  How can we who are married, or we who are under the direction of our parents, imitate such a life?

It is answered, Just as you may imitate the life of our blessed Saviour and His Apostles.  The circumstances of our Saviour's life, and the state and condition of His Apostles, were more different from yours than that of Miranda's is; and yet their life, the purity and perfection of their behaviour, is the common example that is proposed to all Christians.

It is their spirit, therefore, their piety, their love of God, that you are to imitate, and not the particular form of their life.

Act under God as they did; direct your common actions to that end which they did; glorify your proper state with such love of God, such charity to your neighbour, such humility and self-denial, as they did; and then, though you are only teaching your own children, and St. Paul is converting whole nations, yet you are following his steps, and acting after his example.

Do not think, therefore, that you cannot or need not be like Miranda because you are not in her state of life; for as the same spirit and temper would have made Miranda a saint, though she had been forced to labour for a maintenance, so if you will but aspire after her spirit and temper, every form and condition of life will furnish you with sufficient means of employing it.

Miranda is what she is, because she does everything in the Name, and with regard to her duty to God; and when you do the same you will be exactly like her, though you are never so different from her in the outward state of your life.

You are married, you say, therefore you have not your time and fortune in your power as she has.

It is very true; and therefore you cannot spend so much time, nor so much money, in the manner that she does.

But now Miranda's perfection does not consist in this, that she spends so much time, or so much money, in such a manner, but that she is careful to make the best use of all that time, and all that fortune, which God has put into her hands.  Do you, therefore, make the best use of all that time and money which is in your disposal, and then you are like Miranda.

If she has two hundred pounds a year, and you have only

two mites, have you not the more reason to be exceeding exact CHAP. IX. in the wisest use of them? If she has a great deal of time, and you have but a little, ought you not to be the more watchful and circumspect, lest that little should be lost?

You say if you were to imitate the cleanly plainness and cheapness of her dress, you should offend your husbands.

First, Be very sure that this is true, before you make it an excuse.

Secondly, If your husbands do really require you to patch your faces, to expose your breasts naked, and to be fine and expensive in all your apparel, then take these two resolutions:

First, To forbear from all this as soon as your husbands will permit you.

Secondly, To use your utmost endeavours to recommend yourselves to their affections by such solid virtues as may correct the vanity of their minds, and teach them to love you for such qualities as will make you amiable in the sight of God and His holy angels.

As to this doctrine concerning the plainness and modesty of dress, it may perhaps be thought by some to be sufficiently confuted by asking whether all persons are to be clothed in the same manner?

These questions are generally put by those who had rather perplex the plainest truths than be obliged to follow them.

Let it be supposed that I had recommended an universal plainness of diet. Is it not a thing sufficiently reasonable to be universally recommended? But would it thence follow that the nobleman and the labourer were to live upon the same food?

Suppose I had pressed an universal temperance, does not religion enough justify such a doctrine? But would it, therefore, follow that all people were to drink the same liquors, and in the same quantity?

In like manner, though plainness and sobriety of dress is recommended to all, yet it does by no means follow that all are to be clothed in the same manner.

Now what is the particular rule with regard to temperance? How shall particular persons that use different liquors, and in different quantities, preserve their temperance?

Is not this the rule? Are they not to guard against indulgence, to make their use of liquors a matter of conscience, and allow of no refreshments but such as are consistent with the strictest rules of Christian sobriety?

Now transfer this rule to the matter of apparel, and all questions about it are answered.

Let everyone but guard against the vanity of dress, let them but make their use of clothes a matter of conscience, let them but desire to make the best use of their money, and then every one has a rule that is sufficient to direct them in every state of life. This rule will no more let the great be vain in their dress than intemperate in their liquors; and yet will leave it as lawful to have some difference in their apparel as to have some difference in their drink.

But now will you say that you may use the finest richest wines, when and as you please; that you may be as expensive in them as you have a mind, because different liquors are allowed? If not, how can it be said that you may use clothes as you please, and wear the richest things you can get, because the bare difference of clothes is lawful?

For as the lawfulness of different liquors leaves no room nor any excuse for the smallest degree of intemperance in drinking, so the lawfulness of different apparel leaves no room nor any excuse for the smallest degrees of vanity in dress.

To ask what is vanity in dress is no more a puzzling question than to ask what is intemperance in drinking. And though religion does not here state the particular measure for all individuals, yet it gives such general rules as are a sufficient direction in every state of life.

He that lets religion teach him that the end of drinking is only so far to refresh our spirits as to keep us in good health, and make soul and body fitter for all the offices of a holy and pious life, and that he is to desire to glorify God by a right use of this liberty, will always know what intemperance is in his particular state.

So he that lets religion teach him that the end of clothing is only to hide our shame and nakedness, and to secure our bodies from the injuries of weather, and that he is to desire to glorify God by a sober and wise use of this necessity, will always know what vanity of dress is in his particular state.

And he that thinks it a needless nicety to talk of the religious use of apparel has as much reason to think it a needless nicety to talk of the religious use of liquors. For luxury and indulgence in dress is as great an abuse as luxury and indulgence in eating and drinking. And there is no avoiding either of them but by making religion the strict measure of our allowance in both cases. And there is nothing in religion to excite a man to this pious exactness in one case, but what is as good a motive to the same exactness in the other.

Farther, as all things that are lawful are not therefore expedient, so there are some things lawful in the use of liquors and apparel, which, by abstaining from them for pious ends, may be made means of great perfection.

Thus, for instance, if a man should deny himself such use of liquors as is lawful; if he should refrain from such expense in his drink as might be allowed without sin; if he should do this, not only for the sake of a more pious self-denial, but that he might be able to relieve and refresh the helpless, poor, and sick; if another should abstain from the use of that which is lawful in dress; if he should be more frugal and mean in his habit than the necessities of religion absolutely require; if he should do this, not only as a means of a better humility, but that he may be more able to clothe other people; these persons might be said to do that which was highly suitable to the true spirit, though not absolutely required by the letter of the law of Christ.

For if those who give a cup of cold water to a disciple of Christ shall not lose their reward, how dear must they be to Christ, who often give themselves water that they may be able to give wine to the sick and languishing members of Christ's body!

But to return. All that has been here said to married women may serve for the same instruction to such as are still under the direction of their parents.

Now though the obedience which is due to parents does not oblige them to carry their virtues no higher than their parents require them, yet their obedience requires them to submit to their direction in all things not contrary to the laws of God.

If, therefore, your parents require you to live more in the fashion and conversation of the world, or to be more expensive in your dress and person, or to dispose of your time otherwise than suits with your desires after greater perfection, you must submit, and bear it as your cross till you are at liberty to follow the higher counsels of Christ, and have it in your power to choose the best ways of raising your virtue to its greatest height.

Now although, whilst you are in this state, you may be obliged to forego some means of improving your virtue, yet there are

CHAP. IX. some others to be found in it that are not to be had in a life of more liberty.

For if in this state where obedience is so great a virtue, you comply in all things lawful, out of a pious, tender sense of duty, then those things which you thus perform are, instead of being hindrances of your virtue, turned into means of improving it.

What you lose by being restrained from such things as you would choose to observe, you gain by that excellent virtue of obedience in humbly complying against your temper.

Now what is here granted is only in things lawful, and therefore the diversion of our English stage is here excepted, being elsewhere proved, as I think, to be absolutely unlawful.[2]

Thus much to show how persons under the direction of others may imitate the wise and pious life of Miranda.

But as for those who are altogether in their own hands, if the liberty of their state makes them covet the best gifts, if it carries them to choose the most excellent ways, if they, having all in their own power, should turn the whole form of their life into a regular exercise of the highest virtues, happy are they who have so learned Christ.

All persons cannot receive this saying.   They that are able to receive it, let them receive it, and bless that Spirit of God which has put such good motions into their hearts.

God may be served and glorified in every state of life.   But as there are some states of life more desirable than others, that more purify our natures, that more improve our virtues, and dedicate us unto God in a higher manner, so those who are at liberty to choose for themselves seem to be called by God to be more eminently devoted to His service.

Ever since the beginning of Christianity there hath been two orders or ranks of people amongst good Christians.

The one that feared and served God in the common offices of a secular worldly life.

The other, renouncing the common business and common enjoyments of life, as riches, marriage, honours, and pleasures, devoted themselves to voluntary poverty, virginity, devotion, and retirement, that by this means they might live wholly unto God in the daily exercise of a divine and heavenly life.

[2] See Law on *The Absolute Unlawfulness of Stage Entertainments*, pub. in 1726.  He also dwells strongly on the subject in his *Treatise of Christian Perfection*, which immediately preceded the *Serious Call*.

This testimony I have from the famous ecclesiastical historian, Eusebius,[3] who lived at the time of the first general council, when the faith of our Nicene creed was established, when the Church was in its greatest glory and purity, when its bishops were so many holy fathers and eminent saints.

"Therefore," saith he, "there hath been instituted in the Church of Christ two ways or manners of living: the one, raised above the ordinary state of nature and common ways of living, rejects wedlock, possessions, and worldly goods, and, being wholly separate and removed from the ordinary conversation of common life, is appropriated and devoted solely to the worship and service of God, through an exceeding degree of heavenly love.

"They who are of this order of people seem dead to the life of this world, and having their bodies only upon earth, are, in their minds and contemplations, dwelling in heaven, from whence, like so many heavenly inhabitants, they look down upon human life, making intercessions and oblations to Almighty God for the whole race of mankind. And this not with the blood of beasts, or the fat, or smoke, and burning of bodies, but with the highest exercises of true piety, with cleansed and purified hearts, and with a whole form of life strictly devoted to virtue. These are their sacrifices which they continually offer unto God, imploring His mercy and favour for themselves and their fellow-creatures.

"Christianity receives this as the perfect manner of life.

"The other is of a lower form, and, suiting itself more to the condition of human nature, admits of chaste wedlock, the care of children and family, of trade and business, and goes through all the employments of life under a sense of piety and fear of God.

"Now they who have chosen this manner of life have their set times for retirement and spiritual exercises, and particular days are set apart for their hearing and learning the Word of God. And this order of people are considered as in the second state of piety." (Euseb. *Dem. Evan.* l. i, c. 8.)

Thus this learned historian.

If, therefore, persons of either sex, moved with the life of Miranda and desirous of perfection, should unite themselves into little societies,[4] professing voluntary poverty, virginity, retirement,

---

[3] There were two eminent fathers of the church named Eusebius, *viz.* Eusebius of Cæsarea and Eusebius of Nicomedia. The historian quoted in the text was the former.

[4] Like the 'united societies' of John Wesley, though he did not recommend nor practise 'virginity and retirement,' nor, quite in Law's sense, 'voluntary poverty.'

and devotion, living upon bare necessaries, that some might be relieved by their charities, and all be blessed with their prayers, and benefited by their example; or if, for want of this, they should practise the same manner of life in as high a degree as they could by themselves, such persons would be so far from being chargeable with any superstition, or blind devotion, that they might be justly said to restore that piety which was the boast and glory of the Church when its greatest saints were alive.

Now as this learned historian observes, that it was an exceeding great degree of heavenly love that carried these persons so much above the common ways of life to such an eminent state of holiness, so it is not to be wondered at that the religion of Jesus Christ should fill the hearts of many Christians with this high degree of love.

For a religion that opens such a scene of glory, that discovers things so infinitely above all the world, that so triumphs over death, that assures us of such mansions of bliss, where we shall so soon be as the angels of God in heaven, what wonder is it if such a religion, such truths and expectations, should, in some holy souls, destroy all earthly desires, and make the ardent love of heavenly things be the one continual passion of their hearts?

If the religion of Christians is founded upon the infinite humiliation, the cruel mockings and scourgings, the prodigious sufferings, the poor, persecuted life, and painful death of a crucified Son of God, what wonder is it if many humble adorers of this profound mystery, many affectionate lovers of a crucified Lord, should renounce their share of worldly pleasures, and give themselves up to a continual course of mortification and self-denial, that thus suffering with Christ here they may reign with Him hereafter?

If truth itself hath assured us that there is but one thing needful, what wonder is it that there should be some amongst Christians so full of faith as to believe this in the highest sense of the words, and to desire such a separation from the world that their care and attention to the one thing needful may not be interrupted?

If our blessed Lord hath said, "If thou wilt be perfect, go and sell that thou hast, and give to the poor, and thou shalt have treasure in heaven, and come and follow Me," what wonder is it that there should be amongst Christians some such zealous followers of Christ so intent upon heavenly treasure, so desirous

of perfection, that they should renounce the enjoyment of their CHAP. IX.
estates, choose a voluntary poverty, and relieve all the poor that
they are able?

If the chosen vessel, St. Paul, hath said, "He that is unmarried
careth for the things that belong to the Lord, how he may please
the Lord": and that "there is this difference also between a wife
and a virgin: the unmarried woman careth for the things of the
Lord, that she may be holy both in body and spirit"; what wonder
is it if the purity and perfection of the virgin state hath been
the praise and glory of the Church in its first and purest ages?
that there have always been some so desirous of pleasing
God, so zealous after every degree of purity and perfection, so
glad of every means of improving their virtue, that they have
renounced the comforts and enjoyments of wedlock to trim their
lamps, to purify their souls, and wait upon God in a state of
perpetual virginity?

And if in these our days, we want examples of these
several degrees of perfection; if neither clergy[5] nor laity are
enough of this spirit; if we are so far departed from it that a
man seems, like St. Paul at Athens, a setter forth of strange
doctrines, when he recommends self-denial, renunciation of the
world, regular devotion, retirement, virginity, and voluntary
poverty, it is because we are fallen into an age where the love
not only of many, but of most, is waxed cold.

I have made this little appeal to antiquity, and quoted these
few passages of Scripture, to support some uncommon practices
in the life of Miranda; and to show that her highest rules of
holy living, her devotion, self-denial, renunciation of the world,
her charity, virginity, and voluntary poverty, are founded on the
sublimest counsels of Christ and His Apostles, suitable to the
high expectations of another life, proper instances of a heavenly
love, and all followed by the greatest saints of the best and
purest ages of the Church.

"He that hath ears to hear, let him hear."

---

[5] Law was a very strong advocate of clerical celibacy, and perhaps even more so in his later, mystic stage, than when he wrote the *Serious Call*.

# CHAPTER X.

*Showing how all orders and ranks of men and women of all ages are obliged to devote themselves unto God.*

CHAP. X. I HAVE in the foregoing chapters gone through the several great instances of Christian devotion, and shown that all the parts of our common life, our employments, our talents, and gifts of fortune, are all to be made holy and acceptable unto God by a wise and religious use of every thing, and by directing our actions and designs to such ends as are suitable to the honour and glory of God.

I shall now show that this regularity of devotion, this holiness of common life, this religious use of everything that we have, is a devotion that is the duty of all orders of Christian people.

FULVIUS has had a learned education, and taken his degrees in the university; he came from thence that he might be free from any rules of life. He takes no employment upon him, nor enters into any business, because he thinks that every employment or business calls people to the careful performance and just discharge of its several duties. When he is grave, he will tell you that he did not enter into holy orders, because he looks upon it to be a state that requires great holiness of life, and that it does not suit his temper to be so good. He will tell you that he never intends to marry, because he cannot oblige himself to that regularity of life and good behaviour which he takes to be the duty of those that are at the head of a family. He refused to be God-father to his nephew, because he will have no trust of any kind to answer for.

Fulvius thinks that he is conscientious in this conduct, and is, therefore, content with the most idle, impertinent, and careless life.

He has no religion, no devotion, no pretences to piety. He lives by no rules, and thinks all is very well, because he is neither a priest, nor a father, nor a guardian, nor has any employment CHAP. X. or family to look after.

But, Fulvius, you are a rational creature, and, as such, are as much obliged to live according to reason[1] and order as a priest is obliged to attend at the altar, or a guardian to be faithful to his trust; if you live contrary to reason, you do not commit a small crime, you do not break a small trust; but you break the law of your nature, you rebel against God, Who gave you that nature, and put yourself amongst those whom the God of reason and order will punish as apostates and deserters.

Though you have no employment, yet, as you are baptized into the profession of Christ's religion, you are as much obliged to live according to the holiness of the Christian spirit, and perform all the promises made at your baptism as any man is obliged to be honest and faithful in his calling. If you abuse this great calling, you are not false in a small matter; but you abuse the precious blood of Christ, you crucify the Son of God afresh, you neglect the highest instances of divine goodness, you disgrace the Church of God, you blemish the body of Christ, you abuse the means of grace and the promises of glory; and it will be more tolerable for Tyre and Sidon at the day of judgment than for you.

It is, therefore, great folly for any one to think himself at liberty to live as he pleases, because he is not in such a state of life as some others are. For if there is anything dreadful in the abuse of any trust, if there is anything to be feared for the neglect of any calling, there is nothing more to be feared than the wrong use of our reason, nor anything more to be dreaded than the neglect of our Christian calling, which is not to serve the little uses of a short life, but to redeem souls unto God,[2] to fill heaven with saints, and finish a kingdom of eternal glory unto God.

No man, therefore, must think himself excused from the exactness of piety and morality because he has chosen to be idle and independent in the world; for the necessities of a reasonable and holy life are not founded in the several conditions and

[1] In his later days Law would have modified what he says about living according to reason, but not in the same direction in which the Evangelicals would have modified, or rather rejected, it.

[2] 'To redeem souls unto God,' would be one of the expressions which led to the charge that the *Serious Call* was not a 'Gospel' treatise. It is Christ, not the Christian calling, that, strictly speaking, redeems souls unto God.

CHAP. X. employments of this life, but in the immutable nature of God and the nature of man. A man is not to be reasonable and holy because he is a priest or the father of a family; but he is to be a pious priest and a good father because piety and goodness are the laws of human nature. Could any man please God without living according to reason and order, there would be nothing displeasing to God in an idle priest or a reprobate father. He, therefore, that abuses his reason is like him who abuses the priesthood; and he that neglects the holiness of the Christian life is as the man that disregards the most important trust.

If a man was to choose to put out his eyes rather than enjoy the light and see the works of God; if he should voluntarily kill himself by refusing to eat and drink; every one would own that such a one was a rebel against God, who justly deserved His highest indignation. You would not say that this was only sinful in a priest or a master of a family, but in every man, as such.

Now wherein does the sinfulness of this behaviour consist? Does it not consist in this, that he abuses his nature, and refuses to act that part for which God had created him? But if this be true, then all persons who abuse their reason, that act a different part from that for which God created them, are, like this man, rebels against God, and, on the same account, subject to His wrath.

Let us suppose that this man, instead of putting out his eyes, had only employed them in looking at ridiculous things, or shut them up in a sleep; that instead of starving himself to death by not eating at all, he should turn every meal into a feast, and eat and drink like an epicure; could he be said to have lived more to the glory of God? could he any more be said to act the part for which God had created him, than if he had put out his eyes and starved himself to death?

Now do but suppose a man acting unreasonably; do but suppose him extinguishing his reason, instead of putting out his eyes, and living in a course of folly and impertinence[3] instead of starving himself to death, and then you have found as great a rebel against God.

For he that puts out his eyes, or murders himself, has only this guilt, that he abuses the powers that God has given him; that he

[3] 'Impertinence,' that is, a course not in accordance with the ends of our being.

refuses to act that part for which he was created, and puts him- CHAP. X.
self into a state that is contrary to the divine will.  And surely
this is the guilt of every one that lives an unreasonable, unholy,
and foolish life.

As, therefore, no particular state, or private life, is an excuse for
the abuse of our bodies or self-murder, so no particular state or
private life is an excuse for the abuse of our reason, or the
neglect of the holiness of the Christian religion.  For surely it is
as much the will of God that we should make the best use of our
rational faculties, that we should conform to the purity and
holiness of Christianity, as it is the will of God that we should
use our eyes, and eat and drink for the preservation of our lives.

Till, therefore, a man can show that he sincerely endeavours to
live according to the will of God, to be that which God requires
him to be ; until he can show that he is striving to live according
to the holiness of the Christian religion ; whosoever he be, or
wheresoever he be, he has all that to answer for, that they have,
who refuse to live, who abuse the greatest trusts, and neglect the
highest calling in the world.

Everybody acknowledges that all orders of men are to be
equally and exactly honest and faithful ; there is no exception to
be made in these duties for any private or particular state of life.
Now if we would but attend to the reason and nature of things ;
if we would but consider the nature of God, and the nature of
man, we should find the same necessity for every other right use
of our reason, for every grace or religious temper of the Christian
life.  We should find it as absurd to suppose that one man
must be exact in piety and another need not, as to suppose
that one man must be exact in honesty, but another need
not.  For Christian humility, sobriety, devotion, and piety are
as great and necessary parts of a reasonable life as justice and
honesty.

And, on the other hand, pride, sensuality, and covetousness
are as great disorders of the soul, are as high an abuse of our
reason, and as contrary to God, as cheating and dishonesty.

Theft and dishonesty seem indeed to vulgar eyes to be greater
sins, because they are so hurtful to civil society, and are so
severely punished by human laws.

But if we consider mankind in a higher view, as God's order
or society of rational beings, that are to glorify Him by the right
use of their reason, and by acting conformably to the order of

their nature, we shall find that every temper that is equally contrary to reason and order, that opposes God's ends and designs, and disorders the beauty and glory of the rational world, is equally sinful in man, and equally odious to God. This would show us that the sin of sensuality is like the sin of dishonesty, and renders us as great objects of the divine displeasure.

Again, if we consider mankind in a further view as a redeemed order of fallen spirits, that are baptized into a fellowship with the Son of God; to be temples of the Holy Ghost; to live according to His holy inspirations; to offer to God the reasonable sacrifice of an humble, pious, and thankful life; to purify themselves from the disorders of their fall;[4] to make a right use of the means of grace in order to be sons of eternal glory. If we look at mankind in this true light, then we shall find that all tempers that are contrary to this holy society, that are abuses of this infinite mercy; all actions that make us unlike to Christ, that disgrace His body, that abuse the means of grace and oppose our hopes of glory, have everything in them that can make us for ever odious unto God. So that though pride and sensuality, and other vices of a like kind, do not hurt civil society as cheating and dishonesty do, yet they hurt that society, and oppose those ends which are greater and more glorious in the eyes of God than all the societies that relate to this world.

Nothing, therefore, can be more false than to imagine, that because we are private persons that have taken upon us no charge or employment of life, that therefore we may live more at large, indulge our appetites, and be less careful of the duties of piety and holiness; for it is as good an excuse for cheating and dishonesty. Because he that abuses his reason, that indulges himself in lust and sensuality, and neglects to act the wise and reasonable part of a true Christian, has everything in his life to render him hateful to God, that is to be found in cheating and dishonesty.

If, therefore, you rather choose to be an idle epicure than to be unfaithful; if you rather choose to live in lust and sensuality than to injure your neighbour in his goods; you have made no better a provision for the favour of God than he that rather chooses to rob a house than to rob a Church.

---

[4] 'To purify themselves from the disorders of their fall,' is another expression which is out of accord with the Evangelical theology, which would hold that no man can 'purify himself,' but must be purified from above.

For the abusing of our own nature is as great a disobedience CHAP. X.
against God as the injuring our neighbour; and he that wants
piety towards God has done as much to damn himself as he that
wants honesty towards men. Every argument, therefore, that
proves it necessary for all men in all stations of life to be truly
honest, proves it equally necessary for all men in all stations of
life to be truly holy and pious, and do all things in such a
manner as is suitable to the glory of God.

Again, another argument to prove that all orders of men are
obliged to be thus holy and devout in the common course of
their lives, in the use of everything that they enjoy, may be taken
from our obligation to prayer.

It is granted that prayer is a duty that belongs to all states and
conditions of men; now if we inquire into the reason why no
state of life is to be excused from prayer, we shall find it as good
a reason why every state of life is to be made a state of piety and
holiness in all its parts.

For the reason why we are to pray unto God, and praise Him
with hymns and psalms of thanksgiving, is this; because we are
to live wholly unto God, and glorify Him all possible ways.
It is not because the praises of words, or forms of thanksgiving,
are more particularly parts of piety, or more the worship of God
than other things; but it is because they are possible ways of
expressing our dependence, our obedience and devotion to God.
Now if this be the reason of verbal praises and thanksgivings to
God, because we are to live unto God all possible ways, then
it plainly follows that we are equally obliged to worship and
glorify God in all other actions that can be turned into acts of
piety and obedience to Him; and as actions are of much more
significancy than words, it must be a much more acceptable
worship of God to glorify Him in all the actions of our common
life than with any little form of words at any particular
times.

Thus, if God is to be worshipped with forms of thanksgiving,
he that makes it a rule to be content and thankful in every part
and accident of his life, because it comes from God, praises God
in a much higher manner than he that has some set time for
singing of psalms. He that dares not say an ill-natured word,
or do an unreasonable thing, because he considers God as everywhere present, performs a better devotion than he that dares not
miss the Church. To live in the world as a stranger and a

CHAP. X. pilgrim, using all its enjoyments as if we used them not, making all our actions so many steps towards a better life, is offering a better sacrifice to God than any forms of holy and heavenly prayers.

To be humble in all our actions, to avoid every appearance of pride and vanity, to be meek and lowly in our words, actions, dress, behaviour, and designs, in imitation of our blessed Saviour, is worshipping God in a higher manner than they who have only times to fall low on their knees in devotions. He that contents himself with necessaries that he may give the remainder to those that want it; that dares not to spend any money foolishly, because he considers it as a talent from God which must be used according to His will; praises God with something that is more glorious than songs of praise.

He that has appointed times for the use of wise and pious prayers performs a proper instance of devotion; but he that allows himself no times, nor any places, nor any actions, but such as are strictly conformable to wisdom and holiness, worships the divine nature with the most true and substantial devotion. For who does not know that it is better to be pure and holy than to talk about purity and holiness? Nay, who does not know that a man is to be reckoned no further pure, or holy, or just, than as he is pure, and holy, and just in the common course of his life? But if this be plain, then it is also plain that it is better to be holy than to have holy prayers.

Prayers, therefore, are so far from being a sufficient devotion that they are the smallest parts of it. We are to praise God with words and prayers because it is a possible way of glorifying God, Who has given us such faculties as may be so used. But then as words are but small things in themselves; as times of prayer are but little, if compared with the rest of our lives; so that devotion, which consists in times and forms of prayer, is but a very small thing if compared to that devotion which is to appear in every other part and circumstance of our lives.

Again, as it is an easy thing to worship God with forms of words, and to observe times of offering them unto Him, so it is the smallest kind of piety.[5]

And, on the other hand, as it is more difficult to worship God with our substance, to honour Him with the right use of our time,

---

[5] It should be remembered in reading this and what follows that (as was said in the Introduction) it was written in a church-going but easy-living age.

to offer to Him the continual sacrifice of self-denial and mortifi- cation; as it requires more piety to eat and drink only for such ends as may glorify God, to undertake no labour, nor allow of any diversion but where we can act in the name of God; as it is most difficult to sacrifice all our corrupt tempers, correct all our passions, and make piety to God the rule and measure of all the actions of our common life; so the devotion of this kind is a much more acceptable service unto God than those words of devotion which we offer to Him either in the Church or in our closet.

Every sober reader will easily perceive that I do not intend to lessen the true and great value of prayers, either public or private; but only to show him that they are certainly but a very slender part of devotion when compared to a devout life.

To see this in a yet clearer light, let us suppose a person to have appointed times for praising God with psalms and hymns, and to be strict in the observation of them; let it be supposed also that in his common life he is restless and uneasy, full of murmurings and complaints at everything, never pleased but by chance, as his temper happens to carry him, but murmuring and repining at the very seasons, and having something to dislike in everything that happens to him. Now can you conceive anything more absurd and unreasonable than such a character as this? Is such an one to be reckoned thankful to God because he has forms of praise which he offers to Him? Nay, is it not certain that such forms of praise must be so far from being an acceptable devotion to God, that they must be abhorred as an abomination? Now the absurdity which you see in this instance is the same in any other part of our life; if our common life hath any contrariety to our prayers, it is the same abomination as songs of thanksgiving in the mouths of murmurers.

Bended knees, whilst you are clothed with pride; heavenly petitions, whilst you are hoarding up treasures upon earth; holy devotions, whilst you live in the follies of the world; prayers of meekness and charity, whilst your heart is the seat of spite and resentment; hours of prayer, whilst you give up days and years to idle diversions, impertinent visits, and foolish pleasures; are as absurd, unacceptable service to God, as forms of thanksgiving from a person that lives in repinings and discontent.

So that unless the common course of our lives be according to the common spirit of our prayers, our prayers are so far from

CHAP. X. being a real or sufficient degree of devotion that they become an empty lip-labour, or, what is worse, a notorious hypocrisy.

Seeing, therefore, we are to make the spirit and temper of our prayers the common spirit and temper of our lives, this may serve to convince us that all orders of people are to labour and aspire after the same utmost perfection of the Christian life.[6] For as all Christians are to use the same holy and heavenly devotions, as they are all with the same earnestness to pray for the Spirit of God, so is it a sufficient proof that all orders of people are, to the utmost of their power, to make their life agreeable to that one Spirit for which they are all to pray.

As certain, therefore, as the same holiness of prayers requires the same holiness of life; so certain is it that all Christians are called to the same holiness of life.

A soldier or a tradesman is not called to minister at the altar, or preach the Gospel; but every soldier or tradesman is as much obliged to be devout, humble, holy, and heavenly-minded in all the parts of his common life, as a clergyman is obliged to be zealous, faithful, and laborious in all parts of his profession.

And all this for this one plain reason, because all people are to pray for the same holiness, wisdom, and divine tempers, and to make themselves as fit as they can for the same heaven.

All men, therefore, as men, have one and the same important[7] business, to act up to the excellency of their rational nature, and to make reason and order the law of all their designs and actions. All Christians, as Christians, have one and the same calling, to live according to the excellency of the Christian spirit, and to make the sublime precepts of the Gospel the rule and measure of all their tempers in common life. The one thing needful to one is the one thing needful to all.

The merchant is no longer to hoard up treasures upon earth; the soldier is no longer to fight for glory; the great scholar is no longer to pride himself in the depths of science; but they must all, with one spirit, "count all things but loss, for the excellency of the knowledge of Christ Jesus."

The fine lady must teach her eyes to weep, and be clothed

---

[6] ' Aspire after ... perfection.' This was the well-known view of Law's *quondam* disciple, John Wesley, and led to a long and heated controversy between his followers and the Calvinists; at least it was one of the points of dispute in that controversy.

[7] Law here uses the term 'rational nature' as equivalent to our 'higher nature,' and 'reason' as equivalent to 'right reason'—that is, reason as opposed to unreason, not reason as opposed to faith.

with humility; the polite gentleman must exchange the gay thoughts of wit and fancy for a "broken and a contrite heart." The man of quality must so far renounce the dignity of his birth as to think himself miserable till he is born again; servants must consider their service as done unto God; masters must consider their servants as their brethren in Christ, that are to be treated as their fellow-members of the mystical body of Christ.

Young ladies must either devote themselves to piety, prayer, self-denial, and all good works, in a virgin state of life; or else marry, to be holy, sober, and prudent in the care of a family, bringing up their children in piety, humility, and devotion, and abounding in all other good works to the utmost of their state and capacity. They have no choice of anything else, but must devote themselves to God in one of these states. They may choose a married or a single life; but it is not left to their choice whether they will make either state a state of holiness, humility, devotion, and all other duties of the Christian life. It is no more left in their power, because they have fortunes, or are born of rich parents, to divide themselves betwixt God and the world, or take such pleasures as their fortune will afford them, than it is allowable for them to be sometimes chaste and modest, and sometimes not.

They are not to consider how much religion may secure them a fair character, or how they may add devotion to an impertinent, vain, and giddy life; but must look into the spirit and temper of their prayers, into the nature and end of Christianity; and then they will find that, whether married or unmarried, they have but one business upon their hands; to be wise, and pious, and holy, not in little modes and forms of worship, but in the whole turn of their minds, in the whole form of all their behaviour, and in the daily course of their common life.

Young gentlemen must consider what our blessed Saviour said to the young gentleman in the Gospel. He bid him "Sell all that he had, and give to the poor." Now though this text should not oblige all people to sell all, yet it certainly obliges all kinds of people to employ all their estates in such wise, reasonable, and charitable ways as may sufficiently show that all that they have is devoted to God, and that no part of it is kept from the poor to be spent in needless, vain, and foolish expenses.

If, therefore, young gentlemen propose to themselves a life of pleasure and indulgence, if they spend their estates in high living, in luxury and intemperance, in state and equipage, in pleasures and diversions, in sports and gaming, and such-like wanton gratifications of their foolish passions, they have as much reason to look upon themselves to be angels as to be disciples of Christ.

Let them be assured that it is the one only business of a Christian gentleman to distinguish himself by good works, to be eminent in the most sublime virtues of the Gospel, to bear with the ignorance and weakness of the vulgar, to be a friend and patron to all that dwell about him, to live in the utmost heights of wisdom and holiness, and show, through the whole course of his life, a true religious greatness of mind. They must aspire after such a gentility as they might have learnt from seeing the blessed Jesus, and show no other spirit of a gentleman but such as they might have got by living with the holy Apostles. They must learn to love God with all their heart, with all their soul, and with all their strength, and their neighbour as themselves; and then they have all the greatness and distinction that they can have here, and are fit for an eternal happiness in heaven hereafter.

Thus in all orders and conditions, either of men or women, this is the one common holiness which is to be the common life of all Christians.

The merchant is not to leave devotion to the clergyman, nor the clergyman to leave humility to the labourer; women of fortune are not to leave it to the poor of their sex to be discreet, chaste, keepers at home, to adorn themselves in modest apparel, shamefacedness, and sobriety; nor poor women leave it to the rich to attend at the worship and service of God. Great men must be eminent for true poverty of spirit, and people of a low and afflicted state must greatly rejoice in God.

The man of strength and power is to forgive, and pray for, his enemies, and the innocent sufferer who is chained in prison must, with Paul and Silas, at midnight sing praises to God. For God is to be glorified, holiness is to be practised, and the spirit of religion is to be the common spirit of every Christian in every state and condition of life.

For the Son of God did not come from above to add an external form of worship to the several ways of life that are in the world, and so to leave people to live as they did before, in such tempers and enjoyments as the fashion and spirit of the world approves. But as He came down from heaven, altogether divine and heavenly in His own nature, so it was to call mankind to a divine and heavenly life; to the highest change of their whole nature and temper; to be born again of the Holy Spirit; to walk in the wisdom and light and love of God; and to be like Him to the utmost of their power; to renounce all the most plausible ways of the world, whether of greatness, business, or pleasure; to a mortification of all their most agreeable passions; and to live in such wisdom, and purity, and holiness, as might fit them to be glorious in the enjoyment of God to all eternity.

Whatever, therefore, is foolish, ridiculous, vain, or earthly, or sensual in the life of a Christian, is something that ought not to be there; it is a spot and a defilement that must be washed away with tears of repentance. But if anything of this kind runs through the course of our whole life, if we allow ourselves in things that are either vain, foolish, or sensual, we renounce our profession.

For as sure as Jesus Christ was wisdom and holiness, as sure as He came to make us like Himself, and to be baptized into His Spirit, so sure is it that none can be said to keep to their Christian profession but they who, to the utmost of their power, live a wise, and holy, and heavenly life. This, and this alone, is Christianity, an universal holiness in every part of life, a heavenly wisdom in all our actions, not conforming to the spirit and temper of the world, but turning all worldly enjoyments into means of piety and devotion to God.

But now, if this devout state of heart, if these habits of inward holiness, be true religion, then true religion is equally the duty and happiness of all orders of men; for there is nothing to recommend it to one, that is not the same recommendation of it to all states of people.

If it be the happiness and glory of a bishop to live in this devout spirit, full of these holy tempers, doing everything as unto God, it is as much the glory and happiness of all men and women, whether young or old, to live in the same spirit. And whoever can find any reasons why an ancient bishop should be intent upon divine things, turning all his life into the highest exercises of piety, wisdom, and devotion, will find them so many reasons why he should, to the utmost of his power, do the same himself.

If you say that a bishop must be an eminent example of Christian holiness, because of his high and sacred calling, you

CHAP. X. say right. But if you say that it is more to his advantage to be exemplary than it is yours, you greatly mistake. For there is nothing to make the highest degrees of holiness desirable to a bishop, but what makes them equally desirable to every young person of every family.

For an exalted piety, high devotion, and the religious use of everything, is as much the glory and happiness of one state of life as it is of another.

Do but fancy in your mind what a spirit of piety you would have in the best bishop in the world, how you would have him love God, how you would have him imitate the life of our Saviour and His Apostles, how you would have him live above the world, shining in all the instances of a heavenly life, and then you have found out that spirit, which you ought to make the spirit of your own life.

I desire every reader to dwell awhile upon this reflection, and perhaps he will find more conviction from it than he imagines. Everyone can tell how good and pious he would have some people to be; everyone knows how wise and reasonable a thing it is in a bishop to be entirely above the world, and be an example of Christian perfection. As soon as you think of a wise and ancient bishop, you fancy some exalted degree of piety, a living example of all those holy tempers which you find described in the Gospel.

Now if you ask yourself, What is the happiest thing for a young clergyman to do? you must be forced to answer, that nothing can be so happy and glorious for him as to be like that excellent holy bishop.

If you go on and ask, What is the happiest thing for any young gentleman or his sisters to do? The answer must be the same; that nothing can be so happy or glorious for them as to live in such habits of piety, in such exercises of a divine life as this good old bishop does. For everything that is great and glorious in religion is as much the true glory of every man or woman as it is the glory of any bishop. If high degrees of divine love, if fervent charity, if spotless purity, if heavenly affection, if constant mortification, if frequent devotion be the best and happiest way of life for any Christian, it is so for every Christian.

Consider, again, if you were to see a bishop in the whole course of his life living below his character, conforming to all the foolish tempers of the world, and governed by the same cares and fears which govern vain and worldly men, what would you think of CHAP. X. him? Would you think that he was only guilty of a small mistake? No; you would condemn him as erring in that which is not only the most, but the only, important matter that relates to him. Stay awhile in this consideration till your mind is fully convinced how miserable a mistake it is in a bishop to live a careless worldly life.

Whilst you are thinking in this manner, turn your thoughts towards some of your acquaintance, your brother or sister, or any young person. Now if you observe the common course of their lives to be not according to the doctrines of the Gospel, if you see that their way of life cannot be said to be a sincere endeavour to enter in at the strait gate, you see something that you are to condemn in the same degree and for the same reasons. They do not commit a small mistake, but are wrong in that which is their all, and mistake their true happiness as much as that bishop does who neglects the high duties of his calling. Apply this reasoning to yourself; if you find yourself living an idle, indulgent, vain life, choosing rather to gratify your passions than to live up to the doctrines of Christianity and practise the plain precepts of our blessed Lord, you have all that blindness and unreasonableness to charge upon yourself that you can charge upon any irregular bishop.

For all the virtues of the Christian life, its perfect purity, its heavenly tempers, are as much the sole rule of your life as the sole rule of the life of a bishop. If you neglect these holy tempers, if you do not eagerly aspire after them, if you do not show yourself a visible example of them, you are as much fallen from your true happiness, you are as great an enemy to yourself, and have made as bad a choice as that bishop that chooses rather to enrich his family than to be like an Apostle. For there is no reason why you should not think the highest holiness, the most heavenly tempers, to be the duty and happiness of a bishop, but what is as good a reason why you should think the same tempers to be the duty and happiness of all Christians. And as the wisest bishop in the world is he who lives in the greatest heights of holiness, who is most exemplary in all the exercises of a divine life, so the wisest youth, the wisest woman, whether married or unmarried, is she that lives in the highest degrees of Christian holiness, and all the exercises of a divine and heavenly life.

# CHAPTER XI.

*Showing how great devotion fills our lives with the greatest peace and happiness that can be enjoyed in this world.*

CHAP. XI. SOME people will perhaps object that all these rules of holy living unto God in all that we do are too great a restraint upon human life; that it will be made too anxious a state by thus introducing a regard to God in all our actions; and that, by depriving ourselves of so many seemingly innocent pleasures, we shall render our lives dull, uneasy, and melancholy.

To which it may be answered:

First, That these rules are prescribed for, and will certainly procure a quite contrary end. That instead of making our lives dull and melancholy, they will render them full of content and strong satisfactions. That by these rules we only change the childish satisfactions of our vain and sickly passions for the solid enjoyments and real happiness of a sound mind.

Secondly, That as there is no foundation for comfort in the enjoyments of this life, but in the assurance that a wise and good God governeth the world, so the more we find out God in every thing, the more we apply to Him in every place, the more we look up to Him in all our actions, the more we conform to His will, the more we act according to His wisdom, and imitate His goodness, by so much the more do we enjoy God, partake of the divine nature, and heighten and increase all that is happy and comfortable in human life.

Thirdly, He that is endeavouring to subdue and root out of his mind all those passions of pride, envy, and ambition, which religion opposes, is doing more to make himself happy, even in this life, than he that is contriving means to indulge them.

For these passions are the causes of all the disquiets and vexations of human life; they are the dropsies and fevers of our minds, vexing them with false appetites, and restless cravings after such things as we do not want, and spoiling our taste for those things which are our proper good.

Do but imagine that you somewhere or other saw a man that proposed reason as the rule of all his actions; that had no desires but after such things as nature wants and religion approves; that was as pure from all the motions of pride, envy, and covetousness as from thoughts of murder; that in this freedom from worldly passions he had a soul full of divine love, wishing and praying that all men may have what they want of worldly things, and be partakers of eternal glory in the life to come.

Do but fancy a man living in this manner, and your own conscience will immediately tell you that he is the happiest man in the world, and that it is not in the power of the richest fancy to invent any higher happiness in the present state of life.

And, on the other hand, if you suppose him to be in any degree less perfect, if you suppose him but subject to one foolish fondness or vain passion, your own conscience will again tell you that he so far lessens his own happiness, and robs himself of the true enjoyment of his other virtues. So true it is, that the more we live by the rules of religion, the more peaceful and happy do we render our lives.

Again, as it thus appears that real happiness is only to be had from the greatest degrees of piety, the greatest denials of our passions, and the strictest rules of religion, so the same truth will appear from a consideration of human misery. If we look into the world and view the disquiets and troubles of human life, we shall find that they are all owing to our violent and irreligious passions.

Now all trouble and uneasiness is founded in the want of something or other. Would we, therefore, know the true cause of our troubles and disquiets, we must find out the cause of our wants, because that which creates and increaseth our wants does in the same degree create and increase our troubles and disquiets.

God Almighty has sent us into the world with very few wants. Meat and drink and clothing are the only things necessary in life; and as these are only our present needs so the present world is well furnished to supply these needs.

If a man had half the world in his power, he can make no more of it than this; as he wants it only to support an animal

CHAP. XI. life so is it unable to do anything else for him, or to afford him any other happiness.

This is the state of man, born with few wants and into a large world very capable of supplying them. So that one would reasonably suppose that men should pass their lives in content and thankfulness to God, at least that they should be free from violent disquiets and vexations, as being placed in a world that has more than enough to relieve all their wants.

But if to all this we add, that this short life, thus furnished with all that we want in it, is only a short passage to eternal glory, where we shall be clothed with the brightness of angels and enter into the joys of God, we might still more reasonably expect that human life should be a state of peace and joy and delight in God. Thus it would certainly be if reason had its full power over us.

But, alas! though God and nature and reason make human life thus free from wants and so full of happiness, yet our passions, in rebellion against God, against nature and reason, create a new world of evils, and fill human life with imaginary wants and vain disquiets.

The man of pride has a thousand wants, which only his own pride has created; and these render him as full of trouble as if God had created him with a thousand appetites without creating anything that was proper to satisfy them. Envy and ambition have also their endless wants, which disquiet the souls of men, and by their contradictory motions render them as foolishly miserable as those that want to fly and creep at the same time.

Let but any complaining, disquieted man tell you the ground of his uneasiness, and you will plainly see that he is the author of his own torment, that he is vexing himself at some imaginary evil, which will cease to torment him as soon as he is content to be that which God and nature and reason require him to be.

If you should see a man passing his days in disquiet because he could not walk upon the water, or catch birds as they fly by him, you would readily confess that such a one might thank himself for such uneasiness. But now if you look into all the most tormenting disquiets of life, you will find them all thus absurd, where people are only tormented by their own folly, and vexing themselves at such things as no more concern them, nor are any more their proper good, than walking upon the water or catching birds.

What can you conceive more silly and extravagant than to CHAP. XI. suppose a man racking his brains, and studying night and day how to fly? wandering from his own house and home, wearying himself with climbing upon every ascent, cringing and courting everybody he meets to lift him from the ground, bruising himself with continual falls, and at last breaking his neck? And all this from an imagination that it would be glorious to have the eyes of people gazing up at him, and mighty happy to eat and drink and sleep at the top of the highest trees in the kingdom. Would you not readily own that such a one was only disquieted by his own folly?

If you ask what it signifies to suppose such silly creatures as these as are nowhere to be found in human life?

It may be answered that wherever you see an ambitious man, there you see this vain and senseless flyer.

Again, if you should see a man that had a large pond of water,[1] yet living in continual thirst, not suffering himself to drink half a draught for fear of lessening his pond; if you should see him wasting his time and strength in fetching more water to his pond; always thirsty, yet always carrying a bucket of water in his hand, watching early and late to catch the drops of rain, gaping after every cloud, and running greedily into every mire and mud in hopes of water, and always studying how to make every ditch empty itself into his pond; if you should see him grow grey and old in these anxious labours, and at last end a careful,[2] thirsty life by falling into his own pond; would you not say that such a one was not only the author of all his own disquiets, but was foolish enough to be reckoned amongst idiots and madmen? But yet, foolish and absurd as this character is, it does not represent half the follies and absurd disquiets of the covetous man.

I could now easily proceed to show the same effects of all our other passions, and make it plainly appear that all our miseries, vexations, and complaints are entirely of our own making, and that, in the same absurd manner as in these instances of the

---

[1] This illustration of 'The Pond' was versified by Law's devoted admirer, John Byrom. It is an extreme instance of Law's favourite argument, the *reductio ad absurdum* ; but, given Law's premises, it would be hard to show that his conclusion was not perfectly logical. The story of the pond should be remembered by the student as one of Law's most characteristic illustrations.

[2] 'Careful,' that is, full of care and anxiety.

CHAP. XI. covetous and ambitious man.   Look where you will, you will
see all worldly vexations but like the vexation of him who was
always in mire and mud in search of water to drink, when he
had more at home than was sufficient for an hundred horses.

COELIA is always telling you how provoked she is, what intolerable shocking things happen to her, what monstrous usage she
suffers, and what vexations she meets with everywhere.   She tells
you that her patience is quite worn out, and there is no bearing
the behaviour of people.   Every assembly that she is at sends
her home provoked; something or other has been said or done
that no reasonable, well-bred person ought to bear.   Poor people
who want her charity are sent away with hasty answers, not
because she has not a heart to part with any money, but because
she is too full of some trouble of her own to attend to the
complaints of others.   Coelia has no business upon her hands
but to receive the income of a plentiful fortune; but yet, by
the doleful turn of her mind, you would be apt to think that
she had neither food nor lodging.   If you see her look more
pale than ordinary, if her lips tremble when she speaks to you,
it is because she is just come from a visit, where Lupus took
no notice at all of her, but talked all the time to Lucinda, who
has not half her fortune.   When cross accidents have so disordered her spirits that she is forced to send for the doctor to
make her able to eat; she tells him, in great anger at Providence,
that she never was well since she was born, and that she envies
every beggar that she sees in health.

This is the disquiet life of Coelia, who has nothing to torment
her but her own spirit.

If you would inspire her with a Christian humility, you need do
no more to make her as happy as any person in the world.   This
virtue would make her thankful to God for half so much health as
she has had, and help her to enjoy more for the time to come.
This virtue would keep off tremblings of the spirits, and loss of
appetite, and her blood would need nothing else to sweeten it.

I have just touched upon these absurd [3] characters for no other
end but to convince you in the plainest manner that the strictest
rules of religion are so far from rendering a life dull, anxious, and
uncomfortable (as is above objected), that, on the contrary, all
the miseries, vexations, and complaints that are in the world

[3] That is, not so much ridiculous, as unreasonable.   In this sense the Latin equivalent 'absurdus' is fre-quently used by Tacitus and Sallust.

are all owing to the want of religion, being directly caused by CHAP. XI. those absurd passions which religion teaches us to deny.

For all the wants which disturb human life, which make us uneasy to ourselves, quarrelsome with others, and unthankful to God ; which weary us in vain labours and foolish anxieties ; which carry us from project to project, and from place to place in a poor pursuit of we know not what, are the wants which neither God, nor nature, nor reason hath subjected us to, but are solely infused into us by pride, envy, ambition, and covetousness.

So far, therefore, as you reduce your desires to such things as nature and reason require ; so far as you regulate all the motions of your heart by the strict rules of religion, so far you remove yourself from that infinity of wants and vexations which torment every heart that is left to itself.

Most people indeed confess that religion preserves us from a great many evils, and helps us in many respects to a more happy enjoyment of ourselves ; but then they imagine that this is only true of such a moderate share of religion as only gently restrains us from the excesses of our passions.[4]  They suppose that the strict rules and restraints of an exalted piety are such contradictions to our nature as must needs make our lives dull and uncomfortable.

Although the weakness of this objection sufficiently appears from what hath been already said, yet I shall add one more word to it.

This objection supposes that religion moderately practised adds much to the happiness of life, but that such heights of piety as the perfection of religion requireth have a contrary effect.

It supposes, therefore, that it is happy to be kept from the excesses of envy, but unhappy to be kept from other degrees of envy ; that it is happy to be delivered from a boundless ambition, but unhappy to be without a more moderate ambition.

---

[4] 'Moderation' was the virtue on which most stress was laid in the popular religion of the eighteenth century. Readers of Addison will remember how, in *The Guardian*, he represents the Church as in its happiest state when it stood between the extremes of fanaticism or 'enthusiasm' and irreligion, when, to use his own illustration, the Church thermometer stood at 'temperate.' Law, who was in many respects the exact antipodes of Addison, wages internecine war against the notion that Christianity was to be regarded as a happy mean between two extremes.  In his *Answer to Dr. Trapp on the Danger of being Righteous Overmuch*, he dwells most fully and directly upon the subject ; but the idea that there can be no extreme, so far as religion is concerned, runs all through the *Serious Call*, and should be specially noted by the student.

CHAP. XI. It supposes also that the happiness of life consists in a mixture of virtue and vice, a mixture of ambition and humility, charity and envy, heavenly affection and covetousness. All which is as absurd as to suppose that it is happy to be free from excessive pains, but unhappy to be without more moderate pains; or that the happiness of health consisted in being partly sick and partly well.

For if humility be the peace and rest of the soul, then no one has so much happiness from humility as he who is the most humble. If excessive envy is a torment of the soul, he most perfectly delivers himself from torment who most perfectly extinguishes every spark of envy. If there is any peace and joy in doing any action according to the will of God, he who brings the most of his actions to this rule does most of all increase the peace and joy of his life.

And thus it is in every virtue; if you act up to every degree of it the more happiness you have from it.[5] And so of every vice; if you only abate its excesses you do but little for yourself; but if you reject it in all degrees then you feel the true ease and joy of a reformed mind.

As, for example, if religion only restrains the excesses of revenge, but lets the spirit still live within you in lesser instances, your religion may have made your life a little more outwardly decent, but not made you at all happier or easier in yourself. But if you have once sacrificed all thoughts of revenge, in obedience to God, and are resolved to return good for evil at all times, that you may render yourself more like to God, and fitter for His mercy in the kingdom of love and glory, this is a height of virtue that will make you feel its happiness.

Secondly, As to those satisfactions and enjoyments which an exalted piety requireth us to deny ourselves, this deprives us of no real comfort of life.

For, first, piety requires us to renounce no ways of life where we can act reasonably, and offer what we do to the glory of God. All ways of life, all satisfactions and enjoyments that are within these bounds, are no way denied us by the strictest rules of piety. Whatever you can do or enjoy, as in the presence of God, as His servant, as His rational creature that has received reason

---

[5] Those who are acquainted with Aristotle's *Ethics* will observe here that Law entirely repudiates 'The Doctrine of the Mean' as applicable to Christian virtues.

and knowledge from Him; all that you can perform conformably CHAP. XI. to a rational nature and the will of God; all this is allowed by the laws of piety. And will you think that your life will be uncomfortable unless you may displease God, be a fool and mad, and act contrary to that reason and wisdom which He has implanted in you?

And as for those satisfactions which we dare not offer to a holy God, which are only invented by the folly and corruption of the world, which inflame our passions, and sink our souls into grossness and sensuality, and render us incapable of the divine favour either here or hereafter, surely it can be no uncomfortable state of life to be rescued by religion from such self-murder, and to be rendered capable of eternal happiness.

Let us suppose a person, destitute of that knowledge which we have from our senses, placed somewhere alone by himself in the midst of a variety of things which he did not know how to use; that he has by him bread, wine, water, golden dust, iron, chains, gravel, garments, fire, etc. Let it be supposed that he has no knowledge of the right use of these things, nor any direction from his senses how to quench his thirst, or satisfy his hunger, or make any use of the things about him. Let it be supposed that in his drought he puts golden dust into his eyes; when his eyes smart he puts wine into his ears; that in his hunger he puts gravel into his mouth; that in pain he loads himself with the iron chains; that, feeling cold, he puts his feet in the water; that, being frightened at the fire, he runs away from it; that being weary, he makes a seat of his bread.[6] Let it be supposed that through his ignorance of the right use of the things that are about him he will plainly torment himself whilst he lives, and at last die, blinded with dust, choked with gravel, and loaded with irons. Let it be supposed that some good being came to him, and showed him the nature and use of all the things that were about him, and gave him such strict rules of using them as would certainly, if

[6] To appreciate the force of these very striking illustrations, it should be remembered that, as moderation was one, so 'reasonableness' was another popular watchword of the eighteenth century. Law, by these illustrations, shows that the godless were acting, not only against the rules of piety, but against the most ordinary rules of reason. *The Reasonableness of Christianity* of John Locke gave the key-note to the theology of the century. Law disagreed *in toto* with Locke, both in his theology and his philosophy, but he desired to show that, tried by the law of 'reasonableness,' entire devotion to God was the only course fitted for a Christian. The whole chapter is a striking comment on the text, 'Godliness has the promise of the life that now is, as well as of that which is to come.'

observed, make him the happier for all that he had, and deliver him from the pains of hunger, and thirst, and cold.

Now could you with any reason affirm that those strict rules of using those things that were about him had rendered that poor man's life dull and uncomfortable?

Now this is in some measure a representation of the strict rules of religion; they only relieve our ignorance, save us from tormenting ourselves, and teach us to use every thing about us to our proper advantage.

Man is placed in a world full of variety of things; his ignorance makes him use many of them as absurdly as the man that put dust in his eyes to relieve his thirst, or put on chains to remove pain.

Religion, therefore, here comes in to his relief, and gives him strict rules of using every thing that is about him; that by so using them suitably to his own nature and the nature of the things, he may have always the pleasure of receiving a right benefit from them. It shows him what is strictly right in meat, drink, and clothes; and that he has nothing else to expect from the things of this world but to satisfy such wants of his own, and then to extend his assistance to all his brethren, that, as far as he is able, he may help all his fellow-creatures to the same benefit from the world that he hath.

It tells him that this world is incapable of giving him any other happiness, and that all endeavours to be happy in heaps of money, or acres of land, in fine clothes, rich beds, stately equipage, and show and splendour, are only vain endeavours, ignorant attempts after impossibilities; these things being no more able to give the least degree of happiness than dust in the eyes can cure thirst, or gravel in the mouth satisfy hunger; but, like dust and gravel misapplied, will only serve to render him more unhappy by such an ignorant misuse of them.

It tells him that although this world can do no more for him than satisfy these wants of the body, yet that there is a much greater good prepared for man than eating, drinking, and dressing; that it is yet invisible to his eyes, being too glorious for the apprehension of flesh and blood, but reserved for him to enter upon as soon as this short life is over, where, in a new body formed to an angelic likeness, he shall dwell in the light and glory of God to all eternity.

It tells him that this state of glory will be given to all those who make a right use of the things of this present world, who CHAP. XI. do not blind themselves with golden dust, or eat gravel, or groan under loads of iron of their own putting on; but use bread, water, wine, and garments for such ends as are according to nature and reason, and who with faith and thankfulness worship the kind Giver of all that they enjoy here, and hope for hereafter.

Now can any one say that the strictest rules of such a religion as this debar us of any of the comforts of life?[7]    Might it not as justly be said of those rules which only hindered a man from choking himself with gravel?    For the strictness of these rules only consists in the exactness of their rectitude.

Who would complain of the severe strictness of a law that, without any exception, forbade the putting of dust into our eyes? Who could think it too rigid that there were no abatements? Now this is the strictness of religion; it requires nothing of us strictly or without abatements, but where every degree of the thing is wrong, where every indulgence does us some hurt.

If religion forbids all instances of revenge without any exception, it is because all revenge is of the nature of poison; and though we do not take so much as to put an end to life, yet, if we take any at all, it corrupts the whole mass of blood, and makes it difficult to be restored to our former health.

If religion commands a universal charity, to love our neighbour as ourselves, to forgive and pray for all our enemies without any reserve, it is because all degrees of love are degrees of happiness that strengthen and support the divine life of the soul, and are as necessary to its health and happiness as proper food is necessary to the health and happiness of the body.

If religion has laws against laying up treasures upon earth, and commands us to be content with food and raiment, it is because every other use of the world is abusing it to our own vexation, and turning all its conveniences into snares and traps to destroy us.    It is because this plainness and simplicity of life

[7] Law was called 'an ascetic'; and so he was in the literal sense of the word, for he lived and recommended a life strictly according to rule.    But he differed *in toto* from those ascetics who thought it a duty to make this life as miserable and uncomfortable as possible, that their minds might be fixed the more steadily upon the happiness of the life to come.    In the passage which follows he shows that the strictest rules of living, which he strives to enforce, so far from taking away the comforts of the present life, only add to them; and in his own life at King's Cliffe, though he framed it according to the principles of the *Serious Call*, he did not affect singularity, nor hold aloof from all society, but was an affable and agreeable neighbour, and hospitable in his way.

CHAP. XI. secures us from the cares and pains of restless pride and envy, and makes it easier to keep that straight road that will carry us to eternal life.

If religion saith, "Sell that thou hast, and give to the poor," it is because there is no other natural or reasonable use of our riches, no other way of making ourselves happier for them; it is because it is as strictly right to give others that which we do not want ourselves as it is right to use so much as our own wants require.[8] For if a man has more food than his own nature requires, how base and unreasonable is it to invent foolish ways of wasting it, and make sport for his own full belly, rather than let his fellow-creatures have the same comfort from food which he hath had? It is so far, therefore, from being a hard law of religion to make this use of our riches, that a reasonable man would rejoice in that religion which teaches him to be happier in that which he gives away than in that which he keeps for himself; which teaches him to make spare food and raiment be greater blessings to him than that which feeds and clothes his own body.

If religion requires us sometimes to fast and deny our natural appetites, it is to lessen that struggle and war that is in our nature; it is to render our bodies fitter instruments of purity, and more obedient to the good motions of divine grace; it is to dry up the springs of our passions that war against the soul, to cool the flame of our blood, and render the mind more capable of divine meditations. So that although these abstinences give some pain to the body, yet they so lessen the power of bodily appetites and passions, and so increase our taste of spiritual joys, that even these severities of religion, when practised with discretion, add much to the comfortable enjoyment of our lives.[9]

If religion calleth us to a life of watching and prayer, it is because we live amongst a crowd of enemies, and are always in need of the assistance of God. If we are to confess and bewail our sins, it is because such confessions relieve the mind and restore it to ease, as burdens and weights taken off the shoulders

---

[8] This was the extent of Law's charity, lavish as it seemed. He would give 'others that which he did not want himself.' But his wants were contracted into a much narrower compass than most people's; the supply of plain food and plain dress left him a very wide margin for the exercise of Christian benevolence.

[9] Observe Law's quaint, but surely very true, description of the results of fasting and self-denial. They are not only good for the soul, but 'add much to the comfortable enjoyment of our lives.'

relieve the body, and make it easier to itself. If we are to be CHAP. XI. frequent and fervent in holy petitions, it is to keep us steady in the sight of our true good, and that we may never want the happiness of a lively faith, a joyful hope, and well-grounded trust in God. If we are to pray often, it is that we may be often happy in such secret joys as only prayer can give, in such communications of the divine presence as will fill our minds with all the happiness that beings not in heaven are capable of.

Was there anything in the world more worth our care, was there any exercise of the mind or any conversation with men that turned more to our advantage than this intercourse with God, we should not be called to such a continuance in prayer. But if a man considers what it is that he leaves when he retires to devotion, he will find it no small happiness to be so often relieved from doing nothing, or nothing to the purpose, from dull idleness, unprofitable labour, or vain conversation. If he considers that all that is in the world, and all that is doing in it, is only for the body and bodily enjoyments, he will have reason to rejoice at those hours of prayer, which carry him to higher consolations, which raise him above these poor concerns, which open to his mind a scene of greater things, and accustom his soul to the hope and expectation of them.

If religion commands us to live wholly unto God and to do all to His glory, it is because every other way is living wholly against ourselves, and will end in our own shame and confusion of face.

As everything is dark that God does not enlighten; as everything is senseless that has not its share of knowledge from Him; as nothing lives but by partaking of life from Him; as nothing exists but because He commands it to be; so there is no glory or greatness but what is of the glory or greatness of God.

We indeed may talk of human glory as we may talk of human life or human knowledge; but as we are sure that human life implies nothing of our own but a dependent living in God, or enjoying so much life in God, so human glory, whenever we find it, must be only so much glory as we enjoy in the glory of God.

This is the state of all creatures, whether men or angels; as they make not themselves, so they enjoy nothing from themselves; if they are great, it must be only as great receivers of the gifts of God; their power can only be so much of the divine power acting in them; their wisdom can only be so much of the divine wisdom shining within them; and their light and glory only so much of the light and glory of God shining upon them.

As they are not men or angels, because they had a mind to be so themselves, but because the will of God formed them to be what they are, so they cannot enjoy this or that happiness of men or angels because they have a mind to it, but because it is the will of God that such things be the happiness of men and such things the happiness of angels. But now if God be thus all in all; if His will is thus the measure of all things and all natures; if nothing can be done but by His power; if nothing can be seen but by a light from Him; if we have nothing to fear but from His justice; if we have nothing to hope for but from His goodness; if this is the nature of man, thus helpless in himself; if this is the state of all creatures, as well those in heaven as those on earth; if they are nothing, can do nothing, can suffer no pain, nor feel any happiness, but so far, and in such degrees, as the power of God does all this; if this be the state of things, then how can we have the least glimpse of joy and comfort, how can we have any peaceful enjoyment of ourselves, but by living wholly unto that God, using and doing everything conformably to His will? A life thus devoted unto God, looking wholly unto Him in all our actions, and doing all things suitably to His glory, is so far from being dull and uncomfortable that it creates new comforts in everything that we do.

On the contrary, would you see how happy they are who live according to their own wills, who cannot submit to the dull and melancholy business of a life devoted unto God, look at the man in the parable to whom his lord had given one talent.

He could not bear the thoughts of using his talent according to the will of him from whom he had it, and therefore he chose to make himself happier in a way of his own. "Lord," says he, "I knew thee that thou art an hard man, reaping where thou hadst not sown, and gathering where thou hadst not strawed. And I was afraid, and went and hid thy talent in the earth. Lo, there thou hast that is thine."

His lord, having convicted him out of his own mouth, despatches him with this sentence, "Cast the unprofitable servant into outer darkness; there shall be weeping and gnashing of teeth." (St. Matt. xxv. 24.)

Here you see how happy this man made himself by not acting CHAP. XI.
wholly according to his lord's will. It was, according to his
own account, a happiness of murmuring and discontent. "I
knew thee," says he, "that thou wast an hard man." It was
a happiness of fears and apprehensions. "I was," says he,
"afraid." It was a happiness of vain labours and fruitless tra-
vails. "I went," says he, "and hid thy talent"; and, after
having been a while the sport of foolish passions, tormenting
fears, and fruitless labours, he is rewarded with darkness, eternal
weeping, and gnashing of teeth.

Now this is the happiness of all those who look upon a strict
and exalted piety, that is, a right use of their talent, to be a
dull and melancholy state of life.

They may live a while free from the restraints and directions
of religion, but instead thereof they must be under the absurd
government of their passions. They must, like the man in the
parable, live in murmurings and discontents, in fears and apprehensions. They may avoid the labour of doing good, of spending
their time devoutly, of laying up treasures in heaven, of clothing
the naked, of visiting the sick; but then they must, like this
man, have labours and pains in vain, that tend to no use or
advantage, that do no good either to themselves or others; they
must travel, and labour, and work, and dig to hide their talent
in the earth. They must, like him, at their Lord's coming be
convicted out of their own mouths, be accused by their own
hearts, and have everything that they have said and thought of
religion be made to show the justice of their condemnation to
eternal darkness, weeping, and gnashing of teeth.

This is the purchase that they make who avoid the strictness
and perfection of religion, in order to live happily.

On the other hand, would you see a short description of the
happiness of a life rightly employed, wholly devoted to God,
you must look at the man in the parable to whom his lord
had given five talents. "Lord," says he, "Thou deliveredst unto
me five talents; behold, I have gained besides them five talents
more. His lord said unto him, Well done, thou good and
faithful servant; thou hast been faithful over a few things, I
will make thee ruler over many things; enter thou into the joy
of thy lord."

Here you see a life that is wholly intent upon the improvement of the talents, that is devoted wholly unto God, is a state

CHAP. XI. of happiness, prosperous labours, and glorious success. Here are not, as in the former case, any uneasy passions, murmurings, vain fears, and fruitless labours. The man is not toiling and digging in the earth for no end nor advantage; but his pious labours prosper in his hands, his happiness increases upon him, the blessing of five becomes the blessing of ten talents, and he is received with a "Well done, good and faithful servant, enter thou into the joy of thy lord."

Now as the case of these men in the parable left nothing else to their choice but either to be happy in using their gifts to the glory of the Lord, or miserable by using them according to their own humours and fancies, so the state of Christianity leaves us no other choice.

All that we have, all that we are, all that we enjoy, are only so many talents from God; if we use them to the ends of a pious and holy life, our five talents will become ten, and our labours will carry us into the joy of our Lord; but if we abuse them to the gratification of our own passions, sacrificing the gifts of God to our own pride and vanity, we shall live here in vain labours and foolish anxieties, shunning religion as a melancholy thing, accusing our Lord as a hard master, and then fall into everlasting misery.

We may for a while amuse ourselves with names, and sounds, and shadows of happiness; we may talk of this or that greatness and dignity; but if we desire real happiness, we have no other possible way to it but by improving our talents, by so holily and piously using the powers and faculties of men in this present state, that we may be happy and glorious in the powers and faculties of angels in the world to come.

How ignorant, therefore, are they of the nature of religion, of the nature of man, and the nature of God, who think a life of strict piety and devotion to God to be a dull uncomfortable state; when it is so plain and certain that there is neither comfort nor joy to be found in anything else!

# CHAPTER XII.

*The happiness of a life wholly devoted unto God, further proved from the vanity, the sensuality, and the ridiculous, poor enjoyments, which they are forced to take up with who live according to their own humours. This represented in various characters.*

WE may still see more of the happiness of a life devoted unto God, by considering the poor contrivances for happiness, and the contemptible ways of life, which they are thrown into, who are not under the directions of a strict piety, but seeking after happiness by other methods.

If one looks at their lives who live by no rule but their own humours and fancies; if one sees but what it is which they call joy, and greatness, and happiness; if one sees how they rejoice and repent, change and fly from one delusion to another; one shall find great reason to rejoice that God hath appointed a strait and narrow way that leadeth unto life, and that we are not left to the folly of our own minds, or forced to take up with such shadows of joy and happiness as the weakness and folly of the world has invented. I say invented, because those things which make up the joy and happiness of the world are mere inventions, which have no foundation in nature and reason, are no way the proper good or happiness of man, no way perfect either in his body or his mind, or carry him to his true end.

As for instance, when a man proposes to be happy in ways of ambition, by raising himself to some imaginary heights above other people; this is truly an invention of happiness which has no foundation in nature, but is as mere a cheat of our own making as if a man should intend to make himself happy by climbing up a ladder.

If a woman seeks for happiness from fine colours or spots upon her face, from jewels and rich clothes, this is as merely an in-

CH. XII. vention of happiness, as contrary to nature and reason as if she should propose to make herself happy by painting a post, and putting the same finery upon it.[1]   It is in this respect that I call these joys and happiness of the world mere inventions of happiness, because neither God, nor nature, nor reason, hath appointed them as such; but whatever appears joyful, or great, or happy in them, is entirely created or invented by the blindness and vanity of our own minds.

And it is on these inventions of happiness that I desire you to cast your eye, that you may thence learn how great a good religion is, which delivers you from such a multitude of follies and vain pursuits as are the torment and vexation of minds that wander from their true happiness in God.

Look at FLATUS,[2] and learn how miserable they are who are left to the folly of their own passions.

Flatus is rich and in health, yet always uneasy, and always searching after happiness.   Every time you visit him you find some new project in his head; he is eager upon it, as something that is more worth his while, and will do more for him than any thing that is already past.   Every new thing so seizes him, that if you were to take him from it, he would think himself quite undone.   His sanguine temper and strong passions promise him so much happiness in everything, that he is always cheated, and is satisfied with nothing.

At his first setting out in life, fine clothes were his delight, his inquiry was only after the best tailors and peruke-makers, and he had no thoughts of excelling in anything but dress.   He spared no expense, but carried every nicety to its greatest height.

---

[1] The raciness and great appropriateness of Law's two illustrations should be noted.   A man who seeks happiness by climbing the heights of ambition is no wiser than he who seeks it by climbing up a ladder, and a woman who seeks it by painting her face and wearing fine clothes is no wiser than she who seeks it by painting and dressing up a post.   These are good specimens of Law's somewhat grim humour.

[2] The character of Flatus is supposed by some to be taken from Law's pupil, Edward Gibbon, father of the historian; but the same objections which apply to Flavia and Miranda apply also to Flatus.   It is true that Edward Gibbon was, like Flatus, of a restless and fickle temper; it is amusing to read John Byrom's complaints of the difficulty he found in getting him to give his attention to shorthand, which was one of his short-lived schemes (see *Byrom's Journal* for Jan. 30, 1730, and following days); but at the time when Law wrote the *Serious Call*, E. Gibbon was little more than a boy, who had just entered upon his unsatisfactory University career.   His early life might give promise that he would turn out a Flatus, and thus might possibly suggest to Law the character of Flatus; but was there any need of such suggestion when the character itself was sufficiently obvious?

But this happiness not answering his expectations, he left off his CH. XII.
brocades, put on a plain coat, railed at fops and beaux, and gave
himself up to gaming with great eagerness.

This new pleasure satisfied him for some time; he envied no
other way of life. But being by the fate of play drawn into a
duel, where he narrowly escaped his death, he left off the dice,
and sought for happiness no longer amongst the gamesters.

The next thing that seized his wandering imagination was the
diversions of the town; and for more than a twelvemonth you
heard him talk of nothing but ladies, drawing-rooms, birth-nights,
plays, balls, and assemblies. But growing sick of these, he had
recourse to hard drinking. Here he had many a merry night,
and met with stronger joys than any he had felt before. Here
he had thoughts of setting up his staff, and looking out no
farther; but unluckily falling into a fever, he grew angry at all
strong liquors, and took his leave of the happiness of being
drunk.

The next attempt after happiness carried him into the field;
for two or three years nothing was so happy as hunting; he
entered upon it with all his soul, and leaped more hedges and
ditches than had ever been known in so short a time. You
never saw him but in a green coat; he was the envy of all that
blow the horn, and always spoke to his dogs in great propriety
of language. If you met him at home on a bad day, you would
hear him blow his horn, and be entertained with the surprising
accidents of the last noble chase. No sooner had Flatus out-done
all the world in the breed and education of his dogs, built
new kennels, new stables, and bought a new hunting-seat, but
he immediately got sight of another happiness, hated the senseless noise and hurry of hunting, gave away his dogs, and was for
some time after deep in the pleasures of building.

Now he invents new kind of dove-cotes, and has such contrivances in his barns and stables as were never seen before;
he wonders at the dulness of the old builders, is wholly bent
upon the improvement of architecture, and will hardly hang a
door in the ordinary way. He tells his friends that he never
was so delighted in anything in his life; that he has more happiness amongst his brick and mortar than ever he had at court;
and that he is contriving how to have some little matter to do
that way as long as he lives.

The next year he leaves his house unfinished, complains to

CH. XII. everybody of masons and carpenters, and devotes himself wholly
to the happiness of riding about.    After this, you can never see
him but on horseback, and so highly delighted with this new
way of life, that he would tell you, give him but his horse and
a clean country to ride in, and you might take all the rest to
yourself.    A variety of new saddles and bridles, and a great
change of horses, added much to the pleasure of this new way
of life.    But, however, having after some time tired both himself
and his horses, the happiest thing he could think of next was to
go abroad and visit foreign countries; and there, indeed, happiness exceeded his imagination, and he was only uneasy that
he had begun so fine a life no sooner.    The next month he
returned home, unable to bear any longer the impertinence of
foreigners.

After this he was a great student for one whole year; he was
up early and late at his Italian grammar, that he might have
the happiness of understanding the opera, whenever he should hear
one, and not to be like those unreasonable people that are pleased
with they know not what.[3]

Flatus is very ill-natured, or otherwise, just as his affairs happen
to be when you visit him; if you find him when some project
is almost worn out, you will find a peevish, ill-bred man; but
if you had seen him just as he entered upon his riding regimen,
or begun to excel in sounding of the horn, you had been saluted
with great civility.

Flatus is now at a full stand, and is doing what he never did in
his life before, he is reasoning and reflecting with himself.    He
loses several days in considering which of his cast-off ways of life
he should try again.

But here a new project comes in to his relief.    He is now living
upon herbs, and running about the country to get himself into as
good wind as any running footman[4] in the kingdom.

I have been thus circumstantial in so many foolish particulars
of this kind of life, because I hope that every particular folly that
you here see will naturally turn itself into an argument for the
wisdom and happiness of a religious life.

---

[3] To appreciate the satire of this
sentence it should be remembered how
very feeble the plots and language of
the early Italian operas are.

[4] For an interesting description of
running footmen, see Sir Walter Scott's
*Bride of Lammermoor*, ch. 21, and
also Note 1, 'Running Footmen,' at
the close of the volume.    The novelist
implies that they existed up to his
own day.

If I could lay before you a particular account of all the circumstances of terror and distress that daily attend a life at sea, the more particular I was in the account, the more I should make you feel and rejoice in the happiness of living upon the land.

In like manner, the more I enumerate the follies, anxieties, delusions, and restless desires which go through every part of a life devoted to human passions and worldly enjoyments, the more you must be affected with that peace, and rest, and solid content, which religion gives to the souls of men.

If you but just cast your eye upon a madman or a fool, it perhaps signifies little or nothing to you; but if you were to attend them for some days, and observe the lamentable madness and stupidity of all their actions, this would be an affecting sight, and would make you often bless yourself for the enjoyment of your reason and senses.

Just so, if you are only told, in the gross, of the folly and madness of a life devoted to the world, it makes little or no impression upon you; but if you are shown how such people live every day; if you see the continual folly and madness of all their particular actions and designs; this would be an affecting sight, and make you bless God for having given you a greater happiness to aspire after.[5]

So that characters of this kind, the more folly and ridicule they have in them, provided that they be but natural, are most useful to correct our minds; and, therefore, are nowhere more proper than in books of devotion and practical piety. And as in several cases we best learn the nature of things by looking at that which is contrary to them, so perhaps we best apprehend the excellency of wisdom by contemplating the wild extravagances of folly.

I shall therefore continue this method a little farther, and endeavour to recommend the happiness of piety to you, by showing you, in some other instances, how miserably and poorly they live who live without it.

But you will perhaps say that the ridiculous, restless life of Flatus is not the common state of those who resign themselves up to live by their own humours, and neglect the strict rules of religion; and that, therefore, it is not so great an argument of the happiness of a religious life as I would make it.

---

[5] That is, a greater happiness even in this life, without taking into account the life to come.

I answer that I am afraid it is one of the most general characters in life; and that few people can read it without seeing
something in it that belongs to themselves. For where shall we
find that wise and happy man who has not been eagerly pursuing
different appearances of happiness, sometimes thinking it was
here and sometimes there?

And if people were to divide their lives into particular stages,
and ask themselves what they were pursuing, or what it was
which they had chiefly in view when they were twenty years old,
what at twenty-five, what at thirty, what at forty, what at fifty,
and so on, till they were brought to their last bed; numbers of
people would find that they had liked, and disliked, and pursued
as many different appearances of happiness as are to be seen in
the life of Flatus.

And thus it must necessarily be more or less with all those who
propose any other happiness than that which arises from a strict
and regular piety.

But, secondly, let it be granted that the generality of people
are not of such restless, fickle tempers as Flatus; the difference
then is only this, Flatus is continually changing and trying something new, but others are content with some one state; they do
not leave gaming and then fall to hunting. But they have so
much steadiness in their tempers, that some seek after no other
happiness but that of heaping up riches; others grow old in the
sports of the field; others are content to drink themselves to
death, without the least inquiry after any other happiness.

Now is there anything more happy or reasonable in such a life
as this than in the life of Flatus? Is it not as great and desirable,
as wise and happy, to be constantly changing from one thing to
another, as to be nothing else but a gatherer of money, a hunter,
a gamester, or a drunkard all your life?

Shall religion be looked upon as a burden, as a dull and
melancholy state, for calling men from such happiness as this, to
live according to the laws of God, to labour after the perfection
of their nature, and prepare themselves for an endless state of
joy and glory in the presence of God?

But turn your eyes now another way, and let the trifling joys,
the gewgaw happiness of FELICIANA, teach you how wise they are,
what delusion they escape, whose hearts and hopes are fixed upon
a happiness in God.

If you were to live with Feliciana but one half year, you would

see all the happiness that she is to have as long as she lives.
She has no more to come but the poor repetition of that which
could never have pleased once, but through a littleness of mind
and want of thought.

She is to be again dressed fine, and keep her visiting day. She
is again to change the colour of her clothes, again to have a new
head, and again put patches on her face. She is again to see
who acts best at the play-house, and who sings finest at the opera.
She is again to make ten visits in a day, and be ten times in a
day trying to talk artfully, easily, and politely about nothing.

She is to be again delighted with some new fashion, and again
angry at the change of some old one. She is to be again at
cards, and gaming at midnight, and again in bed at noon. She
is to be again pleased with hypocritical compliments, and again
disturbed at imaginary affronts. She is to be again pleased with
her good luck at gaming, and again tormented with the loss of
her money. She is again to prepare herself for a birth-night, and
again see the town full of good company. She is again to hear
the cabals and intrigues of the town; again to have secret in-
telligence of private amours, and early notice of marriages,
quarrels, and partings.

If you see her come out of her chariot more briskly than usual,
converse with more spirit, and seem fuller of joy than she was
last week, it is because there is some surprising new dress, or
new diversion just come to town.

These are all the substantial and regular parts of Feliciana's
happiness; and she never knew a pleasant day in her life, but it
was owing to some one or more of these things.

It is for this happiness that she has always been deaf to the
reasonings of religion, that her heart has been too gay and
cheerful to consider what is right or wrong in regard to eternity;
or to listen to the sound of such dull words as wisdom, piety,
and devotion.

It is for fear of losing some of this happiness that she dares
not meditate on the immortality of her soul, consider her relation
to God, or turn her thoughts towards those joys which make
saints and angels infinitely happy in the presence and glory
of God.

But now let it be here observed, that as poor a round of
happiness as this appears, yet most women that avoid the restraints of religion for a gay life must be content with very small

CH. XII. parts of it. As they have not Feliciana's fortune and figure in the world, so they must give away the comforts of a pious life for a very small part of her happiness.

And if you look into the world, and observe the lives of those women, whom no arguments can persuade to live wholly unto God, in a wise and pious employment of themselves, you will find most of them to be such as lose all the comforts of religion, without gaining the tenth part of Feliciana's happiness.[6] They are such as spend their time and fortunes only in mimicking the pleasures of richer people; and rather look and long after than enjoy those delusions, which are only to be purchased by considerable fortunes.

But if a woman of high birth and great fortune, having read the Gospel, should rather wish to be an under servant in some pious family, where wisdom, piety, and great devotion directed all the actions of every day; if she should rather wish this than to live at the top of Feliciana's happiness, I should think her neither mad nor melancholy, but that she judged as rightly of the spirit of the Gospel as if she had rather wished to be poor "Lazarus at the gate," than to be the rich man "clothed in purple and fine linen, and faring sumptuously every day."

But to proceed. Would you know what a happiness it is to be governed by the wisdom of religion, and to be devoted to the joys and hopes of a pious life; look at the poor condition of Succus, whose greatest happiness is a good night's rest in bed, and a good meal when he is up. When he talks of happiness, it is always in such expressions that show you that he has only his bed and his dinner in his thoughts.

This regard to his meals and repose makes Succus order all the rest of his time with relation to them. He will undertake no business that may hurry his spirits, or break in upon his hours of eating and rest. If he reads it shall only be for half an hour, because that is sufficient to amuse the spirits; and he will read something that may make him laugh, as rendering the body fitter for its food and rest. Or if he has at any time a mind to indulge a grave thought, he always has recourse to a useful treatise upon the ancient cookery. Succus is an enemy to all party-matters, having made it an observation that there is as good eating amongst the Whigs as the Tories.

[6] After having shown how utterly worthless Feliciana's happiness was, Law displays a fine humour in the words 'a tenth part of that happiness.'

CH. XII.

He talks coolly and moderately upon all subjects, and is as fearful of falling into a passion as of catching cold, being very positive that they are both equally injurious to the stomach. If you ever see him more hot than ordinary, it is upon some provoking occasion, when the dispute about cookery runs very high, or in the defence of some beloved dish, which has often made him happy. But he has been so long upon these subjects, is so well acquainted with all that can be said on both sides, and has so often answered all objections, that he generally decides the matter with great gravity.

Succus is very loyal, and as soon as ever he likes any wine he drinks the king's health with all his heart. Nothing could put rebellious thoughts into his head, unless he should live to see a proclamation against eating of pheasants' eggs.

All the hours that are not devoted either to repose or nourishment are looked upon by Succus as waste or spare time; for this reason he lodges near a coffee-house [7] and a tavern, that when he rises in the morning he may hear the news, and when he parts at night he may not have far to go to bed. In the morning you always see him in the same place in the coffee-room, and if he seems more attentively engaged than ordinary, it is because some criminal is broke out of Newgate, or some lady was robbed last night, but they cannot tell where. When he has learned all that he can, he goes home to settle the matter with the barber's boy that comes to shave him.

The next waste time that lies upon his hands is from dinner to supper; and if melancholy thoughts ever come into his head it is at this time, when he is often left to himself for an hour or more, and that after the greatest pleasure he knows is just over. He is afraid to sleep, because he has heard it is not healthful at that time, so that he is forced to refuse so welcome a guest.

But here he is soon relieved by a settled method of playing at cards till it is time to think of some little nice matter for supper.

After this Succus takes his glass, talks of the excellency of

[7] Coffee-houses and chocolate-houses were the resort of idlers and newsmongers, and were more like our clubs than our hotels, but not nearly so select and exclusive. Steele tells us in his first number of the *Tatler*, bearing the suggestive motto, ' Quicquid agunt homines,' "that all accounts of gallantry shall be under the article of White's Chocolate - house; poetry, under that of Will's Coffee-house; learning, under the title of Grecian; foreign and domestic news you will have from St. James's Coffee-house."

CH. XII. the English constitution,[8] and praises that Minister the most who keeps the best table.

On a Sunday night you may sometimes hear him condemning the iniquity of the town rakes; and the bitterest thing that he says against them is this, that he verily believes some of them are so abandoned as not to have a regular meal or a sound night's sleep in a week.

At eleven, Succus bids all good night, and parts in great friendship. He is presently in bed, and sleeps till it is time to go to the coffee-house next morning.

If you were to live with Succus for a twelvemonth, this is all that you would see in his life, except a few curses and oaths that he uses as occasion offers.

And now I cannot help making this reflection:

That as I believe the most likely means in the world to inspire a person with true piety was to have seen the example of some eminent professor of religion, so the next thing that is likely to fill one with the same zeal, is to see the folly, the baseness, and poor satisfactions of a life destitute of religion. As the one excites us to love and admire the wisdom and greatness of religion so the other may make us fearful of living without it.

For who can help blessing God for the means of grace, and for the hope of glory, when he sees what variety of folly they sink into, who live without it? Who would not heartily engage in all the labours and exercises of a pious life, be "steadfast, immovable, and always abounding in the work of the Lord," when he sees what dull sensuality, what poor views, what gross enjoyments they are left to, who seek for happiness in other ways?

So that, whether we consider the greatness of religion, or the littleness of all other things, and the meanness of all other enjoyments, there is nothing to be found in the whole nature of things for a thoughtful mind to rest upon but a happiness in the hopes of religion.

Consider now with yourself how unreasonably it is pretended that a life of strict piety must be a dull and anxious state?

[8] 'The excellency of the English Constitution,' and 'Our happy Establishment in Church and State,' were stock phrases in the eighteenth century, which, however, would not at all commend themselves to Law. Though he very rarely obtrudes his political views, he was, from beginning to end, a staunch and uncompromising Jacobite and nonjuror, and there would be something supremely ridiculous to a man of such views, in one of the life and character of Succus, glorying in the English Constitution.

For can it with any reason be said, that the duties and restraints CH. XII. of religion must render our lives heavy and melancholy, when they only deprive us of such happiness as has been here laid before you?

Must it be tedious and tiresome to live in the continual exercise of charity, devotion, and temperance, to act wisely and virtuously, to do good to the utmost of your power, to imitate the divine perfections, and prepare yourself for the enjoyment of God? Must it be dull and tiresome to be delivered from blindness and vanity, from false hopes and vain fears, to improve in holiness, to feel the comforts of conscience in all your actions, to know that God is your friend, that all must work for your good, that neither life nor death, neither men nor devils, can do you any harm; but that all your sufferings and doings that are offered unto God, all your watchings and prayers, and labours of love and charity, all your improvements, are in a short time to be rewarded with everlasting glory in the presence of God; must such a state as this be dull and tiresome for want of such happiness as Flatus or Feliciana enjoys?

Now if this cannot be said, then there is no happiness or pleasure lost by being strictly pious, nor has the devout man anything to envy in any other state of life. For all the art and contrivance in the world, without religion, cannot make more of human life, or carry its happiness to any greater height, than Flatus and Feliciana have done.

The finest wit, the greatest genius upon earth, if not governed by religion, must be as foolish and low and vain in his methods of happiness as the poor Succus.

If you were to see a man duly endeavouring all his life to satisfy his thirst by holding up one and the same empty cup to his mouth, you would certainly despise his ignorance.

But if you should see others of brighter parts and finer understandings ridiculing the dull satisfaction of one cup, and thinking to satisfy their own thirst by a variety of gilt and golden empty cups, would you think that these were ever the wiser, or happier, or better employed for their finer parts?

Now this is all the difference that you can see in the happiness of this life.

The dull and heavy soul may be content with one empty appearance of happiness, and be continually trying to hold one and the same empty cup to his mouth all his life. But then let

CH. XII. the wit, the great scholar, the fine genius, the great statesman, the polite gentleman lay all their heads together, and they can only show you more and various empty appearances of happiness; give them all the world into their hands, let them cut and carve as they please, they can only make a greater variety of empty cups.

So that if you do not think it hard to be deprived of the pleasures of gluttony for the sake of religion, you have no reason to think it hard to be restrained from any other worldly pleasure. For search as deep and look as far as you will, there is nothing here to be found that is nobler or greater than high eating and drinking unless you look for it in the wisdom and laws of religion.

And if all that is in the world are only so many empty cups, what does it signify which you take, or how many you take, or how many you have?

If you would but use yourself to such meditations as these, to reflect upon the vanity of all orders of life without piety, to consider how all the ways of the world are only so many different ways of error, blindness, and mistake you would soon find your heart made wiser and better by it. These meditations would awaken your soul into a zealous desire of that solid happiness which is only to be found in recourse to God.

Examples of great piety are not now common in the world; it may not be your happiness to live within sight of any, or to have your virtue inflamed by their light and fervour. But the misery and folly of worldly men is what meets your eyes in every place, and you need not look far to see how poorly, how vainly men dream away their lives for want of religious wisdom.

This is the reason that I have laid before you so many characters of the vanity of a worldly life, to teach you to make a benefit of the corruption of the age, and that you may be made wise, though not by the sight of what piety is, yet by seeing what misery and folly reigns, where piety is not.[9]

If you would turn your mind to such reflections as these, your own observation would carry this instruction much further, and all your conversation and acquaintance with the world would be a daily conviction to you of the necessity of seeking some greater happiness than all the poor enjoyments this world can give.

[9] The reason which Law gives for drawing so many portraits of worldlings of different kinds may seem an uncharitable one, but the student of the early Georgian era will see only too well the force of it. If he had drawn many pictures of piety, his readers would have found few examples of what he meant in real life; but they would see on all sides of them examples of what he meant them to avoid.

To meditate upon the perfection of the divine attributes, to CH. XII. contemplate the glories of heaven, to consider the joys of saints and angels living for ever in the brightness and glory of the divine presence, these are the meditations of souls advanced in piety, and not so suited to every capacity.[10]

But to see and consider the emptiness and error of all worldly happiness, to see the grossness of sensuality, the poorness of pride, the stupidity of covetousness, the vanity of dress, the delusion of honour, the blindness of our passions, the uncertainty of our lives, and the shortness of all worldly projects; these are meditations that are suited to all capacities, fitted to strike all minds. They require no depth of thought or sublime speculation, but are forced upon us by all our senses, and taught us by almost everything that we see and hear.

This is that "wisdom that crieth, and putteth forth her voice in the streets" (Prov. viii. 1), that standeth at all our doors, that appealeth to all our senses, teaching us in everything and everywhere, by all that we see and all that we hear, by births and burials, by sickness and health, by life and death, by pains and poverty, by misery and vanity, and by all the changes and chances of life, that there is nothing else for man to look after, no other end in nature for him to drive at, but a happiness which is only to be found in the hopes and expectations of religion.

[10] The reason of this, too, is painfully obvious. Law was obliged to strike a low note, because even earnest Christians, in their horror of 'enthusiasm,' were too much of 'the earth, earthy,' before the Evangelical Revival.

# CHAPTER XIII.

*That not only a life of vanity or sensuality, but even the most regular kind of life that is not governed by great devotion, sufficiently shows its miseries, its wants, and emptiness, to the eyes of all the world. This represented in various characters.*

CH. XIII. It is a very remarkable saying of our Lord and Saviour to His disciples in these words, "Blessed are your eyes, for they see, and your ears, for they hear." They teach us two things: First, That the dulness and heaviness of men's minds with regard to spiritual matters is so great that it may justly be compared to the want of eyes and ears.

Secondly, That God has so filled everything and every place with motives and arguments for a godly life, that they who are but so blessed, so happy as to use their eyes and their ears, must needs be affected with them.

Now though this was in a more especial manner the case of those whose senses were witnesses of the life and miracles and doctrines of our blessed Lord, yet it is as truly the case of all Christians at this time. For the reasons of religion, the calls to piety, are so written and engraved upon everything, and present themselves so strongly and so constantly to all our senses in everything that we meet, that they can only be disregarded by eyes that see not and ears that hear not.

What greater motive to a religious life than the vanity, the poorness of all worldly enjoyments; and yet who can help seeing and feeling this every day of his life?

What greater call to look towards God than the pains, the sicknesses, the crosses, and vexations of this life; and yet whose eyes and ears are not daily witnesses of them?

What miracles could more strongly appeal to our senses, or

what message from heaven speak louder to us, than the daily dying and departure of our fellow-creatures?

So that the one thing needful, or the great end of life, is not left to be discovered by fine reasoning and deep reflections, but is pressed upon us in the plainest manner by the experience of all our senses, by everything that we meet with in life.

Let us but intend to see and hear, and then the whole world becomes a book of wisdom and instruction to us all; all that is regular in the order of nature, all that is accidental in the course of things, all the mistakes and disappointments that happen to ourselves, all the miseries and errors that we see in other people, become so many plain lessons of advice to us, teaching us, with as much assurance as an angel from heaven, that we can no ways raise ourselves to any true happiness but by turning all our thoughts, our wishes, and endeavours after the happiness of another life.

It is this right use of the world that I would lead you into by directing you to turn your eyes upon every shape of human folly, that you may thence draw fresh arguments and motives of living to the best and greatest purposes of your creation.

And if you would but carry this intention about you, of profiting by the follies of the world, and of learning the greatness of religion from the littleness and vanity of every other way of life; if, I say, you would but carry this intention in your mind, you would find every day, every place, and every person a fresh proof of their wisdom who choose to live wholly unto God. You would then often return home the wiser, the better, and the more strengthened in religion by everything that has fallen in your way.

OCTAVIUS[1] is a learned, ingenious man, well versed in most parts of literature, and no stranger to any kingdom in Europe. The other day, being just recovered from a lingering fever, he took upon him to talk thus to his friends:

"My glass," says he, "is almost run out, and your eyes see how many marks of age and death I bear about me; but I plainly feel myself sinking away faster than any standers-by imagine. I fully believe that one year more will conclude my reckoning."

The attention of his friends was much raised by such a declaration, expecting to hear something truly excellent from so learned

---

[1] In the sketch of Octavius we have a forecast of that excessive depreciation of human learning, which with Law (himself an essentially learned man) afterwards became an almost ludicrous foible.

CH. XIII. a man, who had but a year longer to live, when Octavius proceeded in this manner:

"For these reasons," says he, "my friends, I have left off all taverns; the wine of those places is not good enough for me in this decay of nature. I must now be nice in what I drink; I cannot pretend to do as I have done; and therefore am resolved to furnish my own cellar with a little of the very best, though it cost me ever so much.

"I must also tell you, my friends, that age forces a man to be wise in many other respects, and makes us change many of our opinions and practices.

"You know how much I have liked a large acquaintance; I now condemn it as an error. Three or four cheerful, diverting companions is all that I now desire; because I find that, in my present infirmities, if I am left alone, or to grave company, I am not so easy to myself."

A few days after Octavius had made this declaration to his friends, he relapsed into his former illness, was committed to a nurse, who closed his eyes before his fresh parcel of wine came in.

Young EUGENIUS, who was present at this discourse, went home a new man, with full resolutions of devoting himself wholly unto God.

"I never" says Eugenius, "was so deeply affected with the wisdom and importance of religion, as when I saw how poorly and meanly the learned Octavius was to leave the world through the want of it.

"How often had I envied his great learning, his skill in language, his knowledge of antiquity, his address, and fine manner of expressing himself upon all subjects! But when I saw how poorly it all ended, what was to be the last year of such a life, and how foolishly the master of all these accomplishments was then forced to talk, for want of being acquainted with the joys and expectations of piety, I was thoroughly convinced that there was nothing to be envied or desired but a life of true piety, nor anything so poor and comfortless as a death without it."

Now as the young Eugenius was thus edified and instructed in the present case; so if you are so happy as to have anything of his thoughtful temper, you will meet with variety of instruction of this kind; you will find that arguments for the wisdom and happiness of a strict piety offer themselves in all places, and appeal to all your senses in the plainest manner.

You will find that all the world preaches to an attentive mind, CH. XIII. and that if you have but ears to hear, almost everything you meet teaches you some lesson of wisdom.

But now, if to these admonitions and instructions, which we receive from our senses, from an experience of the state of human life; if to these we add the lights of religion, those great truths which the Son of God has taught us; it will be then as much past all doubt that there is but one happiness for man, as that there is but one God.

For since religion teaches us that our souls are immortal, that piety and devotion will carry them to an eternal enjoyment of God, and that carnal worldly tempers will sink them into an everlasting misery with damned spirits,[2] what gross nonsense and stupidity is it, to give the name of joy or happiness to any thing but that which carries us to this joy and happiness in God?

Were all to die with our bodies, there might be some pretence for those different sorts of happiness that are so much talked of; but since our all begins at the death of our bodies; since all men are to be immortal, either in misery or happiness, in a world entirely different from this; since they are all hastening hence at all uncertainties as fast as death can cut them down; some in sickness, some in health, some sleeping, some waking, some at midnight, others at cock-crowing, and all at hours that they know not of; is it not certain that no man can exceed another in joy and happiness, but so far as he exceeds him in those virtues which fit him for a happier death?

COGNATUS[3] is a sober, regular clergyman, of good repute in the world and well esteemed in his parish. All his parishioners say he is an honest man, and very notable at making a bargain. The farmers listen to him with great attention when he talks of the properest time of selling corn.

He has been for twenty years a diligent observer of markets, and has raised a considerable fortune by good management.

Cognatus is very orthodox, and full of esteem of our English

[2] In his later life Law would not have used this expression. He became a firm believer in 'the restitution of all things,' though he did not put the doctrine prominently forward lest it should become an encouragement to men to sin. Such passages as these led Gibbon to say that the *Serious Call* was full of 'hell and damnation'; but surely this is an exaggeration; such expressions are very rare.

[3] Cognatus is a character painfully common in the easy-going days of the Georgian era, when too many of the clergy were only a little less, if less, worldly than the laity. There were more Parsons Trulliber than Parsons Adams, though the latter were not rare.

CH. XIII. liturgy; and if he has not prayers on Wednesdays and Fridays,[4] it is because his predecessor had not used the parish to any such custom.

As he cannot serve both his livings himself,[5] he makes it matter of conscience to keep a sober curate upon one of them, whom he hires to take care of all the souls in the parish at as cheap a rate as a sober man can be procured.[6]

Cognatus has been very prosperous all his time, but still he has had the uneasiness and vexations that they have who are deep in worldly business. Taxes, losses, crosses, bad mortgages, bad tenants, and the hardness of the times are frequent subjects of his conversation; and a good or bad season has a great effect upon his spirits.

Cognatus has no other end in growing rich but that he may leave a considerable fortune to a niece whom he has politely educated in expensive finery by what he has saved out of the tithes of two livings.

The neighbours look upon Cognatus as a happy clergyman, because they see him (as they call it) in good circumstances; and some of them intend to dedicate their own sons to the Church, because they see how well it has succeeded with Cognatus, whose father was but an ordinary man.

But now if Cognatus, when he first entered into holy orders, had perceived how absurd[7] a thing it is to grow rich by the Gospel; if he had proposed to himself the example of some primitive father; if he had had the piety of the great St. Austin[8] in his eye, who durst not enrich any of his relations out of the revenue of the Church; if instead of twenty years' care to lay up treasures upon earth he had distributed the income of every year in the most Christian acts of charity and compassion.

If instead of tempting his niece to be proud, and providing her with such ornaments as the Apostle forbids, he had clothed, com-

---

[4] The mention of prayers on Wednesdays and Fridays shows, what is fully borne out from other sources, that 'the prayer days,' as they were then called, were not yet so generally neglected as they afterwards became.

[5] 'Both his livings' points to the growing evil of pluralities.

[6] The position of stipendiary curates was then very hard. £30 a year was the highest stipend for which they could look, and it was often much less, while the amassing of several benefices in one hand rendered their chance of ever being beneficed almost hopeless; there were in consequence far fewer benefices to be disposed of. See Stackhouse's *Miseries and Great Hardships of the Inferior Clergy*, etc., *passim*.

[7] That is, unreasonable.

[8] That is, of course, Augustine, Bishop of Hippo, not Augustine, the first Archbishop of Canterbury.

forted, and assisted numbers of widows, orphans, and distressed, CH. XIII.
who were all to appear for him at the last day.

If instead of the cares and anxieties of bad bonds, troublesome
mortgages, and ill bargains, he had had the constant comfort of
knowing that his treasure was securely laid up, where neither
moth corrupteth nor thieves break through and steal; could it
with any reason be said that he had mistaken the spirit and
dignity of his order, or lessened any of that happiness which is to
be found in his sacred employments?

If instead of rejoicing in the happiness of a second living, he
had thought it as unbecoming the office of a clergyman to
traffic for gain in holy things as to open a shop.

If he had thought it better to recommend some honest labour
to his niece than to support her in idleness by the labours of a
curate; better that she should want fine clothes and a rich husband
than that cures of souls should be farmed about, and brother
clergymen not suffered to live by those altars at which they serve.
If this had been the spirit of Cognatus, could it with any reason
be said that these rules of religion, this strictness of piety, had
robbed Cognatus of any real happiness?   Could it be said that a
life thus governed by the spirit of the Gospel must be dull and
melancholy if compared to that of raising a fortune for a niece?

Now as this cannot be said in the present case, so in every
other kind of life, if you enter into the particulars of it, you
will find that, however easy and prosperous it may seem, yet you
cannot add piety to any part of it without adding so much of a
better joy and happiness to it.

Look now at that condition of life which draws the envy of all
eyes.

NEGOTIUS is a temperate, honest man.   He served his time
under a master of great trade, but has by his own management made it a more considerable business than ever it was
before.   For thirty years last past he has written fifty or sixty
letters in a week, and is busy in corresponding with all parts
of Europe.   The general good of trade seems to Negotius to be
the general good of life; whomsoever he admires, whatever he
commands or condemns either in Church or State, is admired,
commended, or condemned, with some regard to trade.

As money is continually pouring in upon him so he often
lets it go in various kinds of expense and generosity, and sometimes in ways of charity.

 Negotius is always ready to join in any public contribution. If a purse is making at any place where he happens to be, whether it be to buy a plate for a horse-race, or to redeem a prisoner out of jail, you are always sure of having something from him.

He has given a fine ring of bells to a church in the country, and there is much expectation that he will some time or other make a more beautiful front to the market-house than has yet been seen in any place. For it is the generous spirit of Negotius to do nothing in a mean way.

If you ask what it is that has secured Negotius from all scandalous vices, it is the same thing that has kept him from all strictness of devotion, it is his great business. He has always had too many important things in his head, his thoughts have been too much employed, to suffer him to fall either into any courses of rakery, or to feel the necessity of an inward, solid piety.

For this reason, he hears of the pleasures of debauchery and the pleasures of piety with the same indifferency; and has no more desire of living in the one than in the other, because neither of them consist with that turn of mind and multiplicity of business which are his happiness.

If Negotius was asked, What is it which he drives at in life? he would be as much at a loss for an answer as if he was asked what any other person is thinking of. For though he always seems to himself to know what he is doing, and has many things in his head, which are the motives of his actions, yet he cannot tell you of any one general end of life that he has chosen with deliberation as being truly worthy of all his labour and pains.

He has several confused notions in his head, which have been a long time there, such as these, viz., That it is something great to have more business than other people; to have more dealings upon his hands than a hundred of the same profession; to grow continually richer and richer, and to raise an immense fortune before he dies. The thing that seems to give Negotius the greatest life and spirit, and to be most in his thoughts, is an expectation that he has, that he shall die richer than any of his business ever did.

The generality of people when they think of happiness think upon Negotius, in whose life every instance of happiness is supposed to meet; sober, prudent, rich, prosperous, generous, and charitable.

Let us now, therefore, look at this condition in another but truer light.

Let it be supposed that this same Negotius was a painful, laborious man, every day deep in variety of affairs; that he neither drank nor debauched, but was sober and regular in his business. Let it be supposed that he grew old in this course of trading; and that the end and design of all this labour and care, and application to business, was only this, that he might die possessed of more than a hundred thousand pairs of boots and spurs, and as many great-coats.[9]

Let it be supposed that the sober part of the world say of him when he is dead that he was a great and happy man, a thorough master of the business, and had acquired a hundred thousand pairs of boots and spurs when he died.

Now if this was really the case, I believe it would be readily granted that a life of such business was as poor and ridiculous as any that can be invented. But it would puzzle any one to show that a man that has spent all his time and thoughts in business and hurry that he might die, as it is said, worth a hundred thousand pounds, is any whit wiser than he who has taken the same pains to have as many pairs of boots and spurs when he leaves the world.

For if the temper and state of our souls be our whole state; if the only end of life be to die as free from sin and as exalted in virtue as we can; if naked as we came, so naked are we to return, and to stand a trial before Christ and His holy angels, for everlasting happiness or misery; what can it possibly signify what a man had, or had not, in this world? What can it signify what you call those things which a man has left behind him; whether you call them his or any one's else; whether you call them trees or fields, or birds and feathers; whether you call them a hundred thousand pounds, or a hundred thousand pairs of boots and spurs? I say, call them; for the things signify no more to him than the names.

Now it is easy to see the folly of a life thus spent, to fur-

---

[9] Observe this specimen of Law's grim humour, which is at the same time most forcible and apposite. Whether it be a hundred thousand pounds, or a hundred thousand pairs of boots and spurs, or of great-coats that he has amassed, is all the same to a man when he is dead.

CH. XIII. nish a man with such a number of boots and spurs. But yet there needs no better faculty of seeing, no finer understanding, to see the folly of a life spent in making a man a possessor of ten towns before he dies.

For if, when he has got all his towns, or all his boots, his soul is to go to his own place among separate spirits, and his body be laid by in a coffin till the last trumpet calls him to judgment, where the inquiry will be, how humbly, how devoutly, how purely, how meekly, how piously, how charitably, how heavenly we have spoken, thought, and acted, whilst we were in the body; how can we say that he who has worn out his life in raising a hundred thousand pounds has acted wiser for himself than he who has had the same care to procure a hundred thousand of anything else?

But, further, let it now be supposed that Negotius, when he first entered into business, happening to read the Gospel with attention and eyes open, found that he had a much greater business upon his hands than that to which he had served an apprenticeship; that there were things which belonged to man, of much greater importance than all that our eyes can see; so glorious as to deserve all our thoughts; so dangerous as to need all our care; and so certain as never to deceive the faithful labourer.

Let it be supposed that, from reading this book, he had discovered that his soul was more to him than his body; that it was better to grow in the virtues of the soul than to have a large body or a full purse; that it was better to be fit for heaven than to have variety of fine houses upon the earth; that it was better to secure an everlasting happiness than to have plenty of things which he cannot keep; better to live in habits of humility, piety, devotion, charity, and self-denial than to die unprepared for judgment; better to be most like our Saviour, or some eminent saint, than to excel all the tradesmen in the world in business and bulk of fortune.

Let it be supposed that Negotius, believing these things to be true, entirely devoted himself to God at his first setting out in the world, resolving to pursue his business no further than was consistent with great devotion, humility, and self-denial, and for no other ends but to provide himself with a sober subsistence, and to do all the good that he could to the souls and bodies of his fellow-creatures.

Let it, therefore, be supposed that, instead of the continual hurry CH. XIII. of business, he was frequent in his retirements, and a strict observer of all the hours of prayer;[10] that instead of restless desires after more riches, his soul had been full of the love of God and heavenly affection, constantly watching against worldly tempers, and always aspiring after divine grace; that instead of worldly cares and contrivances, he was busy in fortifying his soul against all approaches of sin; that instead of costly show and expensive generosity of a splendid life, he loved and exercised all instances of humility and lowliness; that instead of great treats and full tables, his house only furnished a sober refreshment to those that wanted it.

Let it be supposed that this contentment kept him free from all kinds of envy, that his piety made him thankful to God in all crosses and disappointments, that his charity kept him from being rich by a continual distribution to all objects of compassion.

Now had this been the Christian spirit of Negotius, can any one say that he had lost the true joy and happiness of life by thus conforming to the spirit and living up to the hopes of the Gospel?

Can it be said that a life made exemplary by such virtues as these, which keep heaven always in our sight, which both delight and exalt the soul here and prepare it for the presence of God hereafter, must be poor and dull if compared to that of heaping up riches which can neither stay with us, nor we with them?

It would be endless to multiply examples of this kind to show you how little is lost and how much is gained by introducing a strict and exact piety into every condition of human life.

I shall now, therefore, leave it to your own meditation to carry this way of thinking further, hoping that you are enough directed by what is here said to convince yourself that a true and exalted piety is so far from rendering any life dull and tiresome that it is the only joy and happiness of every condition in the world.

Imagine to yourself some person in a consumption or any other lingering distemper that was incurable.

If you were to see such a man wholly intent upon doing every thing in the spirit of religion, making the wisest use of all his time, fortune, and abilities. If he was for carrying every duty of piety to its greatest height, and striving to have all the advantage that could be had from the remainder of his life. If he avoided all

[10] That is, all the canonical hours.

CH. XIII. business but such as was necessary; if he was averse to all the follies and vanities of the world, had no taste for finery and show, but sought for all his comfort in the hopes and expectations of religion; you would certainly commend his prudence; you would say that he had taken the right method to make himself as joyful and happy as any one can be in a state of such infirmity.

On the other hand, if you should see the same person with trembling hands, short breath, thin jaws, and hollow eyes, wholly intent upon business and bargains as long as he could speak. If you should see him pleased with fine clothes when he could scarce stand to be dressed, and laying out his money in horses and dogs, rather than purchase the prayers of the poor for his soul, which was so soon to be separated from his body, you would certainly condemn him as a weak, silly man.

Now as it is easy to see the reasonableness, the wisdom and happiness of a religious spirit in a consumptive man, so if you pursue the same way of thinking you will as easily perceive the same wisdom and happiness of a pious temper in every other state of life.

For how soon will every man that is in health be in the state of him that is in a consumption? How soon will he want all the same comforts and satisfactions of religion which every dying man wants?

And if it be wise and happy to live piously because we have not above a year to live, is it not being more wise and making ourselves more happy because we may have more years to come? If one year of piety before we die is so desirable, is not more years of piety much more desirable?

If a man had five fixed years to live, he could not possibly think at all, without intending to make the best use of them all. When he saw his stay so short in this world, he must needs think that this was not a world for him; and when he saw how near he was to another world that was eternal, he must surely think it very necessary to be very diligent in preparing himself for it.

Now as reasonable as piety appears in such a circumstance of life, it is yet more reasonable in every circumstance of life to every thinking man.

For who but a madman can reckon that he has five years certain to come?

And if it be reasonable and necessary to deny our worldly tempers and live wholly unto God because we are certain that we are to die at the end of five years, surely it must be more reasonable and necessary for us to live in the same spirit because CH. XIII. we have no certainty that we shall live five weeks.

Again, if we were to add twenty years to the five, which is in all probability more than will be added to the lives of many people who are at man's estate, what a poor thing is this ! how small a difference is there between five and twenty-five years?

It is said that a day is with God as a thousand years, and a thousand years as one day, because in regard to His eternity this difference is as nothing.

Now as we are all created to be eternal, to live in an endless succession of ages upon ages, where thousands and millions of thousands of years will have no proportion to our everlasting life in God, so with regard to this eternal state, which is our real state, twenty-five years is as poor a pittance as twenty-five days.

Now we can never make any true judgment of time as it relates to us without considering the true state of our duration. If we are temporary beings, then a little time may justly be called a great deal in relation to us ; but if we are eternal beings, then the difference of a few years is as nothing.

If we were to suppose three different sorts of rational beings, all of different but fixed duration, one sort that lived certainly only a month, the other a year, and the third a hundred years.

Now if these beings were to meet together and talk about time, they must talk in a very different language ; half an hour to those that were to live but a month must be a very different thing to what it is to those who are to live a hundred years.

As, therefore, time is thus different a thing with regard to the state of those who enjoy it, so if we would know what time is with regard to ourselves, we must consider our state.

Now since our eternal state is as certainly ours as our present state, since we are as certainly to live for ever as we now live at all, it is plain that we cannot judge of the value of any particular time, as to us, but by comparing it to that eternal duration for which we are created.

If you would know what five years signify to a being that was to live a hundred, you must compare five to a hundred and see what proportion it bears to it, and then you will judge right.

So if you would know what twenty years signify to a son of Adam, you must compare it, not to a million of ages, but to an eternal duration to which no number of millions bears any proportion, and then you will judge right by finding it nothing.

Consider, therefore, this : how would you condemn the folly of a man that should lose his share of future glory for the sake of being rich, or great, or praised, or delighted in any enjoyment, only one poor day before he was to die!

But if the time will come when a number of years will seem less to every one than a day does now, what a condemnation must it then be if eternal happiness should appear to be lost for something less than the enjoyment of a day!

Why does a day seem a trifle to us now? It is because we have years to set against it. It is the duration of years that makes it appear as nothing.

What a trifle, therefore, must the years of a man's age appear when they are forced to be set against eternity, when there shall be nothing but eternity to compare them with!

Now this will be the case of every man as soon as he is out of the body; he will be forced to forget the distinctions of days and years, and to measure time, not by the course of the sun, but by setting it against eternity.

As the fixed stars, by reason of our being placed at such distance from them, appear but so many points, so when we, placed in eternity, shall look back upon all time, it will all appear but as a moment.

Then a luxury, an indulgence, a prosperity, a greatness of fifty years will seem to every one that looks back upon it as the same poor short enjoyment as if he had been snatched away in his first sin.

These few reflections upon time are only to show how poorly they think, how miserably they judge, who are less careful of an eternal state, because they may be some years' distance from it, than they would be if they knew they were within a few weeks of it.

# CHAPTER XIV.[1]

*Concerning that part of devotion which relates to times and hours of prayer. Of daily early prayer in the morning. How we are to improve our forms of prayer, and how to increase the spirit of devotion.*

HAVING in the foregoing chapters shown the necessity of a devout spirit or habit of mind in every part of our common life, in the discharge of all our business, in the use of all the gifts of God, I come now to consider that part of devotion which relates to times and hours of prayer.[2]

I take it for granted that every Christian that is in health is up early in the morning, for it is much more reasonable to suppose a person up early because he is a Christian than because he is a labourer, or a tradesman, or a servant, or has business that wants him.[3]

We naturally conceive some abhorrence of a man that is in bed when he should be at his labour or in his shop. We cannot tell how to think anything good of him who is such a slave to drowsiness as to neglect his business for it.

Let this, therefore, teach us to conceive how odious we must appear in the sight of heaven if we are in bed, shut up in sleep and darkness, when we should be praising God, and are such slaves to drowsiness as to neglect our devotions for it.

For if he is to be blamed as a slothful drone that rather chooses the lazy indulgence of sleep than to perform his proper share of

---

[1] With this chapter Law may be said to begin Part II. of his work. Part I. treats of devotion as it concerns our life ; Part II. of devotion as it concerns our worship.

[2] In fixing the canonical hours of prayer, Law shows himself still the strong churchman who had combated Bishop Hoadley ten years before.

[3] Those who were affected by the Evangelical Revival, to which Law gave the first impulse, though he was very far indeed from following its course, laid great stress upon the duty of early rising. John Wesley enjoined his societies to hold meetings at 6 A. M., and complained bitterly when some of them were lax in regard to this rule. He himself rose at 4 A.M., and in most of the biographies of the early evangelical leaders of both sections, mention of the early rising of the hero is made.

CH. XIV. worldly business, how much is he to be reproached that had rather lie folded up in a bed than be raising up his heart to God in acts of praise and adoration?

Prayer is the nearest approach to God, and the highest enjoyment of Him that we are capable of in this life.[4]

It is the noblest exercise of the soul, the most exalted use of our best faculties, and the highest imitation of the blessed inhabitants of heaven.

When our hearts are full of God, sending up holy desires to the throne of grace, we are then in our highest state, we are upon the utmost heights of human greatness; we are not before kings and princes, but in the presence and audience of the Lord of all the world, and can be no higher till death is swallowed up in glory.

On the other hand, sleep is the poorest, dullest refreshment of the body, that is so far from being intended as an enjoyment that we are forced to receive it either in a state of insensibility, or in the folly of dreams.

Sleep is such a dull, stupid state of existence that even amongst mere animals we despise them most which are most drowsy. He, therefore, that chooses to enlarge the slothful indulgence of sleep rather than be early at his devotions to God chooses the dullest refreshment of the body before the highest, noblest employment of the soul; he chooses that state which is a reproach to mere animals rather than that exercise which is the glory of angels.

You will perhaps say, though you rise late, yet you are always careful of your devotions when you are up.

It may be so; but what then? Is it well done of you to rise late because you pray when you are up? Is it pardonable to waste great part of the day in bed because some time after you say your prayers?

It is as much your duty to rise to pray as to pray when you are risen. And if you are late at your prayers, you offer to God the prayers of an idle, slothful worshipper, that rises to prayers as idle servants rise to their labour.

Further, if you fancy that you are careful of your devotions when you are up, though it be your custom to rise late, you

---

[4] This very high estimate of the value of prayer should be set as a balance against Law's opening sentences in the *Serious Call* to the effect that prayer is not the whole of devotion, but only a very small part of it. It is noticeable that Law's brother-nonjuror, Robert Nelson, begins his devotional treatise (*The Practice of True Devotion*) with a similar remark.

deceive yourself, for you cannot perform your devotions as you ought. For he that cannot deny himself this drowsy indulgence, but must pass away good part of the morning in it, is no more prepared for prayer when he is up than he is prepared for fasting, abstinence, or any other self-denial. He may indeed more easily read over a form of prayer than he can perform these duties, but he is no more disposed to enter into the true spirit of prayer than he is disposed to fasting. For sleep thus indulged gives a softness and idleness to all our tempers, and makes us unable to relish anything but what suits with an idle state of mind, and gratifies our natural tempers as sleep does. So that a person that is a slave to this idleness is in the same temper when he is up, and though he is not asleep yet he is under the effects of it, and everything that is idle, indulgent, or sensual pleases him, for the same reason that sleep pleases him ; and, on the other hand, everything that requires care, or trouble, or self-denial, is hateful to him for the same reason that he hates to rise. He that places any happiness in this morning indulgence would be glad to have all the day made happy in the same manner, though not with sleep yet with such enjoyments as gratify and indulge the body in the same manner as sleep does, or at least with such as come as near to it as they can. The remembrance of a warm bed is in his mind all the day, and he is glad when he is not one of those that sit starving in a church.

Now you do not imagine that such a one can truly mortify that body which he thus indulges ; yet you might as well think this as that he can truly perform his devotions, or live in such a drowsy state of indulgence and yet relish the joys of a spiritual life.

For surely no one will pretend to say that he knows and feels the true happiness of prayer who does not think it worth his while to be early at it.

It is not possible in nature for an epicure to be truly devout ; he must renounce this habit of sensuality before he can relish the happiness of devotion.

Now he that turns sleep into an idle indulgence does as much to corrupt and disorder his soul, to make it a slave to bodily appetites, and keep it incapable of all devout and heavenly tempers as he that turns the necessities of eating into a course of indulgence.

A person that eats and drinks too much does not feel such effects from it as those do who live in notorious instances of

CH. XIV. gluttony and intemperance; but yet his course of indulgence, though it be not scandalous in the eyes of the world, nor such as torments his own conscience, is a great and constant hinderance to his improvement in virtue; it gives him "eyes that see not," and "ears that hear not"; it creates a sensuality in the soul, increases the power of bodily passions, and makes him incapable of entering into the true spirit of religion.

Now this is the case of those who waste their time in sleep; it does not disorder their lives, or wound their consciences, as notorious acts of intemperance do; but, like any other more moderate course of indulgence, it silently, and by smaller degrees, wears away the spirit of religion, and sinks the soul into a state of dulness and sensuality.

If you consider devotion only as a time of so much prayer, you may perhaps perform it, though you live in this daily indulgence; but if you consider it as a state of the heart, as a lively fervour of the soul, that is deeply affected with a sense of its own misery and infirmities, and desiring the spirit of God more than all things in the world, you will find that the spirit of indulgence, and the spirit of prayer cannot subsist together. Mortification of all kinds is the very life and soul of piety; but he that has not so small a degree of it, as to be able to be early at his prayers, can have no reason to think that he has taken up his cross, and is following Christ.

What conquest has he got over himself? what right hand has he cut off? what trials is he prepared for? what sacrifice is he ready to offer unto God, who cannot be so cruel to himself as to rise to pray at such a time as the drudging part of the world are content to rise to their labour?

Some people will not scruple to tell you that they indulge themselves in sleep, because they have nothing to do; and that if they had either business or pleasure to rise to, they would not lose so much of their time in sleep. But such people must be told that they mistake the matter; that they have a great deal of business to do; they have a hardened heart to change; they have the whole spirit of religion to get. For, surely, he that thinks devotion to be of less moment than business or pleasure, or that he has nothing to do, because nothing but his prayers want him, may be justly said to have the whole spirit of religion to seek.

You must not, therefore, consider how small a crime it is to rise late, but you must consider how great a misery it is to want the spirit of religion, to have a heart not rightly affected with prayer; and to live in such softness and idleness, as makes you incapable of the most fundamental duties of a truly Christian and spiritual life.

This is the right way of judging of the crime of wasting great part of your time in bed.

You must not consider the thing barely in itself, but what it proceeds from; what virtues it shows to be wanting; what vices it naturally strengthens. For every habit of this kind discovers the state of the soul, and plainly shows the whole turn of your mind.

If our blessed Lord used to pray early before day; if He spent whole nights in prayer; if the devout Anna was day and night in the temple; if St. Paul and Silas at midnight sang praises unto God; if the primitive Christians for several hundred years, besides their hours of prayer in the day-time, met publicly in the churches at midnight to join in psalms and prayers, is it not certain that these practices showed the state of their hearts? Are they not so many plain proofs of the whole turn of their minds?

And if you live in a contrary state, wasting great part of every day in sleep, thinking any time soon enough to be at your prayers, is it not equally certain that this practice as much shows the state of your heart, and the whole turn of your mind?

So that, if this indulgence is your way of life, you have as much reason to believe yourself destitute of the true spirit of devotion, as you have to believe the Apostles and Saints of the primitive Church were truly devout. For as their way of life was a demonstration of their devotion so a contrary way of life is as strong a proof of a want of devotion.

When you read the Scriptures, you see a religion that is all life, and spirit, and joy in God; that supposes our souls risen from earthly desires and bodily indulgences to prepare for another body, another world, and other enjoyments. You see Christians represented as temples of the Holy Ghost, as children of the day, as candidates for an eternal crown, as watchful virgins that have their lamps always burning in expectation of the Bridegroom. But can he be thought to have this joy in God, this care of eternity, this watchful spirit, who has not zeal enough to rise to his prayers?

When you look into the writings and lives of the first Christians, you see the same spirit that you see in the Scriptures. All is reality, life, and action. Watching and prayers, self-denial and mortification, was the common business of their lives.

From that time to this there has been no person like them, eminent for piety, who has not, like them, been eminent for self-denial and mortification. This is the only royal way that leads to a kingdom.

But how far are you from this way of life, or rather how contrary to it, if, instead of imitating their austerity and mortification, you cannot so much as renounce so poor an indulgence as to be able to rise to your prayers? If self-denials and bodily sufferings, if watchings and fastings, will be marks of glory at the day of judgment, where must we hide our heads that have slumbered away our time in sloth and softness?

You perhaps now find some pretences to excuse yourself from that severity of fasting and self-denial, which the first Christians practised. You fancy that human nature is grown weaker, and that the difference of climates may make it not possible for you to observe their methods of self-denial and austerity in these colder countries.

But all this is but pretence; for the change is not in the outward state of things, but in the inward state of our minds. When there is the same spirit in us that there was in the Apostles and primitive Christians, when we feel the weight of religion as they did, when we have their faith and hope, we shall take up our cross and deny ourselves, and live in such methods of mortification as they did.

Had St. Paul lived in a cold country, had he had a constitution made weak with a sickly stomach, and often infirmities, he would have done as he advised Timothy, he would have mixed a little wine with his water.

But still he would have lived in a state of self-denial and mortification. He would have given this same account of himself. "I, therefore, so run, not as uncertainly; so fight I, not as one that beateth the air; but I keep under my body, and bring it into subjection: lest that by any means, when I have preached to others, I myself should be a castaway."

After all, let it now be supposed, that you imagine there is no necessity for you to be so sober and vigilant, so fearful of yourself, so watchful over your passions, so apprehensive of danger, so careful of your salvation as the Apostles were. Let it be CH. XIV. supposed that you imagine that you want less self-denial and mortification to subdue your bodies and purify your souls than they wanted; that you need not have your loins girt and your lamps burning as they had, will you, therefore, live in a quite contrary state? Will you make your life as constant a course of softness and indulgence as theirs was of strictness and self-denial?

If, therefore, you should think that you have time sufficient both for prayer and other duties, though you rise late, yet let me persuade you to rise early, as an instance of self-denial. It is so small a one, that if you cannot comply with it you have no reason to think yourself capable of any other.

If I were to desire you not to study the gratifications of your palate in the niceties of meats and drinks, I would not insist much upon the crime of wasting your money in such a way, though it be a great one; but I would desire you to renounce such a way of life, because it supports you in such a state of sensuality and indulgence as renders you incapable of relishing the most essential doctrines of religion.

For the same reason I do not insist much on the crime of wasting so much of your time in sleep, though it be a great one; but I desire you to renounce this indulgence, because it gives a softness and idleness to your soul, and is so contrary to that lively, zealous, watchful, self-denying spirit, which was not only the spirit of Christ and His Apostles, the spirit of all the saints and martyrs which have ever been amongst men, but must be the spirit of all those who would not sink in the common corruption of the world.

Here, therefore, we must fix our charge against this practice; we must blame it, not as having this or that particular evil, but as a general habit that extends itself through our whole spirit, and supports a state of mind that is wholly wrong.

It is contrary to piety, not as accidental slips and mistakes in life are contrary to it, but in such a manner as an ill habit of body is contrary to health.

On the other hand, if you were to rise early every morning as an instance of self-denial, as a method of renouncing indulgence, as a means of redeeming your time and fitting your spirit for prayer, you would find mighty advantages from it. This method, though it seems such a small circumstance of life, would in all probability be a means of great piety. It would keep it constantly in your head that softness and idleness were to be avoided, that self-denial was a part of Christianity. It would teach you to exercise power over yourself, and make you able by degrees to renounce other pleasures and tempers that war against the soul.

This one rule would teach you to think of others; it would dispose your mind to exactness, and be very likely to bring the remaining part of the day under rules of prudence and devotion.

But, above all, one certain benefit from this method you will be sure of having; it will best fit and prepare you for the reception of the Holy Spirit. When you thus begin the day in the spirit of religion, renouncing sleep, because you are to renounce softness and redeem your time; this disposition, as it puts your heart into a good state so it will procure the assistance of the Holy Spirit; what is so planted and watered will certainly have an increase from God. You will then speak from your heart, your soul will be awake, your prayers will refresh you like meat and drink, you will feel what you say, and begin to know what saints and holy men have meant by fervours of devotion.

He that is thus prepared for prayer, who rises with these dispositions, is in a very different state from him who has no rules of this kind, who rises by chance, as he happens to be weary of his bed, or is able to sleep no longer. If such a one prays only with his mouth; if his heart feels nothing of that which he says; if his prayers are only things of course; if they are a lifeless form of words, which he only repeats because they are soon said; there is nothing to be wondered at in all this, for such dispositions are the natural effects of such a state of life.

Hoping, therefore, that you are now enough convinced of the necessity of rising early to your prayers, I shall proceed to lay before you a method of daily prayer.

I do not take upon me to prescribe to you the use of any particular forms of prayer, but only to show the necessity of praying at such times and in such a manner.

You will here find some helps how to furnish yourself with such forms of prayer as shall be useful to you. And if you are such a proficient in the spirit of devotion that your heart is always ready to pray in its own language, in this case I press no necessity of borrowed forms.

For though I think a form of prayer very necessary and ex-

pedient for public worship,[5] yet if any one can find a better way of CH. XIV.
raising his heart unto God in private than by prepared forms of
prayer, I have nothing to object against it, my design being only
to assist and direct such as stand in need of assistance.

Thus much, I believe, is certain, that the generality of Christians ought to use forms of prayer at all the regular times of
prayer.  It seems right for every one to begin with a form of
prayer ; and if, in the midst of his devotion, he finds his heart
ready to break forth into new and higher strains of devotion, he
should leave his form for a while, and follow those fervours of his
heart till it again wants the assistance of his usual petitions.

This seems to be the true liberty of private devotion ; it should
be under the direction of some form, but not so tied down to it
but that it may be free to take such new expressions as its present
fervours happen to furnish it with, which sometimes are more
affecting, and carry the soul more powerfully to God, than any
expressions that were ever used before.

All people that have ever made any reflections upon what
passes in their own hearts must know that they are mighty
changeable in regard to devotion.  Sometimes our hearts are so
awakened, have such strong apprehensions of the divine presence,
are so full of deep compunction for our sins, that we cannot
confess them in any language but that of tears.

Sometimes the light of God's countenance shines so bright
upon us, we see so far into the invisible world, we are so affected
with the wonders of the love and goodness of God, that our
hearts worship and adore in a language higher than that of words,
and we feel transports of devotion which only can be felt.

On the other hand, sometimes we are so sunk into our bodies,
so dull and unaffected with that which concerns our souls, that
our hearts are as much too low for our prayers ; we cannot keep
pace with our forms of confession, or feel half of that in our hearts
which we have in our mouths ; we thank and praise God with
forms of words, but our hearts have little or no share in them.

It is, therefore, highly necessary to provide against this inconstancy of our hearts by having at hand such forms of prayer as
may best suit us when our hearts are in their best state, and also

---

[5] It is a great mistake to suppose
that Law made light of public worship.
He only did not insist upon it, because
he took it for granted, as he was justified in doing, that his readers were not
likely to neglect this duty.  His own
practice was to attend every service,
week-day and Sunday, at his Parish
Church at King's Cliffe, which it was
not usual for nonjurors to do.

CH. XIV. be most likely to raise and stir them up when they are sunk into dulness.   For as words have a power of affecting our hearts on all occasions, as the same thing differently expressed has different effects upon our minds, so it is reasonable that we should make this advantage of language, and provide ourselves with such forms of expressions as are most likely to move and enliven our souls, and fill them with sentiments suitable to them.

The first thing that you are to do when you are upon your knees is to shut your eyes, and, with a short silence, let your soul place itself in the presence of God; that is, you are to use this or some other better method to separate yourself from all common thoughts, and make your hearts as sensible as you can of the divine presence.

Now if this recollection of spirit is necessary, as who can say it is not? then how poorly must they perform their devotions who are always in a hurry, who begin them in haste, and hardly allow themselves time to repeat their very form with any gravity or attention?   Theirs is properly saying prayers, instead of praying.

To proceed.   If you were to use yourself (as far as you can) to pray always in the same place; if you were to reserve that place for devotion, and not allow yourself to do anything common in it; if you were never to be there yourself but in times of devotion; if any little room, (or if that cannot be) if any particular part of a room, was thus used, this kind of consecration of it, as a place holy unto God, would have an effect upon your mind, and dispose you to such tempers as would very much assist your devotion. For by having a place thus sacred in your room, it would in some measure resemble a chapel or house of God.   This would dispose you to be always in the spirit of religion when you were there, and fill you with wise and holy thoughts when you were by yourself.   Your own apartment would raise in your mind such sentiments as you have when you stand near an altar, and you would be afraid of thinking or doing anything that was foolish near that place, which is the place of prayer and holy intercourse with God.[6]

When you begin your petitions, use such various expressions of the attributes of God as may make you most sensible of the greatness and power of the divine nature.

[6] On this, as indeed on all points, to the best of his ability, Law practised what he preached.   His room is still to be seen at the Hall Yard, King's Cliffe, in which there is a little nook marked off, which he used for an oratory, and for no other purpose.

Begin, therefore, in words like these: "O Being of all beings, Fountain of all light and glory, gracious Father of men and angels, Whose universal Spirit is everywhere present, giving life and light and joy to all angels in heaven and all creatures upon earth," etc.

For these representations of the divine attributes, which show us in some degree the majesty and greatness of God, are an excellent means of raising our hearts into lively acts of worship and adoration.

What is the reason that most people are so much affected with this petition in the burial service of our Church: "Yet, O Lord God most holy, O Lord most mighty, O holy and most merciful Saviour, deliver us not into the bitter pains of eternal death"? It is because the joining together so many great expressions gives such a description of the greatness of the Divine Majesty as naturally affects every sensible mind.

Although, therefore, prayer does not consist in fine words or studied expressions, yet as words speak to the soul, as they have a certain power of raising thoughts in the soul, so those words which speak of God in the highest manner, which most fully express the power and presence of God, which raise thoughts in the soul most suitable to the greatness and providence of God, are the most useful, and most edifying in our prayers.

When you direct any of your petitions to our blessed Lord, let it be in some expressions of this kind: "O Saviour of the world, God of God, Light of Light, Thou that art the Brightness of Thy Father's glory, and the express Image of His person; Thou that art the Alpha and Omega, the Beginning and End of all things; Thou that hast destroyed the power of the devil, that hast overcome death; Thou that art entered into the Holy of Holies, that sittest at the right hand of the Father, that art high above all thrones and principalities, that makest intercession for all the world; Thou that art the judge of the quick and dead; Thou that wilt speedily come down in Thy Father's glory to reward all men according to their works, be Thou my light and my peace," etc.

For such representations which describe so many characters of our Saviour's nature and power are not only proper acts of adoration, but will, if they are repeated with attention, fill our hearts with the highest fervours of true devotion.

Again, if you ask any particular grace of our blessed Lord, let it be in some manner like this:

"O Holy Jesus, Son of the most high God, Thou that wert scourged at a pillar, stretched and nailed upon a cross for the sins of the world, unite me to Thy cross, and fill my soul with Thy holy, humble, and suffering spirit. O Fountain of Mercy, Thou that didst save the thief upon the cross, save me from the guilt of a sinful life; Thou that didst cast seven devils out of Mary Magdalene, cast out of my heart all evil thoughts and wicked tempers. O Giver of Life, Thou that didst raise Lazarus from the dead, raise up my soul from the death and darkness of sin. Thou that didst give to Thy Apostles power over unclean spirits, give me power over mine own heart. Thou that didst appear unto Thy disciples when the doors were shut, do Thou appear to me in the secret apartment of my heart. Thou that didst cleanse the lepers, heal the sick, and give sight to the blind, cleanse my heart, heal the disorders of my soul, and fill me with heavenly light."

Now these appeals have a double advantage: First, As they are so many proper acts of our faith, whereby we not only show our belief of the miracles of Christ, but turn them at the same time into so many instances of worship and adoration.

Secondly, As they strengthen and increase the faith of our prayers, by presenting to our mind so many instances of that power and goodness, which we call upon for our own assistance.

For he that appeals to Christ, as casting out devils and raising the dead, has then a powerful motive in his mind to pray earnestly and depend faithfully upon His assistance.

Again, in order to fill your prayers with excellent strains of devotion, it may be of use to you to observe this further rule.

When at any time, either in reading the Scripture or any book of piety, you meet with a passage that more than ordinarily affects your mind, and seems, as it were, to give your heart a new motion towards God, you should try to turn it into the form of a petition, and then give it a place in your prayers.

By this means you would be often improving your prayers, and storing yourself with proper forms of making the desires of your heart known unto God.

At all the stated hours of prayer it will be a great benefit to you to have something fixed and something at liberty in your devotions.

You should have some fixed subject, which is constantly to be the chief matter of your prayer at that particular time; and yet have liberty to add such other petitions as your condition may CH. XIV. then require.

For instance: As the morning is to you the beginning of new life, as God has then given you a new enjoyment of yourself and a fresh entrance into the world, it is highly proper that your first devotions should be a praise and thanksgiving to God as for a new creation; and that you should offer and devote body and soul, all that you are, and all that you have, to His service and glory.

Receive, therefore, every day as a resurrection from death, as a new enjoyment of life; meet every rising sun with such sentiments of God's goodness as if you had seen it, and all things, new created upon your account; and, under the sense of so great a blessing, let your joyful heart praise and magnify so good and glorious a Creator.

Let therefore praise and thanksgiving, and oblation of yourself unto God, be always the fixed and certain subject of your first prayers in the morning; and then take the liberty of adding such other devotions as the accidental difference of your state, or the accidental difference of your heart, shall then make most needful and expedient for you.

For one of the greatest benefits of private devotion consists in rightly adapting our prayers to these two conditions, the difference of our state, and the difference of our hearts.

By the difference of our state is meant the difference of our external state or condition, as of sickness, health, pains, losses, disappointments, troubles, particular mercies, or judgments from God; all sorts of kindnesses, injuries, or reproaches from other people.

Now as these are great parts of our state of life, as they make great difference in it, by continually changing, so our devotion will be made doubly beneficial to us when it watches to receive and sanctify all these changes of our state, and turns them all into so many occasions of a more particular application to God of such thanksgivings, such resignation, such petitions, as our present state more especially requires.

And he that makes every change in his state a reason of presenting unto God some particular petitions suitable to that change, will soon find that he has taken an excellent means, not only of praying with fervour, but of living as he prays.

The next condition, to which we are always to adapt some part of our prayers, is the difference of our hearts, by which is meant

CH. XIV. the different state of the tempers of our hearts, as of love, joy, peace, tranquillity, dulness and dryness of spirit, anxiety, discontent, motions of envy and ambition, dark and disconsolate thoughts, resentments, fretfulness, and peevish tempers.

Now as these tempers, through the weakness of our nature, will have their succession more or less even in pious minds, so we should constantly make the present state of our heart the reason of some particular application to God.

If we are in the delightful calm of sweet and easy passions,[7] of love and joy in God, we should then offer the grateful tribute of thanksgiving to God for the possession of so much happiness, thankfully owning and acknowledging Him as the bountiful Giver of it all.

If, on the other hand, we feel ourselves laden with heavy passions, with dulness of spirit, anxiety, and uneasiness, we must then look up to God in acts of humility, confessing our unworthiness, opening our troubles to Him, beseeching Him in His good time to lessen the weight of our infirmities, and to deliver us from such passions as oppose the purity and perfection of our souls.

Now by thus watching and attending to the present state of our hearts, and suiting some of our petitions exactly to their wants, we shall not only be well acquainted with the disorders of our souls, but also be well exercised in the method of curing them.

By this prudent and wise application of our prayers, we shall get all the relief from them that is possible; and the very changeableness of our hearts will prove a means of exercising a greater variety of holy tempers.

Now by all that has here been said, you will easily perceive that persons careful of the greatest benefit of prayer ought to have a great share in the forming and composing their own devotions.

As to that part of their prayers which is always fixed to one certain subject, in that they may use the help of forms composed by other persons; but in that part of their prayers, which they are always to suit to the present state of their life, and the present state of their heart, there they must let the sense of their own condition help them to such kinds of petition, thanksgiving, or resignation as their present state more especially requires.

---

[7] 'Passion' was used for any strong feeling, not necessarily of suffering or of anger.

"I am doubtful, lest
You break into some merry passion."
(Shakespeare.)

Happy are they who have this business and employment upon CH. XIV. their hands !

And now, if people of leisure, whether men or women, who are so much at a loss how to dispose of their time, who are forced into poor contrivances, idle visits, and ridiculous diversions, merely to get rid of hours that hang heavily upon their hands; if such were to appoint some certain spaces of their time to the study of devotion, searching after all the means and helps to attain a devout spirit; if they were to collect the best forms of devotion, to use themselves to transcribe the finest passages of Scripture prayers; if they were to collect the devotions, confessions, petitions, praises, resignations, and thanksgivings, which are scattered up and down in the Psalms, and range them under proper heads, as so much proper fuel for the flame of their own devotion; if their minds were often thus employed, sometimes meditating upon them, sometimes getting them by heart, and making them as habitual as their own thoughts, how fervently would they pray who came thus prepared to prayer?

And how much better would it be to make this benefit of leisure time than to be dully and idly lost in the poor impertinences[8] of a playing, visiting, wandering life?

How much better would it be to be thus furnished with hymns and anthems of the saints, and teach their souls to ascend to God, than to corrupt, bewilder, and confound their hearts with the wild fancies, the lustful thoughts of a lewd poet?

Now though people of leisure seem called more particularly to this study of devotion, yet persons of much business or labour must not think themselves excused from this, or some better method of improving their devotion.

For the greater their business is, the more need they have of some such method as this to prevent its power over their hearts; to secure them from sinking into worldly tempers, and preserve a sense and taste of heavenly things in their minds. And a little time, regularly and constantly employed to any one use or end, will do great things and produce mighty effects.

And it is for want of considering devotion in this light, as something that is to be nursed and cherished with care, as something that is to be made part of our business, that is to be improved with care and contrivance, by art and method, and a diligent use of the best helps; it is for want of considering it in this light,

---

[8] 'Impertinences,' that is, occupations unsuitable to the true end of our being.

CH. XIV. that so many people are so little benefited by it, and live and
die strangers to that spirit of devotion, which, by a prudent use
of proper means, they might have enjoyed in a high degree.

For though the spirit of devotion is the gift of God, and not
attainable by any mere power of our own, yet it is mostly given,
and never withheld from, those who, by a wise and diligent use of
proper means, prepare themselves for the reception of it.

And it is amazing to see how eagerly men employ their parts,
their sagacity, time, study, application, and exercise; how all
helps are called to their assistance when anything is intended and
desired in worldly matters; and how dull, negligent, and unim-
proved they are, how little they use their parts, sagacity, and
abilities to raise and increase their devotion!

MUNDANUS is a man of excellent parts and clear apprehension.
He is well advanced in age, and has made a great figure in
business. Every part of trade and business that has fallen in his
way has had some improvement from him, and he is always contriving to carry every method of doing anything well to its greatest
height. Mundanus aims at the greatest perfection in everything.
The soundness and strength of his mind, and his just way of
thinking upon things, make him intent upon removing all imperfections.

He can tell you all the defects and errors in all the common
methods, whether of trade, building, or improving land, or manu-
factures. The clearness and strength of his understanding, which
he is constantly improving by continual exercise in these matters,
by often digesting his thoughts in writing, and trying everything
every way, has rendered him a great master of most concerns in
human life.

Thus has Mundanus gone on increasing his knowledge and
judgment as fast as his years came upon him.

The only thing which has not fallen under his improvement,
nor received any benefit from his judicious mind, is his devotion.
This is just in the same poor state it was when he was only six
years of age, and the old man prays now in that little form of words
which his mother used to hear him repeat night and morning.[9]

---

[9] Law would have been the last man
to depreciate the simple piety of child-
hood. He loved children, attended
regularly the schools for poor children
which he founded at King's Cliffe,
and delighted in having his brother
George's children about him; but he
felt that a man's mind was different
from a child's mind, and that prayers
which would be suitable to the latter
would be utterly unsuitable to the
former.

This Mundanus, that hardly ever saw the poorest utensil, or CH. XIV. ever took the meanest trifle into his hand, without considering how it might be made or used to better advantage, has gone all his life long praying in the same manner as when he was a child, without ever considering how much better or oftener he might pray ; without considering how improvable the spirit of devotion is, how many helps a wise and reasonable man may call to his assistance, and how necessary it is that our prayers should be enlarged, varied, and suited to the particular state and condition of our lives.

If Mundanus sees a book of devotion, he passes it by as he does a spelling-book, because he remembers that he learned to pray so many years ago under his mother when he learned to spell.

Now how poor and pitiable is the conduct of this man of sense, who has so much judgment and understanding in everything but that which is the whole wisdom of man?

And how miserably do many people more or less imitate this conduct?

All which seems to be owing to a strange infatuated state of negligence, which keeps people from considering what devotion is. For if they did but once proceed so far as to reflect about it, or ask themselves any questions concerning it, they would soon see that the spirit of devotion was like any other sense or understanding, that is only to be improved by study, care, application, and the use of such means and helps as are necessary to make a man a proficient in any art or science.[10]

CLASSICUS is a man of learning, and well versed in all the best authors of antiquity. He has read them so much that he has entered into their spirit, and can very ingeniously imitate the manner of any of them. All their thoughts are his thoughts, and he can express himself in their language. He is so great a friend to this improvement of the mind that if he lights on a young scholar, he never fails to advise him concerning his studies.[11]

[10] This view of devotion, as a habit to be cultivated like any other habit, would not quite accord with the emotional religion which was aroused by the Evangelical Revival, but it surely is the common-sense view and the philosophical view. It is the application to devotion of the Aristotelian maxim that the ἕξις begets the ἐνέργεια, and the ἐνέργεια strengthens the ἕξις.

[11] The character of Classicus was perhaps more common in the eighteenth than in the nineteenth century. Law, it should be remembered, was a contemporary of Bentley, the first of classical critics, and of Warburton and Hurd, whose friendship was cemented by the study of the classics. 'Scholarship' meant in those days, in common parlance, purely the knowledge of Latin and Greek, and there were many who devoted themselves almost entirely to these studies.

Classicus tells this young man he must not think that he has done enough when he has only learned languages, but that he must be daily conversant with the best authors, read them again and again, catch their spirit by living with them, and that there is no other way of becoming like them, or of making himself a man of taste and judgment.

How wise might Classicus have been, and how much good might he have done in the world, if he had but thought as justly of devotion as he does of learning?

He never, indeed, says anything shocking or offensive about devotion, because he never thinks or talks about it. It suffers nothing from him but neglect and disregard.

The two Testaments would not have had so much as a place amongst his books, but that they are both to be had in Greek.

Classicus thinks that he sufficiently shows his regard for the holy Scripture when he tells you that he has no other books of piety besides them.

It is very well, Classicus, that you prefer the Bible to all other books of piety; he has no judgment that is not thus far of your opinion.

But if you will have no other book of piety besides the Bible, because it is the best, how comes it, Classicus, that you do not content yourself with one of the best books amongst the Greeks and Romans? How comes it that you are so greedy and eager after all of them? How comes it that you think the knowledge of one is a necessary help to the knowledge of the other? How comes it that you are so earnest, so laborious, so expensive of your time and money to restore broken periods and scraps of the ancients?

How comes it that you read so many commentators upon Cicero, Horace, and Homer, and not one upon the Gospel? How comes it that your love of Cicero and Ovid makes you love to read an author that writes like them; and yet your esteem for the Gospel gives you no desire, nay, prevents your reading such books as breathe the very spirit of the Gospel?

How comes it that you tell your young scholar he must not content himself with barely understanding his authors, but must be continually reading them all, as the only means of entering into their spirit, and forming his own judgment according to them?

Why, then, must the Bible lie alone in your study? Is not the spirit of the saints, the piety of the holy followers of Jesus

Christ, as good and necessary a means of entering into the spirit and taste of the Gospel as the reading of the ancients is of entering into the spirit of antiquity?

Is the spirit of poetry only to be got by much reading of poets and orators? And is not the spirit of devotion to be got in the same way by frequently reading the holy thoughts and pious strains of devout men?

Is your young poet to search after every line that may give new wings to his fancy or direct his imagination? And is it not as reasonable for him who desires to improve in the divine life, that is, in the love of heavenly things, to search after every strain of devotion that may move, kindle, and inflame the holy ardour of his soul?

Do you advise your orator to translate the best orations, to commit much of them to memory, to be frequently exercising his talent in this manner, that habits of thinking and speaking justly may be formed in his mind? And is there not the same benefit and advantage to be made by books of devotion? Should not a man use them in the same way, that habits of devotion and aspiring to God in holy thoughts may be well formed in his soul?

Now the reason why Classicus does not think and judge thus reasonably of devotion is owing to his never thinking of it in any other manner than as the repeating a form of words. It never in his life entered into his head to think of devotion as a state of the heart, as an improvable talent of the mind, as a temper that is to grow and increase like our reason and judgment, and to be formed in us by such a regular diligent use of proper means as are necessary to form any other wise habit of mind.

And it is for want of this that he has been content all his life with the bare letter of prayer, and eagerly bent upon entering into the spirit of heathen poets and orators.

And it is much to be lamented that numbers of scholars are more or less chargeable with this excessive folly; so negligent of improving their devotion, and so desirous of other poor accomplishments, as if they thought it a nobler talent to be able to write an epigram in the turn of Martial than to live and think and pray to God in the spirit of St. Austin.

And yet, to correct this temper, and fill a man with a quite contrary spirit, there seems to be no more required than the bare belief of the truth of Christianity.

And if you were to ask Mundanus and Classicus, or any man

CH. XIV. of business or learning, whether piety is not the highest perfection of man, or devotion the greatest attainment in the world, they must both be forced to answer in the affirmative, or else give up the truth of the Gospel.

For to set any accomplishment against devotion, or to think anything or all things in the world can bear any proportion to its excellency, is the same absurdity in a Christian as it would be in a philosopher to prefer a meal's meat to the greatest improvement in knowledge.

For as philosophy professes purely the search and inquiry after knowledge, so Christianity supposes, intends, desires, and aims at nothing else but the raising fallen man to a divine life, to such habits of holiness, such degrees of devotion, as may fit him to enter among the holy inhabitants of the kingdom of heaven.

He that does not believe this of Christianity may be reckoned an infidel; and he that believes thus much has faith enough to give him a right judgment of the value of things, to support him in a sound mind, and enable him to conquer all the temptations which the world shall lay in his way.

To conclude this chapter. Devotion is nothing else but right apprehensions and right affections towards God.[12]

All practices, therefore, that heighten and improve our true apprehensions of God, all ways of life that tend to nourish, raise, and fix our affections upon Him are to be reckoned so many helps and means to fill us with devotion.

As prayer is the proper fuel of this holy flame, so we must use all our care and contrivance to give prayer its full power; as by alms, self-denial, frequent retirements, and holy readings, composing forms for ourselves, or using the best we can get, adding length of time, and observing hours of prayer; changing, improving, and suiting our devotions to the condition of our lives and the state of our hearts.

Those who have most leisure seem more especially called to a more eminent observance of these holy rules of a devout life. And they who, by the necessity of their state, and not through their own choice, have but little time to employ thus, must make the best use of that little they have.

For this is the certain way of making devotion produce a devout life.

[12] Observe the definition of devotion. If you have 'right apprehensions' of (full knowledge you cannot have in this life) and 'right affections towards God,' you cannot fail to be devout.

# CHAPTER XV.

*Of chanting or singing of Psalms in our private devotions. Of the excellency and benefit of this kind of devotion. Of the great effects it hath upon our hearts. Of the means of performing it in the best manner.*

You have seen in the foregoing chapter what means and methods you are to use to raise and improve your devotion, how early you are to begin your prayers, and what is to be the subject of your first devotions in the morning.

There is one thing still remaining that you must be required to observe, not only as fit and proper to be done, but as such as cannot be neglected without great prejudice to your devotions; and that is, to begin all your prayers with a Psalm.

This is so right, is so beneficial to devotion, has so much effect upon our hearts, that it may be insisted upon as a common rule for all persons.

I do not mean that you should read over a Psalm, but that you should chant or sing one of those Psalms which we commonly call the reading Psalms;[1] for singing is as much the proper use of a Psalm as devout supplication is the proper use of a form of prayer, and a Psalm only read is very much like a prayer that is only looked over.

Now the method of chanting a Psalm, such as is used in the colleges, in the universities, and in some churches, is such as all persons are capable of.[2]  The change of the voice in thus chanting

---

[1] At the time when Law wrote, the question whether the old version of Sternhold and Hopkins or the new version of Tate and Brady were preferable was being vehemently discussed. Both versions were commonly called 'the singing Psalms,' in contrast to which the versions in our Bible and in our Prayer Book were called 'the reading Psalms.'

[2] Perhaps some may demur to this dictum.  But, at any rate, it would be easier for those who had no ear for music to chant a 'reading Psalm' after a fashion than to sing to a regular tune a metrical Psalm, or one of those hymns of Watts or Doddridge which were then coming into fashion, and which were soon to be increased in rich abundance by Law's own disciples, John and Charles Wesley.  Moreover, it would be more in accordance with Law's constant standard, that of the early church.

163

of a Psalm is so small and natural that everybody is able to do it, and yet sufficient to raise and keep up the gladness of our hearts.

You are, therefore, to consider this chanting of a Psalm as a necessary beginning of your devotions, as something that is to awaken all that is good and holy within you, that is to call your spirits to their proper duty, to set you in your best posture towards heaven, and tune all the powers of your soul to worship and adoration.

For there is nothing that so clears a way for your prayers, nothing that so disperses dulness of heart, nothing that so purifies the soul from poor and little passions, nothing that so opens heaven, or carries your heart so near it, as these songs of praise.

They create a sense and delight in God, they awaken holy desires, they teach you how to ask, and they prevail with God to give. They kindle a holy flame, they turn your heart into an altar, your prayers into incense, and carry them as a sweet-smelling savour to the throne of grace.

The difference between singing and reading a Psalm will easily be understood if you consider the difference between reading and singing a common song that you like. Whilst you only read it, you only like it, and that is all; but as soon as you sing it, then you enjoy it, you feel the delight of it, it has got hold of you, your passions keep pace with it, and you feel the same spirit within you that seems to be in the words.

If you were to tell a person that has such a song that he need not sing it, that it was sufficient to peruse it, he would wonder what you mean, and would think you as absurd as if you were to tell him that he should only look at his food to see whether it was good, but need not eat it; for a song of praise not sung is very like any other good thing not made use of.

You will perhaps say that singing is a particular talent that belongs only to particular people, and that you have neither voice nor ear to make any music.

If you had said that singing is a general talent, and that people differ in that as they do in all other things, you had said something much truer.

For how vastly do people differ in the talent of thinking, which is not only common to all men, but seems to be the very essence of human nature! How readily do some people reason upon everything! and how hardly do others reason upon anything!

How clearly do some people discourse upon the most abstruse CH. XV. matters! and how confusedly do others talk upon the plainest subjects!

Yet no one desires to be excused from thought or reason or discourse, because he has not these talents as some people have them.    But it is full as just for a person to think himself excused from thinking upon God, from reasoning about his duty to Him, or discoursing about the means of salvation, because he has not these talents in any fine degree; this is full as just as for a person to think himself excused from singing the praises of God because he has not a fine ear or a musical voice.

For as it is speaking, and not graceful speaking, that is a required part of prayer; as it is bowing, and not genteel bowing, that is a proper part of adoration; so it is singing, and not artful fine singing, that is a required way of praising God.

If a person was to forbear praying because he had an odd tone in his voice, he would have as good an excuse as he has that forbears from singing Psalms because he has but little management of his voice.    And as a man's speaking his prayers, though in an odd tone, may yet sufficiently answer all the ends of his own devotion, so a man's singing of a Psalm, though not in a very musical way, may yet sufficiently answer all the ends of rejoicing in and praising God.

Secondly, This objection might be of some weight if you were desired to sing to entertain other people, but is not to be admitted in the present case, where you are only required to sing the praises of God as a part of your private devotion.

If a person that has a very ill voice and a bad way of speaking was desired to be the mouth of a congregation, it would be a very proper excuse for him to say that he had not a voice or a way of speaking that was proper for prayer; but he would be very absurd if, for the same reason, he should neglect his own private devotions.

Now this is exactly the case of singing Psalms.    You may not have the talent of singing so as to be able to entertain other people, and, therefore, it is reasonable to excuse yourself from it; but if, for that reason, you should excuse yourself from this way of praising God, you would be guilty of a great absurdity; because singing is no more required for the music that is made by it than prayer is required for the fine words that it contains, but as it is the natural and proper expression of a heart rejoicing in God.

Our blessed Saviour and His Apostles sang a hymn,[3] but it may reasonably be supposed that they rather rejoiced in God than made fine music.

Do but so live that your heart may truly rejoice in God, that it may feel itself affected with the praises of God, and then you will find that this state of your heart will neither want a voice nor ear to find a tune for a Psalm. Everyone at some time or other finds himself able to sing in some degree; there are some times and occasions of joy that make all people ready to express their sense of it in some sort of harmony. The joy that they feel forces them to let their voice have a part in it.

He, therefore, that saith he wants a voice or an ear to sing a Psalm mistakes the case; he wants that spirit that really rejoices in God; the dulness is in his heart and not in his ear; and when his heart feels a true joy in God, when it has a full relish of what is expressed in the Psalms, he will find it very pleasant to make the motions of his voice express the motions of his heart.

Singing, indeed, as it is improved into an art, as it signifies the running of the voice through such or such a compass of notes, and keeping time with a studied variety of changes, is not natural, nor the effect of any natural state of the mind; so, in this sense, it is not common to all people any more than those antic[4] and invented motions which make fine dancing are common to all people.

But singing, as it signifies a motion of the voice suitable to the motions of the heart, and the changing of its tone according to the meaning of the words which we utter, is as natural and common to all men as it is to speak high when they threaten in anger, or to speak low when they are dejected and ask for a pardon.

All men, therefore, are singers in the same manner as all men think, speak, laugh, and lament. For singing is no more an invention than grief or joy are inventions.

Every state of the heart naturally puts the body into some state that is suitable to it, and is proper to show it to other people. If a man is angry or disdainful, no one need instruct

[3] The 'hymn' was probably a 'reading Psalm,' a part of the great Hallel (Psalms cxvi.-cxviii.), and therefore the reference is especially apposite to Law's design.

[4] 'Antic' is here used, as it is in Shakespeare ("come hither cover'd with an antic face,") and other old writers, as an adjective, not as it is now, as a substantive; but the sense is entirely the same. Addison speaks of "the antic postures of a merry-Andrew" (*Freeholder*).

him how to express these passions by the tone of his voice. The state of his heart disposes him to a proper use of his voice.

If there are but few singers of divine songs, if people want to be exhorted to this part of devotion, it is because there are but few whose hearts are raised to that height of piety as to feel any emotions of joy and delight in the praises of God.

Imagine to yourself that you had been with Moses when he was led through the Red Sea; that you had seen the waters divide themselves, and stand on an heap on both sides; that you had seen them held up till you had passed through, then let fall upon your enemies; do you think that you should then have wanted a voice or an ear to have sung with Moses, "The Lord is my strength and my song, and He is become my salvation," etc.? I know your own heart tells you that all people must have been singers upon such an occasion. Let this, therefore, teach you that it is the heart that tunes a voice to sing the praises of God; and that if you cannot sing these same words now with joy, it is because you are not so affected with the salvation of the world by Jesus Christ as the Jews were, or you yourself would have been, with their deliverance at the Red Sea.

That it is the state of the heart that disposes us to rejoice in any particular kind of singing may be easily proved from variety of observations upon human nature. An old debauchee may, according to the language of the world, have neither voice nor ear, if you only sing a Psalm or a song in praise of virtue to him; but yet, if in some easy tune you sing something that celebrates his former debauches, he will then, though he has no teeth in his head, show you that he has both a voice and an ear to join in such music. You then awaken his heart, and he as naturally sings to such words as he laughs when he is pleased. And this will be the case in every song that touches the heart; if you celebrate the ruling passion of any man's heart, you put his voice in tune to join with you.

Thus if you can find a man whose ruling temper is devotion, whose heart is full of God, his voice will rejoice in those songs of praise which glorify that God Who is the joy of his heart, though he has neither voice nor ear for other music. Would you, therefore, delightfully perform this part of devotion, it is not so necessary to learn a tune, or practise upon notes, as to prepare your heart; for, as our blessed Lord saith, Out of the heart proceed evil thoughts, murders, etc., so it is equally true that out of

CH. XV. the heart proceed holy joys, thanksgiving, and praise. If you can once say with David, "My heart is fixed; O God, my heart is fixed," it will be very easy and natural to add, as he did, "I will sing, and give praise," etc.

Secondly, Let us now consider another reason for this kind of devotion. As singing is a natural effect of joy in the heart so it has also a natural power of rendering the heart joyful.

The soul and body are so united that they have each of them power over one another in their actions. Certain thoughts and sentiments in the soul produce such and such motions or actions in the body; and on the other hand, certain motions and actions of the body have the same power of raising such and such thoughts and sentiments in the soul. So that as singing is the natural effect of joy in the mind, so it is as truly a natural cause of raising joy in the mind.

As devotion of the heart naturally breaks out into outward acts of prayer, so outward acts of prayer are natural means of raising the devotion of the heart.

It is thus in all states and tempers of the mind; as the inward state of the mind produces outward actions suitable to it, so those outward actions have the like power of raising an inward state of mind suitable to them.

As anger produces angry words, so angry words increase anger.

So that, if we barely consider human nature, we shall find that singing or chanting the Psalms is as proper and necessary to raise our hearts to a delight in God as prayer is proper and necessary to excite in us the spirit of devotion. Every reason for one is in all respects as strong a reason for the other.

If, therefore, you would know the reason and necessity of singing Psalms, you must consider the reason and necessity of praising and rejoicing in God, because singing of Psalms is as much the true exercise and support of this spirit of thanksgiving as prayer is the true exercise and support of the spirit of devotion. And you may as well think that you can be as devout as you ought without the use of prayer as that you can rejoice in God as you ought without the practice of singing Psalms. Because this singing is as much the natural language of praise and thanksgiving as prayer is the natural language of devotion.

The union of soul and body is not a mixture of their substances, as we see bodies united and mixed together, but consists solely in the mutual power that they have of acting upon one another.

If two persons were in such a state of dependence upon one another that neither of them could act, or move, or think, or feel, or suffer, or desire anything without putting the other into the same condition, one might properly say that they were in a strict union, although their substances were not united together.

Now this is the union of the soul and body; the substance of the one cannot be mixed or united with the other, but they are held together in such a state of union that all the actions and sufferings of the one are at the same time the actions and sufferings of the other. The soul has no thought or passion but the body is concerned in it; the body has no action or motion but what in some degree affects the soul.

Now as it is the sole will of God that is the reason and cause of all the powers and effects which you see in the world; as the sun gives light and heat, not because it has any natural power of so doing; as it is fixed in a certain place and other bodies moving about it, not because it is in the nature of the sun to stand still, and in the nature of other bodies to move about it; but merely because it is the will of God that they should be in such a state. As the eye is the organ or instrument of seeing, not because the skins and coats and humours of the eye have a natural power of giving sight; as the ears are the organs or instruments of hearing, not because the make of the ear has any natural power over sounds, but merely because it is the will of God that seeing and hearing should be thus received; so in like manner it is the sole will of God, and not the nature of a human soul or body, that is the cause of this union betwixt the soul and the body.

Now if you rightly apprehend this short account of the union of the soul and body, you will see a great deal into the reason and necessity of all the outward parts of religion.

This union of our souls and bodies is the reason both why we have so little and so much power over ourselves. It is owing to this union that we have so little power over our souls; for as we cannot prevent the effects of external objects upon our bodies, as we cannot command outward causes, so we cannot always command the inward state of our minds; because, as outward objects act upon our bodies without our leave so our bodies act upon our minds by the laws of the union of the soul and the body. And thus you see it is owing to this union that we have so little power over ourselves.

On the other hand, it is owing to this union that we have so

CH. XV. much power over ourselves.   For as our souls in a great measure
depend upon our bodies, and as we have great power over our
bodies; as we can command our outward actions and oblige ourselves to such habits of life as naturally produce habits in the
soul; as we can mortify our bodies, and remove ourselves from
objects that inflame our passions, so we have a great power over
the inward state of our souls.   Again, as we are masters of our
outward actions; as we can force ourselves to outward acts of
reading, praying, singing, and the like; and as all these bodily
actions have an effect upon the soul; as they naturally tend to
form such and such tempers in our hearts; so, by being masters
of these outward bodily actions, we have great power over the
inward state of the heart.

And thus it is owing to this union that we have so much power
over ourselves.

Now from this you may also see the necessity and benefit of
singing Psalms, and of all the outward acts of religion; for if the
body has so much power over the soul, it is certain that all such
bodily actions as affect the soul are of great weight in religion,
not as if there were any true worship or piety in the actions
themselves, but because they are proper to raise and support that
spirit which is the true worship of God.

Though, therefore, the seat of religion is in the heart, yet since
our bodies have a power over our hearts, since outward actions
both proceed from and enter into the heart, it is plain that outward actions have a great power over that religion which is seated
in the heart.

We are, therefore, as well to use outward helps as inward
meditation in order to beget and fix habits of piety in our hearts.

This doctrine may be easily carried too far; for by calling in
too many outward means of worship, it may degenerate into
superstition; as on the other hand, some have fallen into the
contrary extreme.   For because religion is justly placed in the
heart, some have pursued that notion so far as to renounce vocal
prayer and other outward acts of worship, and have resolved
all religion into a quietism or mystic intercourses with God in
silence.[5]

[5] It may be thought that, as Law,
not many years after he wrote the
*Serious Call*, became a (so-called)
mystic, he would retract what he
here writes about 'quietism or mystic

intercourses with God in silence.' But
I believe he would have held the same
sentiments to the end of his life.   He
conceived an intense admiration of the
spirituality and ardent piety shown in

Now these are two extremes equally prejudicial to true religion, and ought not to be objected either against internal or external worship. As you ought not to say that I encourage that quietism by placing religion in the heart, so neither ought you to say that I encourage superstition by showing the benefit of outward acts of worship.

For since we are neither all soul nor all body, seeing none of our actions are either separately of the soul or separately of the body; seeing we have no habits but such as are produced by the actions both of our souls and bodies; it is certain that if we would arrive at habits of devotion or delight in God, we must not only meditate and exercise our souls, but we must practise and exercise our bodies to all such outward actions as are conformable to these inward tempers.

If we would truly prostrate our souls before God, we must use our bodies to postures of lowliness; if we desire true fervours of devotion, we must make prayer the frequent labour of our lips; if we would banish all pride and passion from our hearts, we must force ourselves to all outward actions of patience and meekness; if we would feel inward motions of joy and delight in God, we must practise all the outward acts of it, and make our voices call upon our hearts.

Now, therefore, you may plainly see the reason and necessity of singing of Psalms; it is because outward actions are necessary to support inward tempers, and, therefore, the outward act of joy is necessary to raise and support the inward joy of the mind.

If any people were to leave off prayer because they seldom find the motions of their heart answering the words which they speak, you would charge them with great absurdity. You would think it very reasonable that they should continue their prayers, and be strict in observing all times of prayer, as the most likely means of removing the dulness and indevotion of their hearts.

Now this is very much the case as to singing of Psalms; people often sing without finding any inward joy suitable to the words which they speak; therefore they are careless of it, or wholly

the writings of the mystics, from the pseudo - Dionysius the Areopagite, downwards; and he was fascinated in an extraordinary degree by the utterances of Jacob Behmen (Böhme). But he never became a 'quietist,' and he never had the slightest sympathy with the 'stillness' of the Moravians, which was so offensive to the Wesleys.

neglect it, not considering that they act as absurdly as he that should neglect prayer because his heart was not enough affected with it. For it is certain that this singing is as much the natural means of raising motions of joy in the mind as prayer is the natural means of raising devotion.

I have been the longer upon this head because of its great importance to true religion. For there is no state of mind so holy, so excellent, and so truly perfect as that of thankfulness to God, and consequently nothing is of more importance in religion than that which exercises and improves this habit of mind.

A dull, uneasy, complaining spirit, which is sometimes the spirit of those that seem careful of religion, is yet of all tempers the most contrary to religion, for it disowns that God which it pretends to adore. For he sufficiently disowns God who does not adore Him as a Being of infinite goodness.

If a man does not believe that all the world is as God's family, where nothing happens by chance, but all is guided and directed by the care and providence of a Being that is all love and goodness to all His creatures; if a man do not believe this from his heart, he cannot be said truly to believe in God. And yet he that has this faith has faith enough to overcome the world, and always be thankful to God. For he that believes that everything happens to him for the best cannot possibly complain for the want of something that is better.

If, therefore, you live in murmurings and complaints, accusing all the accidents of life, it is not because you are a weak, infirm creature, but it is because you want the first principle of religion, a right belief in God. For as thankfulness is an express acknowledgment of the goodness of God towards you, so repinings and complaints are as plain accusations of God's want of goodness towards you.

On the other hand, would you know who is the greatest saint in the world? It is not he who prays most or fasts most; it is not he who gives most alms, or is most eminent for temperance, chastity, or justice; but it is he who is always thankful to God, who wills everything that God willeth, who receives everything as an instance of God's goodness, and has a heart always ready to praise God for it.

All prayer and devotion, fastings and repentance, meditation and retirement, all sacraments and ordinances, are but so many means to render the soul thus divine, and conformable to the will of God, and to fill it with thankfulness and praise for everything that comes from God. This is the perfection of all virtues; and all virtues that do not tend to it or proceed from it are but so many false ornaments of a soul not converted unto God.

You need not, therefore, now wonder that I lay so much stress upon singing a Psalm at all your devotions, since you see it is to form your spirit to such joy and thankfulness to God as is the highest perfection of a divine and holy life.

If anyone would tell you the shortest, surest way to all happiness and all perfection, he must tell you to make it a rule to yourself to thank and praise God for everything that happens to you. For it is certain that whatever seeming calamity happens to you, if you thank and praise God for it, you turn it into a blessing. Could you, therefore, work miracles, you could not do more for yourself than by this thankful spirit, for it heals with a word speaking, and turns all that it touches into happiness.

If, therefore, you would be so true to your eternal interest as to propose this thankfulness as the end of all your religion; if you would but settle it in your mind that this was the state that you were to aim at by all your devotions, you would then have something plain and visible to walk by in all your actions, you would then easily see the effect of your virtues, and might safely judge of your improvement in piety. For so far as you renounce all selfish tempers and motions of your own will, and seek for no other happiness but in the thankful reception of everything that happens to you, so far you may be safely reckoned to have advanced in piety.

And although this be the highest temper that you can aim at, though it be the noblest sacrifice that the greatest saint can offer unto God, yet it is not tied to any time, or place, or great occasion, but is always in your power, and may be the exercise of every day. For the common events of every day are sufficient to discover and exercise this temper, and may plainly show you how far you are governed in all your actions by this thankful spirit.

And for this reason I exhort you to this method in your devotion, that every day may be made a day of thanksgiving, and that the spirit of murmur and discontent may be unable to enter into the heart, which is so often employed in singing the praises of God.

It may perhaps after all be objected that although the great benefit and excellent effects of this practice are very apparent, yet it seems not altogether so fit for private devotions, since it can hardly be pcrformed without making our devotions public to other people, and seems also liable to the charge of sounding a trumpet at our prayers.

It is therefore answered, First, That great numbers of people have it in their power to be as private as they please; such persons, therefore, are excluded from this excuse, which, however it may be so to others, is none to them.    Therefore let such take the benefit of this excellent devotion.

Secondly, Numbers of people are by the necessity of their state, as servants, apprentices, prisoners, and families in small houses, forced to be continually in the presence or sight of somebody or other.

Now are such persons to neglect their prayers because they cannot pray without being seen?    Are they not rather obliged to be more exact in them, that others may not be witnesses of their neglect, and so be corrupted by their example?

Now what is here said of devotion may surely be said of this chanting a Psalm, which is only a part of devotion.

The rule is this : Do not pray that you may be seen of men, but if your confinement obliges you to be always in the sight of others, be more afraid of being seen to neglect than of being seen to have recourse to prayer.

Thirdly, The short of the matter is this.    Either people can use such privacy in this practice as to have no hearers, or they cannot.    If they can, then this objection vanishes as to them; and if they cannot, they should consider their confinement and the necessities of their state as the confinement of a prison; and then they have an excellent pattern to follow; they may imitate St. Paul and Silas, who sang praises to God in prison, though we are expressly told that the prisoners heard them.    They, therefore, did not refrain from this kind of devotion for fear of being heard by others.    If, therefore, anyone is in the same necessity, either in prison or out of prison, what can he do better than to follow this example?

I cannot pass by this place of Scripture without desiring the pious reader to observe how strongly we are here called upon to this use of Psalms, and what a mighty recommendation of it the practice of these two great saints is.

In this their great distress in prison, in chains, under the sore-
ness of stripes, in the horror of night, the divinest, holiest thing
they could do was to sing praises unto God.

And shall we, after this, need any exhortation to this holy
practice? Shall we let the day pass without such thanksgivings
as they would not neglect in the night? Shall a prison, chains,
and darkness furnish them with songs of praise, and shall we
have no singings in our closets?

Further, let it also be observed that while these two holy men
were thus employed in the most exalted part of devotion, doing
that on earth which angels do in heaven, that "the foundations
of the prison were shaken, all the doors were opened, and every
one's bands were loosed" (Acts xvi. 26).

And shall we now ask for motives to this divine exercise when,
instead of arguments, we have here such miracles to convince us
of its mighty power with God?

Could God by a voice from heaven more expressly call us to
these songs of praise than by thus showing us how He hears,
delivers, and rewards those that use them?

But this by the way. I now return to the objection in hand,
and answer, Fourthly, That the privacy of our prayers is not
destroyed by our having, but by our seeking, witnesses of them.

If, therefore, nobody hears you but those you cannot separate
yourself from, you are as much in secret, and "your Father Who
seeth in secret" will as truly reward your secrecy, as if you were
seen by Him alone.

Fifthly, Private prayer, as it is opposed to prayer in public,
does not suppose that no one is to have any witness of it. For
husbands and wives, brothers and sisters, parents and children,
masters and servants, tutors and pupils are to be witnesses to one
another of such devotion as may truly and properly be called
private. It is far from being a duty to conceal such devotion
from such near relations.

In all these cases, therefore, where such relations sometimes
pray together in private and sometimes apart by themselves, the
chanting of a Psalm can have nothing objected against it.

Our blessed Lord commands us, when we fast, to "anoint our
heads and wash our faces, that we appear not unto men to fast,
but unto our Father which is in secret."

But this only means that we must not make public ostentation
to the world of our fasting.

For if no one was to fast in private, or could be said to fast in private, but he that had no witnesses of it, no one could keep a private fast but he that lived by himself, for every family must know who fasts in it. Therefore the privacy of fasting does not suppose such a privacy as excludes everybody from knowing it, but such a privacy as does not seek to be known abroad.

Cornelius, the devout centurion, of whom the Scripture saith that he "gave much" and "prayed to God alway" (Acts x. 2), saith unto St. Peter: "Four days ago, I was fasting until this hour."

Now that this fasting was sufficiently private and acceptable to God appears from the vision of an angel with which the holy man was blessed at that time.

But that it was not so private as to be entirely unknown to others appears, as from the relation of it here so from what is said in another place, that he "called two of his household servants, and a devout soldier of them that waited upon him continually." So that Cornelius's fasting was so far from being unknown to his family that the soldiers and they of his household were made devout themselves by continually waiting upon him, that is, by seeing and partaking of his good works.

As, therefore, the privacy or excellency of fasting is not destroyed by being known to some particular persons, neither would the privacy or excellency of your devotions be hurt, though by chanting a Psalm you should be heard by some of your family.

The whole of the matter is this. Great part of the world can be as private as they please; therefore let them use this excellent devotion between God and themselves.

Another great part of the world must and ought to have witnesses of several of their devotions; let them, therefore, not neglect the use of a Psalm at such times as it ought to be known to those with whom they live, that they do not neglect their prayers. For surely there can be no harm in being known to be singing a Psalm at such times as it ought to be known that you are at your prayers.

And if at other times you desire to be in such secrecy at your devotions as to have nobody suspect it, and for that reason forbear your Psalm, I have nothing to object against it, provided that at the known hours of prayer you never omit this practice.

For who would not be often doing that in the day which St. Paul and Silas would not neglect in the middle of the night?

And if, when you are thus singing, it should come into your head how the prison shaked and the doors opened when St. Paul sung, it would do your devotion no harm.

Lastly, Seeing our imaginations have great power over our hearts, and can mightily affect us with their representations, it would be of great use to you if, at the beginning of your devotions, you were to imagine to yourself some such representations as might heat and warm your heart into a temper suitable to those prayers that you are then about to offer unto God.

As thus: before you begin your Psalm of praise and rejoicing in God, make this use of your imagination.

Be still, and imagine to yourself that you saw the heavens open and the glorious choirs of cherubims and seraphims about the throne of God. Imagine that you hear the music of those angelic voices that cease not day and night to sing the glories of Him that is, and was, and is to come.

Help your imagination with such passages of Scripture as these (Rev. vii. 9)—"I beheld, and, lo, in heaven a great multitude, which no man could number, of all nations, and kindreds, and people, and tongues, standing before the throne, and before the Lamb, clothed with white robes, and palms in their hands. And they cried with a loud voice, Salvation to our God which sitteth upon the throne, and unto the Lamb.

"And all the angels stood round about the throne, and fell before the throne on their faces, and worshipped God, saying, Amen: Blessing, and glory, and wisdom, and thanksgiving, and honour, and power, and strength, be unto God for ever and ever. Amen."

Think upon this till your imagination has carried you above the clouds, till it has placed you amongst those heavenly beings, and made you long to bear a part in their eternal music.

If you will but use yourself to this method, and let your imagination dwell upon such representations as these, you will soon find it to be an excellent means of raising the spirit of devotion within you.

Always, therefore, begin your Psalm or song of praise with these imaginations; and at every verse of it imagine yourself amongst those heavenly companions, that your voice is added to theirs, and that angels join with you, and you with them;

and that you with a poor and low voice are singing that on earth which they are singing in heaven.

Again, sometimes imagine that you had been one of those that joined with our blessed Saviour when He sung an Hymn. Strive to imagine to yourself with what majesty He looked; fancy that you had stood close by Him, surrounded with His glory. Think how your heart would have been inflamed, what ecstasies of joy you would have then felt, when singing with the Son of God. Think, again and again, with what joy and devotion you would then have sung, had this been really your happy state, and what a punishment you should have thought it to have been then silent; and let this teach you how to be affected with Psalms and Hymns of thanksgiving.

Again, sometimes imagine to yourself that you saw holy David with his hands upon his harp, and his eyes fixed upon heaven, calling with transport on the creation, sun and moon, light and darkness, day and night, men and angels, to join with his rapturous soul in praising the Lord of heaven.

Dwell upon this imagination till you think you are singing with this divine musician, and let such a companion teach you to exalt your heart unto God in the following Psalm, which you may use constantly first in the morning:

Psalm cxlv.—"I will magnify thee, O God, my King; I will praise Thy name for ever and ever," etc.

These following Psalms, as the 34th, 96th, 103rd, 111th, 146th, 147th, are such as wonderfully set forth the glory of God, and, therefore, you may keep to any one of them at any particular hour as you like; or you may take the finest parts of any Psalms, and so adding them together may make them fitter for your own devotion.

# CHAPTER XVI.

*Recommending devotion at nine o'clock in the morning, called in Scripture the third hour of the day. The subject of these prayers is humility.*

I AM now come to another hour of prayer, which in Scripture is called the third hour of the day; but according to our way of numbering the hours, it is called the ninth hour of the morning.

The devout Christian must at this time look upon himself as called upon by God to renew his acts of prayer, and address himself again to the throne of grace.

There is indeed no express command in Scripture to repeat our devotions at this hour. But then it is to be considered also that neither is there any express command to begin and end the day with prayer. So that if that be looked upon as a reason for neglecting devotion at this hour, it may as well be urged as a reason for neglecting devotion both at the beginning and end of the day.

But if the practice of the saints in all ages of the world, if the customs of the pious Jews and primitive Christians be of any force with us, we have authority enough to persuade us to make this hour a constant season of devotion.[1]

The Scriptures show us how this hour was consecrated to devotion both by Jews and Christians; so that, if we desire to number ourselves amongst those whose hearts were devoted unto God, we must not let this hour pass without presenting us to Him in some solemnities of devotion. And besides this authority for this practice, the reasonableness of it is sufficient to invite us to the observance of it.

For if you were up at a good time in the morning, your first devotions will have been at a proper distance from this hour; you will have been long enough at other business to make it proper for you to return to this greatest of all business, the raising your soul and affections unto God.

[1] That is, the 'Nones' of the primitive Church.

179

But if you have risen so late as to be hardly able to begin your first devotions at this hour, which is proper for your second, you may thence learn that the indulging yourself in the morning sleep is no small matter, since it sets you so far back in your devotions, and robs you of those graces and blessings which are obtained by frequent prayers.

For if prayer has power with God, if it looses the bands of sin, if it purifies the soul, reforms our hearts, and draws down the aids of divine grace, how can that be reckoned a small matter which robs us of an hour of prayer?

Imagine yourself somewhere placed in the air as a spectator of all that passes in the world, and that you saw in one view the devotions which all Christian people offer unto God every day. Imagine that you saw some piously dividing the day and night as the primitive Christians did, and constant at all hours of devotion, singing Psalms, and calling upon God at all those times that saints and martyrs received their gifts and graces from God.

Imagine that you saw others living without any rules as to times and frequency of prayer, and only at their devotions sooner or later, as sleep and laziness happens to permit them.

Now if you were to see this as God sees it, how do you suppose you should be affected with this sight? What judgment do you imagine you should pass upon these different sorts of people? Could you think that those who were thus exact in their rules of devotion got nothing by their exactness? Could you think that their prayers were received just in the same manner, and procured them no more blessings than theirs do who prefer laziness and indulgence to times and rules of devotion?

Could you take the one to be as true servants of God as the other? Could you imagine that those who were thus different in their lives would find no difference in their states after death? Could you think it a matter of indifference, to which of these people you were most like?

If not, let it be now your care to join yourself to that number of devout people, to that society of saints, amongst whom you desire to be found when you leave the world.

And although the bare number and repetition of our prayers is of little value, yet since prayer, rightly and attentively performed, is the most natural means of amending and purifying our hearts; since opportunity and frequency in prayer is as much pressed upon us by Scripture as prayer itself; we may be sure that when we are frequent and importunate in our prayers, we are CH. XVI. taking the best means of obtaining the highest benefits of a devout life.

And on the other hand, they who through negligence, laziness, or any other indulgence render themselves either unable or uninclined [2] to observe rules and hours of devotion, we may be sure that they deprive themselves of those graces and blessings which an exact and fervent devotion procures from God.

Now as this frequency of prayer is founded in the doctrines of Scripture, and recommended to us by the practice of the true worshippers of God, so we ought not to think ourselves excused from it, but where we can show that we are spending our time in such business as is more acceptable to God than these returns of prayer.

Least of all must we imagine that dulness, negligence, indulgence, or diversions can be any pardonable excuses for our not observing an exact and frequent method of devotion.

If you are of a devout spirit, you will rejoice at these returns of prayer, which keep your soul in a holy enjoyment of God, which change your passions into divine love, and fill your heart with stronger joys and consolations than you can possibly meet with in anything else.

And if you are not of a devout spirit, then you are moreover obliged to this frequency of prayer, to train and exercise your heart into a true sense and feeling of devotion.

Now, seeing the holy spirit of the Christian religion, and the example of the saints of all ages, calls upon you thus to divide the day into hours of prayer, so it will be highly beneficial to you to make a right choice of those matters which are to be the subject of your prayers, and to keep every hour of prayer appropriated to some particular subject,[3] which you may alter or enlarge according as the state you are in requires.

---

[2] ' Uninclined,' probably used purposely instead of the more usual ' disinclined,' which would imply a positive repugnance. Law meant something merely negative, ' negligence,' ' laziness,' etc.

[3] It may help the student to have a tabulated form of the particular subjects of devotion for the different hours:

| Hours. | Subject. |
|---|---|
| 6 a.m. | Praise and thanksgiving. |
| 9 a.m. | Humility. |

12 noon. Universal love, with intercessions as an act of universal love.

3 p.m. Resignation and conformity to the will of God.

6 p.m. Self-examination and confession of the sins of the day.

Just before bed-time, Death.

The order is carefully chosen. The morning is to everyone the beginning of a new life, a resurrection from

CH. XVI.

By this means you will have an opportunity of being large and particular in all the parts of any virtue or grace which you then make the subject of your prayers. And by asking for it in all its parts, and making it the substance of a whole prayer once every day, you will soon find a mighty change in your heart, and that you cannot thus constantly pray for all the parts of any virtue every day of your life and yet live the rest of the day contrary to it.

If a worldly-minded man was to pray every day against all the instances of a worldly temper, if he should make a large description of the temptations of covetousness, and desire God to assist him to reject them all, and to disappoint him in all his covetous designs, he would find his conscience so much awakened that he would be forced either to forsake such prayers or to forsake a worldly life.

The same will hold true in any other instance. And if we ask, and have not, 'tis because we ask amiss; because we ask in cold and general forms, such as only name the virtues without describing their particular parts, such as are not enough particular to our condition, and therefore make no change in our hearts. Whereas when a man enumerates all the parts of any virtue in his prayers, his conscience is thereby awakened, and he is frighted at seeing how far short he is of it. And this stirs him up to an ardour in devotion when he sees how much he wants of that virtue which he is praying for.

I have in the last chapter laid before you the excellency of praise and thanksgiving, and recommended that as the subject of your first devotions in the morning.

And because a humble state of soul is the very state of religion, because humility is the life and soul of piety, the foundation and support of every virtue and good work, the best guard and security of all holy affections, I shall recommend humility to you as highly proper to be made the constant subject of your devotions at this

---

death, sleep being "consanguineus lethi" (Virgil, *Aen.* vii. 278). Praise and thanksgiving for this renewal of life are the natural impulses of the pious soul, and, as a correlative, the "oblation of yourself to God." Cf. Canon Bright's beautiful hymn :

"At Thy feet, O Christ, we lay
Thine own gift of this new day."

Humility comes next, because, in Law's racy language, "we may as well think to see without eyes, or live without breath, as to live in the spirit of religion without the spirit of humility." Universal love follows, as the highest grace of Christianity. Then resignation, which Law's contemporary, Bishop Butler, terms "the whole of piety" (see Sermon XIV., on "Love to God" : "Resignation to the will of God is the whole of piety; it includes in it all that is good," etc.). The two last speak for themselves.

third hour of the day, earnestly desiring you to think no day CH. XVI.
safe, or likely to end well, in which you have not thus early put
yourself in this posture of humility, and called upon God to carry
you through the day in the exercise of a meek and lowly spirit.

This virtue is so essential to the right state of our souls that
there is no pretending to a reasonable or pious life without it.
We may as well think to see without eyes, or live without breath,
as to live in the spirit of religion without the spirit of humility.

And although it is thus the soul and essence of all religious
duties, yet is it, generally speaking, the least understood, the least
regarded, the least intended, the least desired and sought after
of all other virtues amongst all sorts of Christians.

No people have more occasion to be afraid of the approaches
of pride than those who have made some advances in a pious
life.  For pride can grow as well upon our virtues as our vices,
and steals upon us on all occasions.

Every good thought that we have, every good action that we
do, lays us open to pride, and exposes us to the assaults of vanity
and self-satisfaction.

It is not only the beauty of our persons, the gifts of fortune,
or our natural talents, and the distinctions of life ; but even our
devotions and alms, our fastings and humiliations, expose us to
fresh and strong temptations of this evil spirit.

And it is for this reason that I so earnestly advise every devout
person to begin every day in this exercise of humility, that he
may go on in safety under the protection of this good guide, and
not fall a sacrifice to his own progress in those virtues which
are to save mankind from destruction.

Humility does not consist in having a worse opinion of ourselves than we deserve, or in abasing ourselves lower than we
really are.[4]   But as all virtue is founded in truth, so humility is
founded in a true and just sense of our weakness, misery, and
sin.   He that rightly feels and lives in this sense of his condition
lives in humility.

[4] Though Law was, what the average theologian of the eighteenth century disliked above all things, ' an
enthusiast,' he was conspicuous for
his common sense.  He knew that
many high-flown expressions of humility were words and nothing more ; those
who used them did not really think
that they were worse than their neighbours.  Unreality was repugnant both
to his theory and to his practice ; so he
is careful to put humility on its right
basis, as the natural outcome of three
things—our weakness, our misery, and
our sin ; if we realised these, there
would be no need of exaggerated expressions of humility ; the bare facts
of the case would be sufficient to
humble us in reality.

CH. XVI.     The weakness of our state appears from our inability to do anything as of ourselves. In our natural state we are entirely without any power; we are indeed active beings, but can only act by a power that is every moment lent us from God.

We have no more power of our own to move a hand or stir a foot than to move the sun or stop the clouds.

When we speak a word, we feel no more power in ourselves to do it than we feel ourselves able to raise the dead. For we act no more within our own power, or by our own strength, when we speak a word or make a sound, than the Apostles acted within their own power, or by their own strength, when a word from their mouth cast out devils and cured diseases.

As it was solely the power of God that enabled them to speak to such purposes so it is solely the power of God that enables us to speak at all.

We indeed find that we can speak, as we find that we are alive; but the actual exercise of speaking is no more in our own power than the actual enjoyment of life.

This is the dependent, helpless poverty of our state; which is a great reason for humility. For since we neither are, nor can do anything of ourselves, to be proud of anything that we are, or of anything that we can do, and to ascribe glory to ourselves for these things, as our own ornaments, has the guilt both of stealing and lying. It has the guilt of stealing, as it gives to ourselves those things which only belong to God. It has the guilt of lying, as it is the denying the truth of our state, and pretending to be something that we are not.

Secondly, Another argument for humility is founded in the misery of our condition.

Now the misery of our condition appears in this, that we use these borrowed powers of our nature to the torment and vexation of ourselves and our fellow-creatures.

God Almighty has entrusted us with the use of reason, and we use it to the disorder and corruption of our nature. We reason ourselves into all kinds of folly and misery, and make our lives the sport of foolish and extravagant passions: seeking after imaginary happiness in all kinds of shapes, creating to ourselves a thousand wants, amusing [5] our hearts with false hopes and fears, using the world worse than irrational animals, envying,

---

[5] 'Amusing,' that is, not merely 'entertaining,' but, in the literal sense of the term, drawing us away from proper and serious thoughts.

vexing, and tormenting one another with restless passions and unreasonable contentions.

Let any man but look back upon his own life, and see what use he has made of his reason, how little he has consulted it, and how less he has followed it. What foolish passions, what vain thoughts, what needless labours, what extravagant projects have taken up the greatest part of his life. How foolish he has been in his words and conversation; how seldom he has done well with judgment, and how often he has been kept from doing ill by accident; how seldom he has been able to please himself, and how often he has displeased others; how often he has changed his counsels, hated what he loved, and loved what he hated; how often he has been enraged and transported at trifles, pleased and displeased with the very same things, and constantly changing from one vanity to another. Let a man but take this view of his own life, and he will see reason enough to confess that pride was not made for man.

Let him but consider that if the world knew all that of him which he knows of himself; if they saw what vanity and passions govern his inside, and what secret tempers sully and corrupt his best actions, he would have no more pretence to be honoured and admired for his goodness and wisdom than a rotten and distempered body to be loved and admired for its beauty and comeliness.

This is so true, and so known to the hearts of almost all people, that nothing would appear more dreadful to them than to have their hearts thus fully discovered to the eyes of all beholders.

And perhaps there are very few people in the world who would not rather choose to die than to have all their secret follies, the errors of their judgments, the vanity of their minds, the falseness of their pretences, the frequency of their vain and disorderly passions, their uneasiness, hatreds, envies, and vexations made known unto the world.

And shall pride be entertained in a heart thus conscious of its own miserable behaviour?

Shall a creature in such a condition, that he could not support himself under the shame of being known to the world in his real state; shall such a creature, because his shame is only known to God, to holy angels, and his own conscience; shall he, in the sight of God and holy angels, dare to be vain and proud of himself?

Thirdly, If to this we add the shame and guilt of sin, we shall find a still greater reason for humility.

No creature that had lived in innocence would have thereby got any pretence for self-honour and esteem; because as a creature, all that it is, or has, or does is from God, and therefore the honour of all that belongs to it is only due to God.

But if a creature that is a sinner, and under the displeasure of the great Governor of all the world, and deserving nothing from Him but pains and punishments for the shameful abuse of his powers; if such a creature pretends to self-glory for anything that he is or does, he can only be said to glory in his shame.

Now how monstrous and shameful the nature of sin is, is sufficiently apparent from that great atonement [6] that is necessary to cleanse us from the guilt of it.

Nothing less has been required to take away the guilt of our sins than the sufferings and death of the Son of God. Had He not taken our nature upon Him, our nature had been for ever separated from God, and incapable of ever appearing before Him.

And is there any room for pride or self-glory whilst we are partakers of such a nature as this?

Have our sins rendered us so abominable and odious to Him that made us, that He could not so much as receive our prayers, or admit our repentance, till the Son of God made Himself man, and became a suffering advocate for our whole race; and can we in this state pretend to high thoughts of ourselves? Shall we presume to take delight in our own worth, who are not worthy so much as to ask pardon for our own sins without the mediation and intercession of the Son of God?

Thus deep is the foundation of humility laid in these deplorable circumstances of our condition, which show that it is as great an offence against truth and the reason of things for a man in this state of things to lay claim to any degrees of glory, as to pretend to the honour of creating himself. If man will

---

[6] In his later phase, though Law still regarded the Atonement as one of the first principles of the Christian system, he utterly repudiated the forensic theory of it; it was not the appeasing of an angry God, but the setting at one, the harmonising, of the disorders and discords of all nature introduced by the Fall. He had probably not as yet reached this stage of thought, but it will be observed that he carefully avoids any expressions which might identify his views on the subject with those of the then popular theology. His later views on the Atonement are expressed most fully in *The Spirit of Love*, which contains the most elaborate statement of his mystic views.

boast of anything as his own, he must boast of his misery and
sin, for there is nothing else but this that is his own property.

Turn your eyes towards heaven, and fancy that you saw what
is doing there; that you saw cherubims and seraphims, and all
the glorious inhabitants of that place, all united in one work;
not seeking glory from one another, not labouring their own
advancement, not contemplating their own perfections, not singing their own praises, not valuing themselves and despising
others; but all employed in one and the same work, all happy
in one and the same joy, "casting down their crowns before
the throne of God, giving glory, and honour, and power to Him
alone" (Rev. iv. 10, 11).

Then turn your eyes to the fallen world, and consider how
unreasonable and odious it must be for such poor worms, such
miserable sinners, to take delight in their own fancied glories,
whilst the highest and most glorious sons of heaven seek for
no other greatness and honour but that of ascribing all honour
and greatness and glory to God alone.

Pride is only the disorder of the fallen world; it has no place
amongst other beings; it can only subsist where ignorance and
sensuality, lies and falsehood, lusts and impurity reign.

Let a man, when he is most delighted with his own figure,
look upon a crucifix,[7] and contemplate our blessed Lord stretched
out and nailed upon a cross; and then let him consider how
absurd it must be for a heart full of pride and vanity to pray
to God, through the sufferings of such a meek and crucified
Saviour.

These are the reflections that you are often to meditate upon,
that you may thereby be disposed to walk before God and man
in such a spirit of humility as becomes the weak, miserable,
sinful state of all that are descended from fallen Adam.

When you have by such general reflections as these convinced
your mind of the reasonableness of humility, you must not content yourself with this, as if you were therefore humble, because
your mind acknowledges the reasonableness of humility, and
declares against pride; but you must immediately enter yourself
into the practice of this virtue like a young beginner, that has
all of it to learn, that can learn but little at a time, and with

---

[7] Another instance of the regret with
which Law, though no Romanist, regarded the loss of many things which
were abolished in the English Church
at the Reformation.

CH. XVI. great difficulty. You must consider that you have not only this virtue to learn, but that you must be content to proceed as a learner in it all your time, endeavouring after greater degrees of it, and practising every day acts of humility, as you every day practise acts of devotion.

You would not imagine yourself to be devout, because in your judgment you approved of prayers, and often declared your mind in favour of devotion. Yet how many people imagine themselves humble enough, for no other reason but because they often commend humility and make vehement declarations against pride.

Cœcus is a rich man, of good birth, and very fine parts. He is fond of dress, curious in the smallest matters that can add any ornament to his person. He is haughty and imperious to all his inferiors, is very full of everything that he says or does, and never imagines it possible for such a judgment as his to be mistaken. He can bear no contradiction, and discovers the weakness of your understanding as soon as ever you oppose him. He changes everything in his house, his habit, and his equipage, as often as anything more elegant comes in his way; Cœcus would have been very religious, but that he always thought he was so.

There is nothing so odious to Cœcus as a proud man; and the misfortune is, that in this he is so very quick-sighted that he discovers in almost everybody some strokes of vanity.

On the other hand, he is exceeding fond of humble and modest persons. Humility, says he, is so amiable a quality, that it forces our esteem wherever we meet with it. There is no possibility of despising the meanest person that has it, or of esteeming the greatest man that wants it.

Cœcus no more suspects himself to be proud than he suspects his want of sense. And the reason of it is because he always finds himself so in love with humility, and so enraged at pride.

It is very true, Cœcus, you speak sincerely when you say you love humility and abhor pride. You are no hypocrite, you speak the true sentiments of your mind; but then take this along with you, Cœcus, that you only love humility and hate pride in other people. You never once in your life thought of any other humility, or of any other pride, than that which you have seen in other people.

The case of Cœcus is a common case; many people live in all

the instances[8] of pride, and indulge every vanity that can enter CH. XVI.
into their minds, and yet never suspect themselves to be governed
by pride and vanity, because they know how much they dislike
proud people, and how mightily they are pleased with humility
and modesty wherever they find them.

All their speeches in favour of humility, and all their railings
against pride are looked upon as so many true exercises and
effects of their own humble spirit.

Whereas in truth these are so far from being proper acts,
or proofs of humility, that they are great arguments of the want of
it.

For the fuller of pride any one is himself, the more impatient
will he be at the smallest instances of it in other people.  And
the less humility any one has in his own mind, the more will
he demand, and be delighted with it in other people.

You must, therefore, act by a quite contrary measure, and
reckon yourself only so far humble as you impose every instance
of humility upon yourself, and never call for it in other people;
so far an enemy to pride as you never spare it in yourself nor
ever censure it in other persons.

Now in order to do this, you need only consider that pride and
humility signify nothing to you, but so far as they are your own;
that they do you neither good nor harm, but as they are the
tempers of your own heart.

The loving, therefore, of humility is of no benefit or advantage
to you, but so far as you love to see all your own thoughts, words,
and actions governed by it.   And the hating of pride does you no
good, is no perfection in you, but so far as you hate to harbour
any degree of it in your own heart.

Now in order to begin and set out well in the practice of
humility, you must take it for granted that you are proud, that you
have all your life been more or less infected with this unreasonable
temper.

You should believe also that it is your greatest weakness that
your heart is most subject to it, that it is so constantly stealing
upon you that you have reason to watch and suspect its
approaches in all your actions.

For this is what most people, especially new beginners in a
pious life, may with great truth think of themselves.

[8] That is, showing in their lives all *exemplum* is used in the same
examples of pride.  The Latin word  sense.

For there is no one vice that is more deeply rooted in our nature, or that receives such constant nourishment from almost everything that we think or do, there being hardly anything in the world that we want or use, or any action or duty of life, but pride finds some means or other to take hold of it. So that at what time soever we begin to offer ourselves to God, we can hardly be surer of anything than that we have a great deal of pride to repent of.

If, therefore, you find it disagreeable to your mind to entertain this opinion of yourself, and that you cannot put yourself amongst those that want to be cured of pride, you may be as sure as if an angel from heaven had told you that you have not only much, but all your humility to seek.

For you can have no greater sign of a more confirmed pride than when you think you are humble enough. He that thinks he loves God enough shows himself to be an entire stranger to that holy passion; so he that thinks he has humility enough shows that he is not so much as a beginner in the practice of true humility.

# CHAPTER XVII.

*Showing how difficult the practice of humility is made by the general spirit and temper of the world. How Christianity requireth us to live contrary to the world.*

EVERY person, when he first applies himself to the exercise of this virtue of humility, must, as I said before, consider himself as a learner, that is to learn something that is contrary to former tempers and habits of mind, and which can only be got by daily and constant practice.

He has not only as much to do as he that has some new art or science to learn, but he has also a great deal to unlearn; he is to forget and lay aside his own spirit, which has been a long while fixing and forming itself; he must forget and depart from abundance of passions and opinions which the fashion, and vogue, and spirit of the world have made natural to him.

He must lay aside his own spirit; because, as we are born in sin, so in pride, which is as natural to us as self-love, and continually springs from it. And this is the reason why Christianity is so often represented as a new birth and a new spirit.

He must lay aside the opinions and passions which he has received from the world, because the vogue and fashion of the world, by which we have been carried away as in a torrent, before we could pass right judgments of the value of things, is, in many respects, contrary to humility; so that we must unlearn what the spirit of the world has taught us before we can be governed by the spirit of humility.

The devil is called in Scripture the prince of this world, because he has great power in it, because many of its rules and principles are invented by this evil spirit, the father of all lies and falsehood, to separate us from God, and prevent our return to happiness.

Now according to the spirit and vogue of this world, whose corrupt air we have all breathed, there are many things that pass

CH. XVII. for great and honourable and most desirable, which yet are so far from being so, that the true greatness and honour of our nature consist in the not desiring them.

To abound in wealth, to have fine houses and rich clothes, to be beautiful in our persons, to have titles of dignity, to be above our fellow-creatures, to command the bows and obeisance of other people, to be looked on with admiration, to overcome our enemies with power, to subdue all that oppose us, to set out ourselves in as much splendour as we can, to live highly and magnificently, to eat and drink, and delight ourselves in the most costly manner, these are the great, the honourable, the desirable things, to which the spirit of the world turns the eyes of all people. And many a man is afraid of standing still, and not engaging in the pursuit of these things, lest the same world should take him for a fool.

The history of the Gospel is chiefly the history of Christ's conquest over this spirit of the world. And the number of true Christians is only the number of those who, following the spirit of Christ, have lived contrary to the spirit of the world.

"If any man hath not the spirit of Christ, he is none of His." Again, "Whosoever is born of God, overcometh the world. Set your affections on things above, and not on things on the earth; for ye are dead, and your life is hid with Christ in God." This is the language of the whole New Testament. This is the mark of Christianity; you are to be dead, that is, dead to the spirit and temper of the world, and live a new life in the Spirit of Jesus Christ.

But notwithstanding the clearness and plainness of these doctrines which thus renounce the world, yet great part of Christians live and die slaves to the customs and temper of the world.

How many people swell with pride and vanity, for such things as they would not know how to value at all, but they are admired in the world?

Would a man take ten years more drudgery in business to add two horses more to his coach but that he knows that the world most of all admires a coach and six?[1] How fearful are many

---

[1] A coach and six was, in Law's day, the usual equipage of the very rich and noble. When coaches, or carriages, as we should call them, were very heavy and cumbrous, and roads atrocious, six horses would not be a merely ostentatious display; they would be necessary for despatch and comfort.

people of having their houses poorly furnished or themselves CH. XVII. meanly clothed for this only reason, lest the world should make no account of them, and place them amongst low and mean people?

How often would a man have yielded to the haughtiness and ill nature of others, and shown a submissive temper, but that he dares not pass for such a poor-spirited man in the opinion of the world?

Many a man would often drop a resentment and forgive an affront but that he is afraid, if he should, the world would not forgive him.

How many would practise Christian temperance and sobriety in its utmost perfection were it not for the censure which the world passes upon such a life?

Others have frequent intentions of living up to the rules of Christian perfection, which they are frighted from by considering what the world would say of them.

Thus do the impressions which we have received from living in the world enslave our minds, that we dare not attempt to be eminent in the sight of God and holy angels for fear of being little in the eyes of the world.

From this quarter arises the greatest difficulty of humility, because it cannot subsist in any mind but so far as it is dead to the world, and has parted with all desires of enjoying its greatness and honours. So that in order to be truly humble, you must unlearn all those notions which you have been all your life learning from this corrupt spirit of the world.

You can make no stand against the assaults of pride, the meek affections of humility can have no place in your soul, till you stop the power of the world over you, and resolve against a blind obedience to its laws.

And when you are once advanced thus far as to be able to stand still in the torrent of worldly fashions and opinions, and examine the worth and value of things which are most admired and valued in the world, you have gone a great way in the gaining of your freedom, and have laid a good foundation for the amendment of your heart.

For as great as the power of the world is, it is all built upon a blind obedience, and we need only open our eyes to get rid of its power.

Ask who you will, learned or unlearned, everyone seems

CH. XVII. to know and confess that the general temper and spirit of the world is nothing else but humour, folly, and extravagance.

Who will not own that the wisdom of philosophy, the piety of religion, was always confined to a small number? And is not this expressly owning and confessing that the common spirit and temper of the world is neither according to the wisdom of philosophy nor the piety of religion?

The world, therefore, seems enough condemned, even by itself, to make it very easy for a thinking man to be of the same judgment.

And, therefore, I hope you will not think it a hard saying that, in order to be humble, you must withdraw your obedience from that vulgar spirit which gives laws to fops and coquettes, and form your judgments according to the wisdom of philosophy and the piety of religion. Who would be afraid of making such a change as this?

Again, To lessen your fear and regard to the opinion of the world, think how soon the world will disregard you, and have no more thought or concern about you than about the poorest animal that died in a ditch.

Your friends, if they can, may bury you with some distinction, and set up a monument to let posterity see that your dust lies under such a stone; and when that is done, all is done. Your place is filled up by another; the world is just in the same state as it was; you are blotted out of its sight, and as much forgotten by the world as if you had never belonged to it.

Think upon the rich, the great, and the learned persons that have made great figures, and been high in the esteem of the world. Many of them died in your time, and yet they are sunk and lost and gone, and as much disregarded by the world as if they had been only so many bubbles of water.

Think again, how many poor souls see heaven lost, and lie now expecting a miserable eternity, for their service and homage to a world that thinks itself every whit as well without them, and is just as merry as it was when they were in it.

Is it, therefore, worth your while to lose the smallest degree of virtue for the sake of pleasing so bad a master and so false a friend as the world is?

Is it worth your while to bow the knee to such an idol as this, that so soon will have neither eyes, nor ears, nor a heart to regard you, instead of serving that great and holy and mighty

God that will make all His servants partakers of His own CH. XVII. eternity?

Will you let the fear of a false world, that has no love for you, keep you from the fear of that God Who has only created you that He may love and bless you to all eternity?

Lastly, You must consider what behaviour the profession of Christianity requireth of you with regard to the world.

Now this is plainly delivered in these words: "Who gave Himself for our sins, that He might deliver us from this present evil world" (Gal. i. 4). Christianity, therefore, implieth a deliverance from this world; and he that professeth it, professeth to live contrary to everything and every temper that is peculiar to this evil world.

St. John declareth this opposition to the world in this manner: "They are of the world: therefore speak they of the world, and the world heareth them. We are of God" (1 St. John iv. 5). This is the description of the followers of Christ; and it is proof enough that no people are to be reckoned Christians in reality, who in their hearts and tempers belong to this world. "We know," saith the same Apostle, "that we are of God, and the whole world lieth in wickedness" (chap. v. ver. 19). Christians, therefore, can no farther know that they are of God than so far as they know they are not of the world; that is, that they do not live according to the ways and spirit of the world. For all the ways and maxims and politics and tempers of the world lie in wickedness. And he is only of God, or born of God in Christ Jesus, who has overcome this world; that is, who has chosen to live by faith, and govern his actions by the principles of a wisdom revealed from God by Christ Jesus.

St. Paul takes it for a certainty, so well known to Christians, that they are no longer to be considered as living in this world, that he thus argues from it, as from an undeniable principle, concerning the abolishing the rites of the Jewish law: "Wherefore if ye be dead with Christ from the rudiments of the world, why, as though living in the world, are ye subject to ordinances?" (Col. ii. 20). Here could be no argument in this, but in the Apostle's taking it for undeniable that Christians knew that their profession required them to have done with all the tempers and passions of this world, to live as citizens of the new Jerusalem, and to have their conversations in heaven.

Our blessed Lord Himself has fully determined this point in

CH. XVII. these words: "They are not of this world, as I am not of this world." This is the state of Christianity with regard to this world. If you are not thus out of, and contrary to the world, you want the distinguishing mark of Christianity; you do not belong to Christ but by being out of the world as He was out of it.[2]

We may deceive ourselves, if we please, with vain and softening comments upon these words, but they are, and will be, understood in their first simplicity and plainness by everyone that reads them in the same spirit that our blessed Lord spoke them. And to understand them in any lower, less significant meaning is to let carnal wisdom explain away that doctrine by which itself was to be destroyed.

The Christian's great conquest over the world is all contained in the mystery of Christ upon the cross. It was there and from thence that He taught all Christians how they were to come out of and conquer the world, and what they were to do in order to be His disciples. And all the doctrines, sacraments, and institutions of the Gospel are only so many explications of the meaning, and applications of the benefit of this great mystery.

And the state of Christianity implieth nothing else but an entire, absolute conformity to that spirit which Christ showed in the mysterious sacrifice of Himself upon the cross.

Every man, therefore, is only so far a Christian as he partakes of this spirit of Christ. It was this that made St. Paul so passionately express himself, "God forbid that I should glory, save in the cross of our Lord Jesus Christ." But why does he glory? Is it because Christ had suffered in his stead, and had excused him from suffering?[3] No, by no means. But it was because his Christian profession had called him to the honour of suffering with Christ, and of dying to the world under reproach and contempt as He had done upon the cross. For he immediately adds, "By Whom the world is crucified unto me, and I unto the world" (Gal. vi. 14). This, you see, was the reason of his

---

[2] Though Law did not, in many respects, follow the course of the Evangelical Revival, of which he was the pioneer, he was thoroughly in accord with it in his view of 'the world,' which, it will be seen, he regarded as essentially opposed to the spirit of Christianity.

[3] Law drew a marked distinction between Christ dying 'in our stead'

($\dot{a}\nu\tau\grave{\iota}$ $\dot{\eta}\mu\hat{\omega}\nu$), and Christ dying 'in our behalf' ($\dot{\upsilon}\pi\grave{\epsilon}\rho$ $\dot{\eta}\mu\hat{\omega}\nu$). His logical mind saw that the former expression would imply that our 'death unto sin,' our 'crucifying the flesh,' etc., was unnecessary, while the latter would not. Christ suffered as our representative rather than as our substitute, that we, too, might suffer with Him.

glorying in the cross of Christ, because it had called him to a like state of death and crucifixion to the world.

Thus was the cross of Christ in St. Paul's days the glory of Christians; not as it signified their not being ashamed to own a Master that was crucified, but as it signified their glorying in a religion which was nothing else but a doctrine of the cross,[4] that called them to the same suffering spirit, the same sacrifice of themselves, the same renunciation of the world, the same humility and weakness, the same patient bearing of injuries, reproaches, and contempts, and the same dying to all the greatness, honours, and happiness of this world which Christ showed upon the cross.

To have a true idea of Christianity we must not consider our blessed Lord as suffering in our stead, but as our representative acting in our name, and with such particular merit as to make our joining with Him acceptable unto God.

He suffered, and was a sacrifice, to make our sufferings and sacrifice of ourselves fit to be received by God. And we are to suffer, to be crucified, to die, to rise with Christ, or else His crucifixion, death, and resurrection will profit us nothing.

The necessity of this conformity to all that Christ did and suffered upon our account is very plain from the whole tenor of Scripture.

First, As to His sufferings: this is the only condition of our being saved by them, if "we suffer with Him, we shall also reign with Him."

Secondly, As to His crucifixion: "Knowing this, that our old man is crucified with Him," etc. (Rom. vi. 6). Here you see, Christ is not crucified in our stead; but, unless our old man be really crucified with Him, the cross of Christ will profit us nothing.

Thirdly, As to the death of Christ, the condition is this: "If we be dead with Christ, we believe that we shall also live with

---

[4] It is curious that Law, a nonjuror, should use here an expression which, at any rate with the earlier nonjurors, had a technical signification. They meant by it, technically, the self-sacrifice they had to make by refusing to take the oaths of allegiance and abjuration. John Kettlewell was the originator of this use of the expression, 'a doctrine of the cross'; and there is no doubt that this is the meaning of the famous clause in Bishop Ken's Will, "And as it (the Church of England) adheres to the doctrine of the cross," which is now so often quoted in a very different sense. Of course, in the text Law uses the term, 'a doctrine of the cross' in its wider signification, not in its technical sense.

Him." If, therefore, Christ be dead alone, if we are not dead with Him, we are as sure, from this Scripture, that we shall not live with Him.

Lastly, As to the resurrection of Christ, the Scripture showeth us how we are to partake of the benefit of it: " If ye be risen with Christ, seek those things which are above, where Christ sitteth on the right hand of God " (Col. iii. 1).

Thus you see how plainly the Scripture sets forth our blessed Lord as our representative, acting and suffering in our name, binding and obliging us to conform to all that He did and suffered for us.[5]

It was for this reason that the holy Jesus said of His disciples, and in them of all true believers, " They are not of this world, as I am not of this world." Because all true believers conforming to the sufferings, crucifixion, death, and resurrection of Christ live no longer after the spirit and temper of this world, but their life is hid with Christ in God.

This is the state of separation from the world to which all orders of Christians are called. They must so far renounce all worldly tempers, be so far governed by the things of another life, as to show that they are truly and really crucified, dead, and risen with Christ. And it is as necessary for all Christians to conform to this great change of spirit, to be thus in Christ new creatures, as it was necessary that Christ should suffer, die, and rise again for our salvation.

How high the Christian life is placed above the ways of this world is wonderfully described by St. Paul in these words: "Wherefore henceforth know we no man after the flesh; yea, though we have known Christ after the flesh, yet henceforth know we Him no more. Therefore if any man be in Christ, he is a new creature : old things are passed away ; behold, all things are become new" (2 Cor. v. 16, 17).

He that feels the force and spirit of these words can hardly bear any human interpretation of them. Henceforth, says he, that is, since the death and resurrection of Christ, the state of Christianity is become so glorious a state that we do not even consider Christ Himself as in the flesh upon earth, but as a God of glory in

---

[5] Observe in this sentence Law's fuller explanation of the light in which he regards Christ's sufferings. From this view of the atonement he never materially diverged, though it is to his later, mystic works that we must look to find his view fully developed.

heaven; we know and consider ourselves not as men in the flesh, CH. XVII. but as fellow-members of a new society that are to have all our hearts, our tempers, and conversation in heaven.

Thus it is that Christianity has placed us out of, and above the world, and we fall from our calling as soon as we fall into the tempers of the world.

Now as it was the spirit of the world that nailed our blessed Lord to the cross, so every man that has the spirit of Christ, that opposes the world as He did, will certainly be crucified by the world some way or other.

For Christianity still lives in the same world that Christ did; and these two will be utter enemies till the kingdom of darkness is entirely at an end.

Had you lived with our Saviour as His true disciple, you had then been hated as He was; and if you now live in His spirit, the world will be the same enemy to you now that it was to Him then.

" If ye were of the world," saith our blessed Lord, " the world would love its own; but because ye are not of the world, but I have chosen you out of the world, therefore the world hateth you " (St. John xv. 19).

We are apt to lose the true meaning of these words by considering them only as an historical description of something that was the state of our Saviour and His disciples at that time. But this is reading the Scripture as a dead letter; for they exactly describe the state of true Christians at this, and all other times, to the end of the world.

For as true Christianity is nothing else but the spirit of Christ, so whether that spirit appear in the person of Christ Himself, or His Apostles, or followers in any age, it is the same thing; whoever hath His spirit will be hated, despised, and condemned by the world as He was.

For the world will always love its own, and none but its own: this is as certain and unchangeable as the contrariety betwixt light and darkness.

When the holy Jesus saith, " If the world hate you," He does not add, by way of consolation, that it may some time or other cease its hatred, or that it will not always hate them; but He only gives this as a reason for their bearing it; " you know that it hated Me before it hated you "; signifying that it was He, that is, His spirit, that by reason of its contrariety to the world, was then and always would be hated by it.

You will perhaps say that the world is now become Christian, at least that part of it where we live; and, therefore, the world is not now to be considered in that state of opposition to Christianity as when it was heathen.[6]

It is granted the world now professeth Christianity; but will any one say that this Christian world is of the spirit of Christ? Are its general tempers the tempers of Christ? Are the passions of sensuality, self-love, pride, covetousness, ambition, and vain-glory less contrary to the spirit of the Gospel now they are amongst Christians, than when they were amongst heathens? Or will you say that the tempers and passions of the heathen world are lost and gone?

Consider, secondly, what you are to mean by the world. Now this is fully described to our hands by St. John. "All that is in the world, the lust of the flesh, the lust of the eyes, and the pride of life," etc. (1 St. John ii. 16). This is an exact and full description of the world. Now, will you say that this world is become Christian? But if all this still subsists, then the same world is now in being, and the same enemy to Christianity, that was in St. John's days.

It was this world that St. John condemned as being not of the Father; whether, therefore, it outwardly professeth or openly persecuteth Christianity, it is still in the same state of contrariety to the true spirit and holiness of the Gospel.

And indeed the world, by professing Christianity, is so far from being a less dangerous enemy than it was before, that it has by its favours destroyed more Christians than ever it did by the most violent persecution.

We must, therefore, be so far from considering the world as in a state of less enmity and opposition to Christianity than it was in the first times of the Gospel, that we must guard against it as a greater and more dangerous enemy now than it was in those times.

It is a greater enemy, because it has greater power over Christians by its favours, riches, honours, rewards, and protections, than it had by the fire and fury of its persecutions.

---

[6] It is very characteristic of Law's thorough-going and uncompromising mind to refuse absolutely to take the 'Christian world' as in any way different from the 'heathen world,' unless it brought forth the plain, practical fruits of Christianity. If there was any difference it was in favour of the latter, which did not sin against so much light and knowledge. He lays very great stress upon this point, because he saw men were in danger of what he would call, 'being amused by an expression.'

It is a more dangerous enemy by having lost its appearance of CH. XVII. enmity. Its outward profession of Christianity makes it no longer considered as an enemy, and, therefore, the generality of people are easily persuaded to resign themselves up to be governed and directed by it.

How many consciences are kept at quiet upon no other foundation but because they sin under the authority of the Christian world?

How many directions of the Gospel lie by unregarded, and how unconcernedly do particular persons read them, for no other reason but because they seem unregarded by the Christian world?

How many compliances do people make to the Christian world without any hesitation or remorse, which, if they had been required of them only by heathens, would have been refused as contrary to the holiness of Christianity?

Who could be content with seeing how contrary his life is to the Gospel, but because he sees that he lives as the Christian world doth?

Who that reads the Gospel would want to be persuaded of the necessity of great self-denial, humility, and poverty of spirit, but that the authority of the world has banished this doctrine of the cross?

There is nothing, therefore, that a good Christian ought to be more suspicious of, or more constantly guard against, than the authority of the Christian world.

And all the passages of Scripture which represent the world as contrary to Christianity, which require our separation from it as from a mammon of unrighteousness, a monster of iniquity, are all to be taken in the same strict sense in relation to the present world.

For the change that the world has undergone has only altered its methods, but not lessened its power of destroying religion.

Christians had nothing to fear from the heathen world but the loss of their lives; but the world become a friend, makes it difficult for them to save their religion.

Whilst pride, sensuality, covetousness, and ambition had only the authority of the heathen world, Christians were thereby made more intent upon the contrary virtues. But when pride, sensuality, covetousness, and ambition have the authority of the Christian world, then private Christians are in the utmost danger

CH. XVII. not only of being shamed out of the practice, but of losing the very notion of the piety of the Gospel.

There is, therefore, hardly any possibility of saving yourself from the present world, but by considering it as the same wicked enemy to all true holiness as it is represented in the Scriptures, and by assuring yourself that it is as dangerous to conform to its tempers and passions, now it is Christian, as when it was heathen.

For only ask yourself, Is the piety, the humility, the sobriety of the Christian world, the piety, the humility, and sobriety of the Christian spirit?  If not, how can you be more undone by any world, than by conforming to that which is Christian?

Need a man do more to make his soul unfit for the mercy of God than by being greedy and ambitious of honour?  Yet how can a man renounce this temper without renouncing the spirit and temper of the world in which you now live?

How can a man be made more incapable of the spirit of Christ than by a wrong value for money; and yet how can he be more wrong in his value of it than by following the authority of the Christian world?

Nay, in every order and station of life, whether of learning or business, either in church or state, you cannot act up to the spirit of religion without renouncing the most general temper and behaviour of those who are of the same order and business as yourself.

And though human prudence seems to talk mighty wisely about the necessity of avoiding particularities, yet he that dares not be so weak as to be particular will be often obliged to avoid the most substantial duties of Christian piety.

These reflections will, I hope, help you to break through those difficulties, and resist those temptations which the authority and fashion of the world have raised against the practice of Christian humility.

# CHAPTER XVIII.

*Showing how the education which men generally receive in their youth makes the doctrines of humility difficult to be practised. The spirit of a better education represented in the character of Paternus.*

ANOTHER difficulty in the practice of humility arises from our education. We are all of us, for the most part, corruptly educated, and then committed to take our course in a corrupt world, so that it is no wonder if examples of great piety are so seldom seen.

Great part of the world are undone by being born and bred in families that have no religion, where they are made vicious and irregular by being like those with whom they first lived.

But this is not the thing I now mean; the education that I here intend is such as children generally receive from virtuous and sober parents, and learned tutors and governors.

Had we continued perfect, as God created the first man, perhaps the perfection of our nature had been a sufficient self-instruction for every one. But as sickness and diseases have created the necessity of medicines and physicians, so the change and disorder of our rational nature has introduced the necessity of education and tutors.

And as the only end of the physician is to restore nature to its own state, so the only end of education is to restore our rational nature to its proper state. Education, therefore, is to be considered as reason borrowed at second hand, which is, as far as it can, to supply the loss of original perfection.[1] And as physic may justly be called the art of restoring health, so education should be considered in no other light than as the art of recovering to man the use of his reason.

[1] The whole of this sentence would be disapproved of by theologians of the Evangelical school. ' Reason borrowed at second hand' would be no advantage in their view, and still less would they agree that education can in any degree 'supply the loss of original perfection.'

Now as the instruction of every art or science is founded upon the discoveries, the wisdom, experience, and maxims of the several great men that have laboured in it; so human wisdom, or right use of our reason, which young people should be called to by their education, is nothing else but the best experience and finest reasonings of men that have devoted themselves to the study of wisdom and the improvement of human nature.

All, therefore, that great saints and dying men, when the fullest of light and conviction, and after the highest improvement of their reason, all that they have said of the necessity of piety, of the excellency of virtue, of their duty to God, of the emptiness of riches, of the vanity of the world; all the sentences, judgments, reasonings, and maxims of the wisest of philosophers, when in their highest state of wisdom, should constitute the common lessons of instruction for youthful minds.

This is the only way to make the young and ignorant part of the world the better for the wisdom and knowledge of the wise and ancient.

An education which is not wholly intent upon this is as much beside the point as an art of physic, that had little or no regard to the restoration of health.

The youths that attended upon Pythagoras, Socrates, Plato, and Epictetus were thus educated. Their every day lessons and instructions were so many lectures upon the nature of man, his true end, and the right use of his faculties; upon the immortality of the soul, its relation to God, the beauty of virtue, and its agreeableness to the divine nature; upon the dignity of reason, the necessity of temperance, fortitude and generosity, and the shame and folly of indulging our passions.[2]

Now as Christianity has, as it were, new created the moral and religious world, and set everything that is reasonable, wise, holy, and desirable in its true point of light, so one would expect that the education of youth should be as much bettered and amended by Christianity as the faith and doctrines of religion are amended by it.

As it has introduced such a new state of things, and so

[2] Although Law had already begun to depreciate 'human learning,' (a depreciation which he carried to a climax in his later years), he shows here, as elsewhere, that he was a thoroughly well-read man himself. What he says of the teaching of Pythagoras, Socrates, Plato, and Epictetus is absolutely true.

fully informed us of the nature of man, the ends of his CH. XVIII.
creation, the state of his condition; as it has fixed all our
goods and evils, taught us the means of purifying our souls,
pleasing God, and becoming eternally happy, one might
naturally suppose that every Christian country abounded with
schools for the teaching not only a few questions and answers
of a Catechism,[3] but for the forming, training, and practising
youths in such an outward course of life as the highest
precepts, the strictest rules, and the sublimest doctrines of
Christianity require.

An education under Pythagoras or Socrates had no other end
but to teach youth to think, judge, act, and follow such rules of
life as Pythagoras or Socrates used.[4]

And is it not as reasonable to suppose that a Christian education should have no other end but to teach youth how to
think, and judge, and act, and live according to the strictest
laws of Christianity?

At least one would suppose that in all Christian schools the
teaching youth to begin their lives in the spirit of Christianity,
in such severity of behaviour, such abstinence, sobriety, humility,
and devotion as Christianity requires should not only be more,
but a hundred times more regarded than any or all things else.

For our education should imitate our guardian angels, suggest
nothing to our minds but what is wise and holy, help us to discover and subdue every vain passion of our hearts, and every false
judgment of our minds.

And it is as sober and reasonable to expect and require all
this benefit of a Christian education as to require that physic
should strengthen all that is right in our nature, and remove
that which is sickly and diseased.

But, alas, our modern education is not of this kind.[5]

---

[3] And not even these, according to
the system of education advocated by
many now in this Christian country.

[4] Let any one read, say, the *Republic
of Plato*, the proper title of which is
Περὶ Δικαιοσύνης, and he will see how
fully justified Law was in making this
assertion.

[5] The state of our public schools
and universities was, perhaps, one of
the weakest points of the eighteenth
century. See the strictures of Gibbon
(*Autobiography*), Cowper (*Tirocinium*), and Gray (*Letters to Mason*)

on the subject. But the particular
system against which Law inveighs
is ten times more rife, in these days of
competitive examinations for everything, than it was in Law's day. It
will be seen that he objects *in toto* to
the plan of appealing to the love of
distinction, the desire of rising above
others. He holds that emulation is
'nothing else but a refinement upon
envy,' that it directly tends to foster
the hateful spirit of pride, and therefore conduces to the destruction of
that which he regards as one of the

CH. XVIII.    The first temper that we try to awaken in children is pride, as dangerous a passion as that of lust. We stir them up to vain thoughts of themselves, and do everything we can to puff up their minds with a sense of their own abilities.

Whatever way of life we intend them for, we apply to the fire and vanity of their minds, and exhort them to everything from corrupt motives. We stir them up to action from principles of strife and ambition, from glory, envy, and a desire of distinction, that they may excel others, and shine in the eyes of the world.

We repeat and inculcate these motives upon them, till they think it a part of their duty to be proud, envious, and vainglorious of their own accomplishments.

And when we have taught them to scorn to be out-done by any, to bear no rival, to thirst after every instance of applause, to be content with nothing but the highest distinctions, then we begin to take comfort in them, and promise the world some mighty things from youths of such a glorious spirit.

If children are intended for holy orders, we set before them some eminent orator whose fine preaching has made him the admiration of the age, and carried him through all the dignities and preferments of the church.

We encourage them to have these honours in their eye, and to expect the reward of their studies from them.

If the youth is intended for a trade, we bid him look at all the rich men of the same trade, and consider how many now

---

highest of Christian graces—humility. It is not easy to answer his arguments on Christian grounds; and it cannot be denied that St. Paul (Gal. v. 19-21) places among 'the works of the flesh' (adding that 'they which do such things shall not inherit the kingdom of God') 'emulations,' which surely is a literal translation of ζῆλοι. 'Emulations' and 'envyings' are put by the apostle in the same category, so Law can plead that he has Scripture on his side. Law, however, seems to me scarcely to take into sufficient account the fact that there may be such a thing as 'generous emulation.' It may be doubted whether, as a matter of fact, in the fresh mind of youth, the rivalry between one boy and another (girls, so far as the eighteenth century went, were out of account, 'high schools' and competitive examinations

being, in that sex, then unknown), *does* tend to produce the evil effects which Law fears; at any rate, whether the advantages which a youth derives from learning to find his own level, which he can find in a public school and in a university more certainly than anywhere else, do not more than counterbalance the disadvantage—and that in the very direction in which Law would lead him. To find his own level tends to make a person, not proud, but humble; and a private education, which, from the nature of the case, cannot so effectually teach the rough lesson of 'give and take,' will be found, except under ideal circumstances, to make a youth think more of himself than the wholesome discipline, especially that which is maintained as 'an unwritten law' by the scholars themselves, in a well ordered public school, will do.

are carried about in their stately coaches who began in the CH. XVIII. same low degree as he now does. We awaken his ambition, and endeavour to give his mind a right turn, by often telling him how very rich such and such a tradesman died.

If he is to be a lawyer, then we set great counsellors, lords, judges, and chancellors before his eyes. We tell him what great fees and great applause attend fine pleading. We exhort him to take fire at these things, to raise a spirit of emulation in himself, and to be content with nothing less than the highest honours of the long robe.

That this is the nature of our best education is too plain to need any proof; and I believe there are few parents but would be glad to see these instructions daily given to their children.[6]

And after all this, we complain of the effects of pride; we wonder to see grown men actuated and governed by ambition, envy, scorn, and a desire of glory, not considering that they were all the time of their youth called upon to all their action and industry upon the same principles.

You teach a child to scorn to be out-done, to thirst for distinction and applause; and is it any wonder that he continues to act all his life in the same manner?

Now if a youth is ever to be so far a Christian as to govern his heart by the doctrines of humility, I would fain know at what time he is to begin it; or if he is ever to begin it at all, why we train him up in tempers quite contrary to it?

How dry and poor must the doctrine of humility sound to a youth that has been spurred up to all his industry by ambition, envy, emulation, and a desire of glory and distinction? And if he is not to act by these principles when he is a man, why do we call him to act by them in his youth?

Envy is acknowledged by all people to be the most un-

[6] Cowper, in his *Tirocinium; or, A Review of Schools*, condemns, as strongly as Law does, the principle of emulation in our public schools, or, as he calls them, "Our public hives of puerile resort."

" A principle whose proud pretensions pass
  Unquestioned, though the jewel be but glass—
That with a world, not often over nice,
Ranks as a virtue, and is yet a vice;
Or rather a gross compound, justly tried,
Of envy, hatred, jealousy, and pride—

Contributes most perhaps to enhance their fame;
And emulation is its specious name.
Boys, once on fire with that contentious zeal,
Feel all the rage that female rivals feel;
The prize of beauty in a woman's eyes
Not brighter than in theirs the scholar's prize.
The spirit of that competition burns
With all varieties of ill by turns!
Each vainly magnifies his own success,
Resents his fellows', wishes it were less;
Exults in his miscarriage, if he fail;
Deems his reward too great, if he prevail;
And labours to surpass him day and night,
Less for improvement than to tickle spite.

generous, base, and wicked passion that can enter into the heart of man.

And is this a temper to be instilled, nourished, and established in the minds of young people?

I know it is said that it is not envy but emulation that is intended to be awakened in the minds of young men.

But this is vainly said. For when children are taught to bear no rival and to scorn to be out-done by any of their age, they are plainly and directly taught to be envious. For it is impossible for any one to have this scorn of being out-done, and this contention with rivals, without burning with envy against all those that seem to excel him, or get any distinction from him. So that what children are taught is rank envy, and only covered with a name of a less odious sound.[7]

Secondly, If envy is thus confessedly bad, and it be only emulation that is endeavoured to be awakened in children, surely there ought to be great care taken that children may know the one from the other. That they may abominate the one as a great crime, whilst they give the other admission into their minds.

But if this were to be attempted, the fineness of the distinction betwixt envy and emulation would show that it was easier to divide them into words than to separate them in action.

For emulation, when it is defined in its best manner, is nothing else but a refinement upon envy, or rather the most plausible part of that black and venomous passion.

And though it is easy to separate them in the notion, yet the most acute philosopher that understands the art of distinguishing ever so well, if he gives himself up to emulation, will certainly find himself deep in envy.

For envy is not an original temper, but the natural, necessary, and unavoidable effect of emulation, or a desire of glory.

So that he who establishes the one in the minds of people necessarily fixes the other there. And there is no other possible way of destroying envy but by destroying emulation or a desire of glory. For the one always rises and falls in proportion to the other.

I know it is said in defence of this method of education that ambition and a desire of glory are necessary to excite young people to industry, and that, if we were to press upon them the

---

[7] For the reason stated in Note 5, I venture to think that the dismal forebodings of Law in this paragraph are far from being always fulfilled.

doctrines of humility, we should deject their minds, and sink them CH. XVIII.
into dulness and idleness.

But these people who say this do not consider that this reason,
if it has any strength, is full as strong against pressing the doctrines
of humility upon grown men, lest we should deject their minds,
and sink them into dulness and idleness.

For who does not see that middle-aged men want as much the
assistance of pride, ambition, and vain-glory, to spur them up to
action and industry, as children do? And it is very certain that
the precepts of humility are more contrary to the designs of such
men, and more grievous to their minds, when they are pressed
upon them, than they are to the minds of young persons.

This reason, therefore, that is given why children should not
be trained up in the principles of true humility is as good a
reason why the same humility should never be required of grown
men.

Thirdly, Let those people who think that children would be
spoiled, if they were not thus educated, consider this.

Could they think that if any children had been educated
by our blessed Lord, or His holy Apostles, that their minds
would have been sunk into dulness and idleness?

Or could they think that such children would not have
been trained up in the profoundest principles of a strict and
true humility? Can they say that our blessed Lord, Who was
the meekest and humblest man that ever was on earth, was
hindered by His humility from being the greatest example of
worthy and glorious actions that ever were done by man?

Can they say that His Apostles, who lived in the humble spirit
of their Master, did therefore cease to be laborious and active
instruments of doing good to all the world?

A few such reflections as these are sufficient to expose all
the poor pretences for an education in pride and ambition.

PATERNUS [8] lived about two hundred years ago; he had but
one son, whom he educated himself in his own house. As they
were sitting together in the garden, when the child was ten years
old, Paternus thus began to him:

---

[8] 'Paternus' is supposed by some to be taken from Law's own father, but without the slightest foundation. Law was scrupulously truthful in small as well as great matters. He would never have represented his father as having 'lived about two hundred years ago,' nor as having 'left an estate which was a great deal more than the necessities of one family require,' nor as having 'taught him Latin and Greek,' which it is hardly likely that a village grocer could have done.

CH. XVIII.    The little time that you have been in the world, my child, you have spent wholly with me; and my love and tenderness to you has made you look upon me as your only friend and benefactor, and the cause of all the comfort and pleasure that you enjoy: your heart, I know, would be ready to break with grief if you thought this was the last day that I should live with you.

But, my child, though you now think yourself mighty happy, because you have hold of my hand, you are now in the hands and under the care of a much greater father and friend than I am, whose love to you is far greater than mine, and from whom you receive such blessings as no mortal can give.

That God Whom you have seen me daily worship, Whom I daily call upon to bless both you and me and all mankind; Whose wondrous acts are recorded in those Scriptures which you constantly read; that God Who created the heavens and the earth; Who brought a flood upon the old world; Who saved Noah in the ark; Who was the God of Abraham, Isaac, and Jacob; Whom Job blessed and praised in the greatest afflictions; Who delivered the Israelites out of the hands of the Egyptians; Who was the protector of righteous Joseph, Moses, Joshua, and holy Daniel; Who sent so many prophets into the world; Who sent His Son Jesus Christ to redeem mankind; this God, Who has done all these great things; Who has created so many millions of men, who lived and died before you were born; with Whom the spirits of good men that are departed this life now live; Whom infinite numbers of angels now worship in heaven; this great God, Who is the creator of worlds, of angels, and men, is your loving father and friend, your good creator and nourisher, from Whom, and not from me, you received your being ten years ago, at the time that I planted that little tender elm which you there see.

I myself am not half the age of this shady oak under which we sit; many of our fathers have sat under its boughs; we have all of us called it ours in our turn, though it stands and drops its masters as it drops its leaves.

You see, my son, this wide and large firmament over our heads, where the sun and moon and all the stars appear in their turns. If you were to be carried up to any of these bodies at this vast distance from us, you would still discover others as much above you as the stars that you see here are above the earth. Were you to go up or down, east or west, north CH. XVIII. or south, you would find the same height without any top, and the same depth without any bottom.

And yet, my child, so great is God, that all these bodies added together are but as a grain of sand in His sight. And yet you are as much the care of this great God and Father of all worlds and all spirits as if He had no son but you, or there were no creature for Him to love and protect but you alone. He numbers the hairs of your head, watches over you sleeping and waking, and has preserved you from a thousand dangers, which neither you nor I know anything of.

How poor my power is, and how little I am able to do for you, you have often seen. Your late sickness has shown you how little I could do for you in that state, and the frequent pains of your head are plain proofs that I have no power to remove them.

I can bring you food and medicines, but have no power to turn them into your relief and nourishment; it is God alone that can do this for you.

Therefore, my child, fear and worship and love God. Your eyes indeed cannot yet see Him. But everything you see are so many marks of His power and presence, and He is nearer to you than anything that you can see.

Take Him for your Lord and Father and Friend; look up unto Him as the fountain and cause of all the good that you have received through my hands, and reverence me only as the bearer and minister of God's good things unto you. And He that blessed my father before I was born will bless you when I am dead.

Your youth and little mind is only yet acquainted with my family, and therefore you think there is no happiness out of it.

But, my child, you belong to a greater family than mine, you are a younger member of the family of this Almighty Father of all nations, Who has created infinite orders of angels and numberless generations of men to be fellow-members of one and the same society in heaven.

You do well to reverence and obey my authority, because God has given me power over you to bring you up in His fear, and to do for you as the holy fathers recorded in Scripture did for their children, who are now in rest and peace with God.

I shall in a short time die, and leave you to God and yourself; and if God forgiveth my sins, I shall go to His Son Jesus Christ, and live amongst patriarchs and prophets, saints and martyrs, where I shall pray for you, and hope for your safe arrival at the same place.

Therefore, my child, meditate on these great things, and your soul will soon grow great and noble by so meditating upon them.

Let your thoughts often leave these gardens, these fields and farms, to contemplate upon God and heaven, to consider upon angels and the spirits of good men living in light and glory.

As you have been used to look to me in all your actions, and have been afraid to do anything unless you first knew my will, so let it now be a rule of your life to look up to God in all your actions, to do everything in His fear, and to abstain from everything that is not according to His will.

Bear Him always in your mind, teach your thoughts to reverence Him in every place, for there is no place where He is not.

God keepeth a book of life, wherein all the actions of all men are written; your name is there, my child, and when you die, this book will be laid open before men and angels, and according as your actions are there found you will either be received to the happiness of those holy men who have died before you, or be turned away amongst wicked spirits that are never to see God any more.

Never forget this book, my son, for it is written, it must be opened, you must see it, and you must be tried by it. Strive therefore to fill it with your good deeds, that the hand-writing of God may not appear against you.

God, my child, is all love, and wisdom, and goodness; and everything that He has made, and every action that He does, is the effect of them all. Therefore you cannot please God, but so far as you strive to walk in love, wisdom, and goodness. As all wisdom, love, and goodness proceeds from God, so nothing but love, wisdom, and goodness can lead to God.

When you love that which God loves, you act with Him, you join yourself to Him; and when you love what He dislikes, then you oppose Him, and separate yourself from Him. This is the true and the right way; think what God loves, and do you love it with all your heart.

First of all, my child, worship and adore God, think of Him magnificently, speak of Him reverently, magnify His providence,

adore His power, frequent His service, and pray unto Him fre- CH. XVIII.
quently and constantly.

Next to this, love your neighbour, which is all mankind, with such tenderness and affection as you love yourself. Think how God loves all mankind, how merciful He is to them, how tender He is of them, how carefully He preserves them, and then strive to love the world as God loves it.

God would have all men to be happy; therefore do you will and desire the same. All men are great instances of divine love, therefore let all men be instances of your love.

But above all, my son, mark this, never do anything through strife, or envy, or emulation, or vain-glory. Never do anything in order to excel other people, but in order to please God, and because it is His will that you should do everything in the best manner you can.

For if it is once a pleasure to you to excel other people, it will by degrees be a pleasure to you to see other people not so good as yourself.

Banish, therefore, every thought of self-pride and self-distinction, and accustom yourself to rejoice in all the excellencies and perfections of your fellow-creatures, and be as glad to see any of their good actions as your own.

For as God is as well pleased with their well-doings as with yours, so you ought to desire that every thing that is wise and holy and good may be performed in as high a manner by other people as by yourself.

Let this, therefore, be your only motive and spur to all good actions, honest industry, and business, to do everything in as perfect and excellent a manner as you can, for this only reason, because it is pleasing to God, Who desires your perfection, and writes all your actions in a book. When I am dead, my son, you will be master of all my estate, which will be a great deal more than the necessities of one family require. Therefore, as you are to be charitable to the souls of men, and wish them the same happiness with you in heaven, so be charitable to their bodies, and endeavour to make them as happy as you upon earth.

As God has created all things for the common good of all men, so let that part of them which is fallen to your share be employed as God would have all employed for the common good of all.

Do good, my son, first of all to those that most deserve it, but remember to do good to all. The greatest sinners receive daily

CH. XVIII. instances of God's goodness towards them; He nourishes and
preserves them, that they may repent and return to Him: do you,
therefore, imitate God, and think no one too bad to receive your
relief and kindness when you see that he wants it.

I am teaching you Latin and Greek, not that you should desire
to be a great critic, a fine poet, or an eloquent orator.  I would
not have your heart feel any of those desires; for the desire of
these accomplishments is a vanity of the mind, and the masters
of them are generally vain men.  For the desire of anything that
is not a real good lessens the application of the mind after that
which is so.

But I teach you these languages, that at proper times you may
look into the history of past ages, and learn the methods of God's
providence over the world; that, reading the writings of the
ancient sages, you may see how wisdom and virtue have been the
praise of great men of all ages, and fortify your mind by their wise
sayings.[9]

Let truth and plainness, therefore, be the only ornament of your
language, and study nothing but how to think of all things as they
deserve, to choose everything that is best, to live according to
reason and order, and to act in every part of your life in conformity to the will of God.

Study how to fill your heart full of the love of God and the love
of your neighbour, and then be content to be no deeper a scholar,
no finer a gentleman, than these tempers will make you.  As true
religion is nothing else but simple nature governed by right reason,[10]
so it loves and requires greater plainness and simplicity of life.
Therefore avoid all superfluous shows of finery and equipage, and
let your house be plainly furnished with moderate conveniences.
Do not consider what your estate can afford, but what right
reason requires.

Let your dress be sober, clean, and modest, not to set out the
beauty of your person, but to declare the sobriety of your mind,
that your outward garb may resemble the inward plainness and
simplicity of your heart.  For it is highly reasonable that you

[9] It was quite in accordance with
Law's principles to recognize fully the
'wisdom and virtue' of the ancient
sages.  Not that he recognized any
wisdom or virtue apart from Christ,
but he held with increasing conviction
that Christ, as "the light of every
one that cometh into the world," influenced and inspired those who had
never heard of Him.

[10] The description of 'true religion'
as 'nothing else but simple nature
governed by right reason,' is utterly
alien to the theology of the Evangelical Revival.

should be one man, all of a piece, and appear outwardly such as CH. XVIII. you are inwardly.

As to your meat and drink, in them observe the highest rules of Christian temperance and sobriety ; consider your body only as the servant and minister of your soul, and only so nourish it as may best perform a humble and obedient service to it.

But, my son, observe this as a most principal thing, which I shall remember you of as long as I live with you.

Hate and despise all human glory, for it is nothing else but human folly. It is the greatest snare and the greatest betrayer that you can possibly admit into your heart.

Love humility in all its instances, practise it in all its parts, for it is the noblest state of the soul of man ; it will set your heart and affections right towards God, and fill you with every temper that is tender and affectionate towards men.

Let every day, therefore, be a day of humility, condescend to all the weakness and infirmities of your fellow-creatures, cover their frailties, love their excellencies, encourage their virtues, relieve their wants, rejoice in their prosperities, compassionate their distress, receive their friendship, overlook their unkindness, forgive their malice, be a servant of servants, and condescend to do the lowest offices to the lowest of mankind.

Aspire after nothing but your own purity and perfection, and have no ambition but to do everything in so reasonable and religious a manner that you may be glad that God is everywhere present, and sees and observes all your actions. The greatest trial of humility is a humble behaviour towards your equals in age, estate, and condition of life. Therefore be careful of all the motions of your heart towards these people. Let all your behaviour towards them be governed by unfeigned love. Have no desire to put any of your equals below you, nor any anger at those that would put themselves above you. If they are proud, they are ill of a very bad distemper ; let them, therefore, have your tender pity, and perhaps your meekness may prove an occasion of their cure. But if your humility should do them no good, it will, however, be the greatest good that you can do to yourself.

Remember that there is but one man in the world with whom you are to have perpetual contention, and be always striving to exceed him, and that is yourself.

The time of practising these precepts, my child, will soon be over with you ; the world will soon slip through your hands, or

CH. XVIII. rather you will soon slip through it; it seems but the other day since I received these same instructions from my dear father that I am now leaving with you. And the God that gave me ears to hear, and a heart to receive what my father said unto me, will, I hope, give you grace to love and follow the same instructions.[11]

Thus did Paternus educate his son.

Can any one now think that such an education as this would weaken and deject the minds of young people, and deprive the world of any worthy and reasonable labours?

It is so far from that, that there is nothing so likely to ennoble and exalt the mind, and prepare it for the most heroical exercise of all virtues.

For who will say that a love of God, a desire of pleasing Him, a love of our neighbour, a love of truth, of reason and virtue, a contemplation of eternity, and the rewards of piety, are not stronger motives to great and good actions than a little uncertain popular praise?

On the other hand, there is nothing in reality that more weakens the mind and reduces it to meanness and slavery, nothing that makes it less master of its own actions, or less capable of following reason, than a love of praise and honour.

For as praise and honour are often given to things and persons where they are not due, as that is generally most praised and honoured, that most gratifies the humours, fashions, and vicious tempers of the world; so he that acts upon the desire of praise and applause must part with every other principle; he must say black is white, put bitter for sweet, and sweet for bitter, and do the meanest, basest things in order to be applauded.

For in a corrupt world, as this is, worthy actions are only to be supported by their own worth, where, instead of being praised and honoured, they are most often reproached and persecuted.

So that to educate children upon a motive of emulation, or a desire of glory in a world where glory itself is false, and most commonly given wrong, is to destroy the natural integrity and fortitude of their minds, and give them a bias which will oftener carry them to base and mean than great and worthy actions.

---

[11] The real tenderness of Law's nature comes out strikingly in this touching address of Paternus. He was a severe and uncompromising, but not, as is sometimes thought, a hard and morose man.

# CHAPTER XIX.

*Showing how the method of educating daughters makes it difficult*
*for them to enter into the spirit of Christian humility. How*
*miserably they are injured and abused by such an education.*
*The spirit of a better education represented in the character*
*of Eusebia.*

THAT turn of mind which is taught and encouraged in the education of daughters makes it exceeding difficult for them to enter into such a sense and practice of humility as the spirit of Christianity requires.

The right education of this sex is of the utmost importance to human life. There is nothing that is more desirable for the common good of all the world. For though women do not carry on the trade and business of the world, yet, as they are mothers and mistresses of families, that have for some time the care of the education of their children of both sorts, they are entrusted with that which is of the greatest consequence to human life. For this reason good or bad women are likely to do as much good or harm in the world as good or bad men in the greatest business of life.

For as the health and strength or weakness of our bodies is very much owing to their methods of treating us when we were young, so the soundness or folly of our minds are not less owing to those first tempers and ways of thinking which we eagerly received from the love, tenderness, authority, and constant conversation of our mothers.

As we call our first language our mother-tongue, so we may as justly call our first tempers our mother-tempers; and perhaps it may be found more easy to forget the language, than to part entirely with those tempers which we learnt in the nursery.

It is, therefore, much to be lamented that this sex, on whom so

CH. XIX. much depends, who have the first forming both of our bodies and our minds, are not only educated in pride, but in the silliest and most contemptible part of it.

They are not indeed suffered to dispute with us the proud prizes of arts and sciences, of learning and eloquence, in which I have much suspicion they would often prove our superiors; but we turn them over to the study of beauty and dress, and the whole world conspires to make them think of nothing else. Fathers and mothers, friends and relations, seem to have no other wish towards the little girl but that she may have a fair skin, a fine shape, dress well, and dance to admiration.

Now, if our fondness for our persons, a desire of beauty, a love of dress, be a part of pride (as surely it is a most contemptible part of it), the first step towards a woman's humility seems to require a repentance of her education.

For it must be owned that, generally speaking, good parents are never more fond of their daughters than when they see them too fond of themselves, and dressed in such a manner as is a great reproach to the gravity and sobriety of the Christian life.

And what makes this matter still more to be lamented is this: that women are not only spoiled by this education, but we spoil that part of the world, which would otherwise furnish most instances of an eminent and exalted piety.

For I believe it may be affirmed that for the most part there is a finer sense, a clearer mind, a readier apprehension, and gentler dispositions in that sex than in the other.[1]

All which tempers, if they were truly improved by proper studies and sober methods of education, would in all probability carry them to greater heights of piety than are to be found amongst the generality of men.

For this reason I speak to this matter with so much openness and plainness, because it is much to be lamented that persons so naturally qualified to be great examples of piety should, by an erroneous education, be made poor and gaudy spectacles of the greatest vanity.

The Church has formerly had eminent saints in that sex, and it may reasonably be thought that it is purely owing to their poor

[1] It is somewhat remarkable that, though Law was essentially 'a man's man,' and though the most signal instances of those who were most deeply influenced by the *Serious Call* were men, not women, he had a most unusually high opinion (for the eighteenth century) of the faculties, both moral and intellectual, of the other sex.

and vain education that this honour of their sex is for the most CH. XIX. part confined to former ages.

The corruption of the world indulges them in great vanity, and mankind seem to consider them in no other view than as so many painted idols that are to allure and gratify their passions; so that if many women are vain, light, gew-gaw creatures, they have this to excuse themselves, that they are not only such as their education has made them, but such as the generality of the world allows them to be.

But then they should consider that the friends to their vanity are no friends of theirs; they should consider that they are to live for themselves, that they have as great a share in the rational nature as men have; that they have as much reason to pretend, and as much necessity to aspire after the highest accomplishments of a Christian and solid virtue as the gravest and wisest among Christian philosophers.

They should consider that they are abused and injured, and betrayed from their only perfection, whenever they are taught that any thing is an ornament in them that is not an ornament in the wisest amongst mankind.

It is generally said that women are naturally of little and vain minds; but this I look upon to be as false and unreasonable as to say that butchers are naturally cruel; for as their cruelty is not owing to their nature, but to their way of life, which has changed their nature; so whatever littleness and vanity is to be observed in the minds of women, it is like the cruelty of butchers, a temper that is wrought into them by that life which they are taught and accustomed to lead.

At least thus much must be said, that we cannot charge any thing upon their nature till we take care that it is not perverted by their education.

And on the other hand, if it were true that they were thus naturally vain and light, then how much more blameable is that education, which seems contrived to strengthen and increase this folly and weakness of their minds? For if it were a virtue in a woman to be proud and vain in herself, we could hardly take better means to raise this passion in her than those that are now used in her education.

MATILDA is a fine woman, of good breeding, great sense and much religion. She has three daughters that are educated by herself. She will not trust them with any one else, or at any

CH. XIX. school, for fear they should learn anything ill. She stays with
the dancing-master all the time he is with them, because she will
hear everything that is said to them. She has heard them read
the Scriptures so often that they can repeat great part of it without
book; and there is scarce a good book of devotion but you may
find it in their closets.

Had Matilda lived in the first ages of Christianity, when it was
practised in the fulness and plainness of its doctrines, she had in
all probability been one of its greatest saints. But as she was
born in corrupt times, where she wants examples of Christian
perfection, and hardly ever saw a piety higher than her own,
so she has many defects, and communicates them all to her
daughters.

Matilda never was meanly dressed in her life; and nothing
pleases her in dress but that which is very rich and beautiful
to the eye.

Her daughters see her great zeal for religion, but then they see
an equal earnestness for all sorts of finery. They see she is not
negligent of her devotion, but then they see her more careful to
preserve her complexion, and to prevent those changes which
time and age threaten her with.

They are afraid to meet her if they have missed the church;
but then they are more afraid to see her if they are not laced
as strait as they can possibly be.

She often shows them her own picture which was taken when
their father fell in love with her. She tells them how distracted he
was with passion at the first sight of her, and that she had never
had so fine a complexion but for the diligence of her good
mother, who took exceeding care of it.

Matilda is so intent upon all the arts of improving their dress,
that she has some new fancy almost every day, and leaves no
ornament untried, from the richest jewel to the poorest flower.
She is so nice and critical in her judgment, so sensible of the
smallest error, that the maid is often forced to dress and undress
her daughters three or four times in a day before she can be
satisfied with it.

As to the patching, she reserves that to herself, for she says,
if they are not stuck on with judgment, they are rather a prejudice
than an advantage to the face.

The children see so plainly the temper of their mother, that
they even affect to be more pleased with dress, and to be more

fond of every little ornament than they really are, merely to gain her favour.

They saw their eldest sister once brought to her tears, and her perverseness severely reprimanded, for presuming to say that she thought it was better to cover the neck than to go so far naked as the modern dress requires.

She stints them in their meals, and is very scrupulous of what they eat and drink, and tells them how many fine shapes she has seen spoiled in her time for want of such care. If a pimple rises in their faces, she is in a great fright, and they themselves are as afraid to see her with it as if they had committed some great sin.

Whenever they begin to look too sanguine[2] and healthful, she calls in the assistance of the doctor; and if physic or issues will keep the complexion from inclining to coarse or ruddy, she thinks them well employed.

By this means they are poor, pale, sickly, infirm creatures, vapoured through want of spirits, crying at the smallest accidents, swooning away at anything that frights them, and hardly able to bear the weight of their best clothes.

The eldest daughter lived as long as she could under this discipline, and died in the twentieth year of her age.

When her body was opened, it appeared that her ribs had grown into her liver, and that her other entrails were much hurt by being crushed together with her stays, which her mother had ordered to be twitched so strait, that it often brought tears into her eyes whilst the maid was dressing her.

Her youngest daughter is run away with a gamester, a man of great beauty, who in dressing and dancing has no superior.

Matilda says she should die with grief at this accident, but that her conscience tells her she has contributed nothing to it herself. She appeals to their closets, to their books of devotion, to testify what care she has taken to establish her children in a life of solid piety and devotion.

Now though I do not intend to say that no daughters are brought up in a better way than this, for I hope there are many that are, yet thus much I believe may be said, that the much greater part of them are not brought up so well, or accustomed to so much religion, as in the present instance.

Their minds are turned as much to the care of their beauty and dress, and the indulgence of vain desires, as in the present case,

[2] That is, ruddy, high complexioned, its literal sense.

without having such rules of devotion to stand against it. So that if solid piety, humility, and a sober sense of themselves is much wanted in that sex, it is the plain and natural consequence of a vain and corrupt education.

And if they are often too ready to receive the first fops, beaux, and fine dancers for their husbands, it is no wonder they should like that in men which they have been taught to admire in themselves.

And if they are often seen to lose that little religion they were taught in their youth, it is no more to be wondered at than to see a little flower choked and killed amongst rank weeds.

For personal pride, and affectation, a delight in beauty and fondness of finery, are tempers that must either kill all religion in the soul, or be themselves killed by it; they can no more thrive together than health and sickness.

Some people that judge hastily will perhaps here say that I am exercising too great a severity against the sex.

But more reasonable persons will easily observe that I entirely spare the sex, and only arraign their education; that I not only spare them, but plead their interest, assert their honour, set forth their perfections, commend their natural tempers, and only condemn that education which is so injurious to their interests, so debases their honour, and deprives them of the benefit of their excellent natures and tempers.

Their education, I profess, I cannot spare; but the only reason is, because it is their greatest enemy, because it deprives the world of so many blessings, and the church of so many saints, as might reasonably be expected from persons so formed by their natural tempers to all goodness and tenderness, and so fitted by the clearness and brightness of their minds, to contemplate, love, and admire everything that is holy, virtuous and divine.

If it should here be said, that I even charge too high upon their education, and they are not so much hurt by it as I imagine:

It may be answered, that though I do not pretend to state the exact degree of mischief that is done by it, yet its plain and natural tendency to do harm is sufficient to justify the most absolute condemnation of it.

But if any one would know how generally women are hurt by this education; if he imagines there may be no personal pride,

or vain fondness of themselves, in those that are patched and CH. XIX.
dressed out with so much glitter of art and ornament:

Let him only make the following experiment wherever he
pleases.

Let him only acquaint any such woman with his opinion
of her—I do not mean that he should tell her to her face, or
do it in any rude public manner; but let him contrive the
most civil, secret, friendly way that he can think of, only to
let her know his opinion, that he thinks she is neither hand-
some, nor dresses well, nor becomes her finery, and I dare
say he will find there are but very few fine dressed women
that will like him never the worse for his bare opinion, though
known to none but themselves; and that he will not be long
without seeing the effects of her resentment.

But if such an experiment would show him that there are
but few such women that could bear with his friendship after
they knew he had such an opinion of them, surely it is time
to complain of and accuse that education which so generally
corrupts their hearts.

For though it is hard to judge of the hearts of people, yet
where they declare their resentment and uneasiness at anything, there they pass the judgment upon themselves. If a
woman cannot forgive a man who thinks she has no beauty,
nor any ornament from her dress, there she infallibly discovers
the state of her own heart, and is condemned by her own, and
not another's judgment.

For we never are angry at others, but when their opinions
of us are contrary to that which we have of ourselves.

A man that makes no pretences to scholarship is never
angry at those that do not take him to be a scholar; so if a
woman had no opinion of her own person and dress, she would
never be angry at those who are of the same opinion with herself.

So that the general bad effects of this education are too much
known to admit of any reasonable doubt.

But how possible it is to bring up daughters in the more
excellent way let the following character declare:

EUSEBIA is a pious widow, well born, and well bred, and has
a good estate for five daughters, whom she brings up as one
intrusted by God, to fit five virgins for the kingdom of heaven.
Her family has the same regulation as a religious house, and
all its orders tend to the support of a constant regular devotion.

She, her daughters, and her maids meet together at all the hours of prayer in the day, and chant Psalms and other devotions, and spend the rest of their time in such good works and innocent diversions as render them fit to return to their Psalms and prayers.

She loves them as her spiritual children, and they reverence her as their spiritual mother, with an affection far above that of the fondest friends.

She has divided part of her estate amongst them, that every one may be charitable out of their own stock, and each of them take it in their turns to provide for the poor and the sick of the parish.

Eusebia brings them up to all kinds of labour that are proper for women, as sewing, knitting, spinning, and all other parts of housewifery; not for their amusement, but that they may be serviceable to themselves and others, and be saved from those temptations which attend an idle life.

She tells them she had rather see them reduced to the necessity of maintaining themselves by their own work than to have riches to excuse themselves from labour. For though, says she, you may be able to assist the poor without your labour, yet by your labour you will be able to assist them more.

If Eusebia has lived as free from sin as it is possible for human nature, it is because she is always watching and guarding against all instances of pride. And if her virtues are stronger and higher than other people's, it is because they are all founded in a deep humility.

My children, says she, when your father died, I was much pitied by my friends, as having all the care of a family and the management of an estate fallen upon me.

But my own grief was founded upon another principle. I was grieved to see myself deprived of so faithful a friend, and that such an eminent example of Christian virtues should be taken from the eyes of his children before they were of an age to love and follow it.

But as to worldly cares, which my friends thought so heavy upon me, they are most of them of our own making, and fall away as soon as we know ourselves.

If a person in a dream is disturbed with strange appearances, his trouble is over as soon as he is awake, and sees that it was the folly of a dream.

Now when a right knowledge of ourselves enters into our

minds, it makes as great a change in all our thoughts and apprehensions as when we awake from the wanderings of a dream.

We acknowledge a man to be mad or melancholy who fancies
himself to be glass, and so is afraid of stirring; or, taking himself
to be wax, dare not let the sun shine upon him.

But, my children, there are things in the world which pass for
wisdom, politeness, grandeur, happiness, and fine breeding which
show as great ignorance of ourselves, and might as justly pass for
thorough madness, as when a man fancies himself to be glass
or ice.

A woman that dares not appear in the world without fine clothes,
that thinks it a happiness to have a face finely coloured, to have a
skin delicately fair, that had rather die than be reduced to poverty
and be forced to work for a poor maintenance, is as ignorant of
herself to the full as he that fancies himself to be glass.

For this reason all my discourse with you has been to acquaint
you with yourselves, and to accustom you to such books and
devotions as may best instruct you in this greatest of all knowledge.

You would think it hard not to know the family into which you
were born, what ancestors you were descended from, and what
estate was to come to you.   But, my children, you may know all
this with exactness, and yet be as ignorant of yourselves as he
that takes himself to be wax.

For though you were all of you born of my body, and bear
your father's name, yet you are all of you pure spirits.   I do not
mean that you have not bodies that want meat and drink, and
sleep and clothing, but that all that deserves to be called you is
nothing else but spirit; a being, spiritual and rational in its
nature, that is as contrary to all fleshly or corporeal beings as life
is contrary to death, that is made in the image of God, to live for
ever, never to cease any more, but to enjoy life and reason and
knowledge and happiness in the presence of God and the society of
angels and glorious spirits to all eternity.

Everything that you call yours besides this spirit is but like
your clothing, something that is only to be used for a while, and
then to end and die and wear away, and to signify no more to you
than the clothing and bodies of other people.

But, my children, you are not only in this manner spirits, but
you are fallen spirits that began your life in a state of corruption
and disorder, full of tempers and passions that blind and darken
the reason of your mind, and incline you to that which is hurtful.

　　Your bodies are not only poor and perishing like your clothes, but they are like infected clothes that fill you with all diseases and distempers, which oppress the soul with sickly appetites and vain cravings.

So that all of us are like two beings that have, as it were, two hearts within us ; with the one we see, and taste, and admire reason, purity, and holiness; with the other we incline to pride, and vanity, and sensual delights.

This internal war we always feel within us more or less ; and if you would know the one thing necessary to all the world it is this : to preserve and perfect all that is rational, holy, and divine in our nature, and to mortify, remove, and destroy all that vanity, pride, and sensuality which springs from corruption of our state.

Could you think, my children, when you look at the world, and see what customs, and fashions, and pleasures, and troubles, and projects, and tempers employ the hearts and time of mankind, that things were thus as I have told you?

But do not you be affected at these things ; the world is in a great dream, and but few people are awake in it.

We fancy that we fall into darkness when we die; but, alas, we are most of us in the dark till then; and the eyes of our souls only then begin to see when our bodily eyes are closing.

You see then your state, my children; you are to honour, improve, and perfect the spirit that is within you, you are to prepare it for the kingdom of heaven, to nourish it with the love of God and of virtue, to adorn it with good works, and to make it as holy and heavenly as you can. You are to preserve it from the errors and vanities of the world; to save it from the corruptions of the body, from those false delights and sensual tempers which the body tempts it with.

You are to nourish your spirits with pious readings and holy meditations, with watchings, fastings, and prayers, that you may taste, and relish, and desire that eternal state which is to begin when this life ends.

As to your bodies, you are to consider them as poor, perishing things that are sickly and corrupt at present, and will soon drop into common dust. You are to watch over them as enemies that are always trying to tempt and betray you, and so never follow their advice and counsel; you are to consider them as the place and habitation of your souls, and so keep them pure, and clean, and decent; you are to consider them as the servants and instru-

ments of action, and so give them food, and rest, and raiment, that CH. XIX.
they may be strong and healthful to do the duties of a charitable,
useful, pious life.

Whilst you live thus, you live like yourselves; and whenever
you have less regard to your souls or more regard to your bodies
than this comes to, whenever you are more intent upon adorning
your persons than upon the perfecting of your souls, you are
much more beside yourselves than he that had rather have a laced
coat than a healthful body.

For this reason, my children, I have taught you nothing that
was dangerous for you to learn; I have kept you from everything
that might betray you into weakness and folly; or make you think
anything fine but a fine mind, anything happy but the favour of
God, or anything desirable but to do all the good you possibly
can.

Instead of the vain, immodest entertainment of plays and
operas, I have taught you to delight in visiting the sick and poor;
what music, and dancing, and diversions are to many in the world,
that prayers, and devotions, and psalms are to you. Your hands
have not been employed in plaiting the hair and adorning your
persons, but in making clothes for the naked. You have not
wasted your fortunes upon yourselves, but have added your labour
to them, for to do more good to other people.

Instead of forced shapes, patched faces, genteel airs, and
affected motions, I have taught you to conceal your bodies with
modest garments, and let the world have nothing to view of you
but the plainness, the sincerity, and humility of all your behaviour.

You know, my children, the high perfection and the great
rewards of virginity; you know how it frees from worldly cares
and troubles, and furnishes means and opportunities of higher
advancements in a divine life; therefore love, and esteem, and
honour virginity; bless God for all that glorious company of holy
virgins that from the beginning of Christianity have, in the several
ages of the Church, renounced the cares and pleasures of matrimony, to be perpetual examples of solitude, contemplation, and
prayer.

But as every one has their proper gift from God, as I look upon
you all to be so many great blessings of a married state, so I leave
it to your choice either to do as I have done, or to aspire after
higher degrees of perfection in a virgin state of life.

I desire nothing, I press nothing upon you, but to make

the most of human life, and to aspire after perfection in whatever state of life you choose.

Never, therefore, consider yourselves as persons that are to be seen, admired, and courted by men; but as poor sinners that are to save yourselves from the vanities and follies of a miserable world, by humility, devotion, and self-denial. Learn to live for your own sakes and the service of God; and let nothing in the world be of any value with you, but that which you can turn into a service to God and a means of your future happiness.

Consider often how powerfully you are called to a virtuous life, and what great and glorious things God has done for you, to make you in love with everything that can promote His glory.

Think upon the vanity and shortness of human life, and let death and eternity be often in your minds; for these thoughts will strengthen and exalt your minds, make you wise and judicious, and truly sensible of the littleness of all human things.

Think of the happiness of prophets and apostles, saints and martyrs, who are now rejoicing in the presence of God, and see themselves possessors of eternal glory. And then think how desirable a thing it is to watch and pray, and do good as they did, that when you die you may have your lot amongst them.

Whether married, therefore, or unmarried, consider yourselves as mothers and sisters, as friends and relations, to all that want your assistance; and never allow yourselves to be idle, whilst others are in want of anything that your hands can make for them.

This useful, charitable, humble employment of yourselves is what I recommend to you with great earnestness, as being a substantial part of a wise and pious life. And besides the good you will thereby do to other people, every virtue of your own heart will be very much improved by it.

For next to reading, meditation, and prayer, there is nothing that so secures our hearts from foolish passions, nothing that preserves so holy and wise a frame of mind, as some useful, humble, employment of ourselves.

Never, therefore, consider your labour as an amusement that is to get rid of your time, and so may be as trifling as you please; but consider it as something that is to be serviceable to yourselves and others, that is to serve some sober ends of life, to save and redeem your time, and make it turn to your account when the works of all people shall be tried by fire.

When you were little, I left you to little amusements, to please yourselves in any things that were free from harm; but as you are now grown up to a knowledge of God and your-selves; as your minds are now acquainted with the worth and value of virtue, and exalted with the great doctrines of religion, you are now to do nothing as children, but despise everything that is poor, or vain, and impertinent; you are now to make the labours of your hands suitable to the piety of your hearts, and employ yourselves for the same ends, and with the same spirit as you watch and pray.

For if there is any good to be done by your labour, if you can possibly employ yourselves usefully to other people, how silly is it, how contrary to the wisdom of religion, to make that a mere amusement, which might as easily be made an exercise of the greatest charity!

What would you think of the wisdom of him, that should employ his time in distilling of waters, and making liquors which nobody could use, merely to amuse himself with variety of their colour and clearness, when, with less labour and expense, he might satisfy the wants of those who have nothing to drink?

Yet he would be as wisely employed as those that are amusing themselves with such tedious works, as they neither need, nor hardly know how to use them when they are finished; when with less labour and expense they might be doing as much good as he that is clothing the naked or visiting the sick.

Be glad, therefore, to know the wants of the poorest people, and let your hands be employed in making such mean and ordinary things for them, as their necessities require. By thus making your labour a gift and service to the poor, your ordinary work will be changed into a holy service, and made as acceptable to God as your devotions.

And as charity is the greatest of all virtues, as it always was the chief temper of the greatest saints; so nothing can make your own charity more amiable in the sight of God than this method of adding your labour to it.

The humility also of this employment will be as beneficial to you as the charity of it. It will keep you from all vain and proud thoughts of your own state and distinction in life, and from treating the poor as creatures of a different species. By accustoming yourselves to this labour and service for the poor, as the representatives of Jesus Christ, you will soon find your heart softened into the greatest meekness and lowliness towards them. You will reverence their estate and condition, think it an honour to serve them, and never be so pleased with yourself as when you are most humbly employed in their service.

This will make you true disciples of your meek Lord and Master, "Who came into the world not to be ministered unto, but to minister"; and though He was Lord of all, and amongst the creatures of His own making, yet was amongst them "as one that serveth."

Christianity has then had its most glorious effects upon your hearts, when it has thus changed your spirit, removed all the pride of life from you, and made you delight in humbling yourselves beneath the lowest of all your fellow-creatures.

Live, therefore, my children, as you have begun your lives, in humble labour for the good of others, and let ceremonious visits and vain acquaintances have as little of your time as you possibly can. Contract no foolish friendships or vain fondnesses for particular persons, but love them most that most turn your love towards God and your compassion towards all the world.

But, above all, avoid the conversation of fine bred fops and beaux, and hate nothing more than the idle discourse, the flattery and compliments of that sort of men, for they are the shame of their own sex, and ought to be the abhorrence of yours.

When you go abroad, let humility, modesty, and a decent carriage be all the state that you take upon you; and let tenderness, compassion, and good nature be all the fine breeding that you show in any place.

If evil speaking, scandal, or backbiting be the conversation where you happen to be, keep your heart and your tongue to yourself; be as much grieved as if you were amongst cursing and swearing, and retire as soon as you can.

Though you intend to marry, yet let the time never come till you find a man that has those perfections which you have been labouring after yourselves, who is likely to be a friend to all your virtues, and with whom it is better to live than to want the benefit of his example.

Love poverty, and reverence poor people,[3] as for many reasons, so particularly for this, because our blessed Saviour was one of the number, and because you may make them all so many friends and advocates with God for you.

Visit and converse with them frequently; you will often find simplicity, innocence, patience, fortitude, and great piety among them; and where they are not so, your good example may amend them.

Rejoice at every opportunity of doing a humble action and exercising the meekness of your minds, whether it be, as the Scripture expresses it, in washing the saints' feet, that is, in waiting upon and serving those that are below you, or in bearing with the haughtiness and ill-manners of those that are your equals or above you. For there is nothing better than humility; it is the fruitful soil of all virtues, and everything that is kind and good naturally grows from it.

Therefore, my children, pray for and practise humility, and reject everything in dress, or carriage, or conversation that has any appearance of pride.

Strive to do everything that is praiseworthy, but do nothing in order to be praised, nor think of any reward for all your labours of love and virtue till Christ cometh with all His holy angels.

And above all, my children, have a care of vain and proud thoughts of your own virtues. For as soon as ever people live different from the common way of the world and despise its vanities, the devil represents to their minds the height of their own perfections, and is content they should excel in good works, provided that he can but make them proud of them.

Therefore watch over your virtues with a jealous eye, and reject every vain thought as you would reject the most wicked imaginations; and think what a loss it would be to you to have the fruit of all your good works devoured by the vanity of your own minds.

Never, therefore, allow yourselves to despise those who do not follow your rules of life, but force your hearts to love them, and pray to God for them, and let humility be always whispering it into your ears that you yourselves will fall from those rules to-morrow, if God should leave you to your own strength and wisdom.

[3] One of the rules at the schools which Law founded at King's Cliffe was that the children were to bow or to curtsey to 'all aged people, whether rich or poor.'

When, therefore, you have spent days and weeks well, do not suffer your hearts to contemplate anything as your own, but give all the glory to the goodness of God, Who has carried you through such rules of holy living as you were not able to observe by your own strength; and take care to begin the next day, not as proficients in virtue that can do great matters, but as poor beginners that want the daily assistance of God to save you from the grossest sins.

Your dear father was a humble, watchful, pious, wise man. Whilst his sickness would suffer him to talk with me, his discourse was chiefly about your education. He knew the benefits of humility, he saw the ruins which pride made in our sex; and, therefore, he conjured me with the tenderest expressions to renounce the fashionable ways of educating daughters in pride and softness, in the care of their beauty and dress, and to bring you all up in the plainest, simplest instances of a humble, holy, and industrious life.

He taught me an admirable rule of humility which he practised all the days of his life, which was this: To let no morning pass without thinking upon some frailty and infirmity of our own that may put us to confusion, make us blush inwardly, and entertain a mean opinion of ourselves.

Think, therefore, my children, that the soul of your good father, who is now with God, speaks to you through my mouth, and let the double desire of your father who is gone, and of me who am with you, prevail upon you to love God, to study your own perfection, to practise humility, and with innocent labour and charity to do all the good that you can to all your fellow-creatures, till God calls you to another life.

Thus did the pious widow educate her daughters.

The spirit of this education speaks so plainly for itself that, I hope, I need say nothing in its justification. If we could see it in life, as well as read of it in books, the world would soon find the happy effects of it.

A daughter thus educated would be a blessing to any family that she came into, a fit companion for a wise man, and make him happy in the government of his family and the education of his children.

And she that either was not inclined, or could not dispose of herself well in marriage, would know how to live to great and excellent ends in a state of virginity.

A very ordinary knowledge of the spirit of Christianity seems to be enough to convince us that no education can be of true advantage to young women but that which trains them up in humble industry, in great plainness of life, in exact modesty of dress, manners, and carriage, and in strict devotion. For what should a Christian woman be but a plain, unaffected, modest, humble creature, averse to everything in her dress and carriage that can draw the eyes of beholders, or gratify the passions of lewd and amorous persons?

How great a stranger must he be to the Gospel who does not know that it requires this to be the spirit of a pious woman.

Our blessed Saviour saith, "Whosoever looketh upon a woman to lust after her hath already committed adultery with her in his heart" (St. Matt. v. 28).

Need an education which turns women's minds to the arts and ornaments of dress and beauty be more strongly condemned than by these words? For surely, if the eye is so easily and dangerously betrayed, every art and ornament is sufficiently condemned that naturally tends to betray it.

And how can a woman of piety more justly abhor and avoid anything than that which makes her person more a snare and temptation to other people? If lust and wanton eyes are the death of the soul, can any women think themselves innocent who, with naked breasts, patched faces, and every ornament of dress, invite the eye to offend?

And as there is no pretence for innocence in such a behaviour, so neither can they tell how to set any bounds to their guilt. For as they can never know how much, or how often they have occasioned sin in other people, so they can never know how much guilt will be placed to their own account.

This, one would think, should sufficiently deter every pious woman from everything that might render her the occasion of loose passions in other people.

St. Paul, speaking of a thing entirely innocent, reasons after this manner: "But take heed lest by any means this liberty of yours become a stumbling-block to those that are weak.—And through thy knowledge thy weak brother perish, for whom Christ died. But when ye sin so against the brethren, and wound their weak conscience, ye sin against Christ. Wherefore, if meat make my brother to offend, I will eat no flesh while the world standeth, lest I make my brother to offend" (1 Cor. viii. 9-13).

Now if this is the spirit of Christianity, if it requires us to abstain from things thus lawful, innocent, and useful, when there is any danger of betraying our weak brethren into any error thereby ; surely it cannot be reckoned too nice or needless a point of conscience for women to avoid such things as are neither innocent nor useful, but naturally tend to corrupt their own hearts and raise ill passions in other people.

Surely every woman of Christian piety ought to say, in the spirit of the Apostle, if patching and paint, or any vain adorning of my person, be a natural means of making weak, unwary eyes to offend, I will renounce all these arts as long as I live, lest I should make my fellow-creatures to offend.

I shall now leave this subject of humility, having said enough, as I hope, to recommend the necessity of making it the constant, chief subject of your devotion at this hour of prayer.

I have considered the nature and necessity of humility, and its great importance to a religious life. I have shown you how many difficulties are formed against it from our natural tempers, the spirit of the world, and the common education of both sexes.

These considerations will, I hope, instruct you how to form your prayers for it to the best advantage, and teach you the necessity of letting no day pass without a serious, earnest application to God for the whole spirit of humility; fervently beseeching Him to fill every part of your soul with it, to make it the ruling, constant habit of your mind, that you may not only feel it, but feel all your other tempers arising from it ; that you may have no thoughts, no desires, no designs, but such as are the true fruits of a humble, meek, and lowly heart.

That you may always appear poor, and little, and mean in your own eyes, and fully content that others should have the same opinion of you.

That the whole course of your life, your expense, your house, your dress, your manner of eating, drinking, conversing, and doing everything may be so many continual proofs of the true unfeigned humility of your heart.

That you may look for nothing, claim nothing, resent nothing ; that you may go through all the actions and accidents of life calmly and quietly, as in the presence of God, looking wholly unto Him, acting wholly for Him; neither seeking vain applause nor resenting neglects or affronts, but doing and receiving everything in the meek and lowly spirit of our Lord and Saviour Jesus Christ.

# CHAPTER XX.

*Recommending devotion at twelve o'clock, called in Scripture the sixth hour of the day. The frequency of devotion equally desirable by all orders of people. Universal love is here recommended to be the subject of prayer at this hour. Of intercession as an act of universal love.*

IT will perhaps be thought by some people that these hours of prayer come too thick, that they can only be observed by people of great leisure, and ought not to be pressed upon the generality of men who have the cares of families, trades, employments; nor upon the gentry, whose state and figure in the world cannot admit of this frequency of devotion, and that it is only fit for monasteries and nunneries, or such people as have no more to do in the world than they have.

To this it is answered,

First, That this method of devotion is not pressed upon any sort of people as absolutely necessary, but recommended to all people as the best, the happiest, and most perfect way of life.

And if a great and exemplary devotion is as much the greatest happiness and perfection of a merchant, a soldier, or a man of quality, as it is the greatest happiness and perfection of the most retired contemplative life, then it is as proper to recommend it without any abatement to one order of men as to another, because happiness and perfection are of the same worth and value to all people.

The gentleman and tradesman may and must spend much of their time differently from the pious monk in the cloister, or the contemplative hermit in the desert; but then, as the monk and hermit lose the ends of retirement unless they make it all serviceable to devotion, so the gentleman and merchant fail of the greatest ends of a social life, and live to their loss in the world, unless devotion be their chief and governing temper.

CH. XX.     It is certainly very honest and creditable for people to engage
in trades and employments; it is reasonable for gentlemen to
manage well their estates and families, and take such recreations as
are proper to their state.   But then every gentleman and tradesman loses the greatest happiness of his creation, is robbed of
something that is greater than all employments, distinctions, and
pleasures of the world, if he does not live more to piety and
devotion than to anything else in the world.

Here are, therefore, no excuses made for men of business and
figure in the world.   First, Because it would be to excuse them from
that which is the greatest end of living, and be only finding so
many reasons for making them less beneficial to themselves, and
less serviceable to God and the world.

Secondly, Because most men of business and figure engage too
far in worldly matters, much farther than the reasons of human
life or the necessities of the world require.

Merchants and tradesmen, for instance, are generally ten times
farther engaged in business than they need, which is so far from
being a reasonable excuse for their want of time for devotion, that
it is their crime, and must be censured as a blameable instance of
covetousness and ambition.

The gentry and people of figure either give themselves up to
state employments, or to the gratifications of their passions in a
life of gaiety and debauchery; and if these things might be
admitted as allowable avocations[1] from devotion, devotion must
be reckoned a poor circumstance of life.

Unless gentlemen can show that they have another God than the
Father of our Lord Jesus Christ, another nature than that which is
derived from Adam, another religion than the Christian, it is in
vain to plead their state, and dignity, and pleasures as reasons for
not preparing their souls for God by a strict and regular devotion.

For since piety and devotion are the common unchangeable
means of saving all the souls in the world that shall be saved, there
is nothing left for the gentleman, the soldier, and the tradesman
but to take care that their several states be, by care and watchfulness, by meditation and prayer, made states of an exact and
solid piety.

If a merchant, having forborne from too great business that he
might quietly attend on the service of God, should therefore die

[1] The literal sense of the word 'avocation'—a calling away from their
proper work.

worth twenty instead of fifty thousand pounds, could any one say that he had mistaken his calling, or gone a loser out of the world?

If a gentleman should have killed fewer foxes, been less frequent at balls, gamings, and merry-meetings, because stated parts of his time had been given to retirement, to meditation and devotion, could it be thought that when he left the world he would regret the loss of those hours that he had given to the care and improvement of his soul?

If a tradesman, by aspiring after Christian perfection, and retiring[2] himself often from his business, should, instead of leaving his children fortunes to spend in luxury and idleness, leave them to live by their own honest labour, could it be said that he had made a wrong use of the world because he had shown his children that he had more regard to that which is eternal than to this which is soon to be at an end?

Since, therefore, devotion is not only the best and most desirable practice in a cloister, but the best and most desirable practice of men as men, and in every state of life, they that desire to be excused from it because they are men of figure, and estates, and business are no wiser than those that should desire to be excused from health and happiness because they were men of figure and estates.

I cannot see why every gentleman, merchant, or soldier should not put these questions seriously to himself:

What is the best thing for me to intend and drive at in all my actions? How shall I do to make the most of human life? What ways shall I wish that I had taken when I am leaving the world?

Now to be thus wise, and to make thus much use of our reason, seems to be but a small and necessary piece of wisdom. For how can we pretend to sense and judgment if we dare not seriously consider, and answer, and govern our lives by that which such questions require of us?

Shall a nobleman think his birth too high a dignity to condescend to such questions as these? Or a tradesman think his business too great to take any care about himself?

Now here is desired no more devotion in any one's life than the answering these few questions requires.

---

[2] The use of the word 'retire' as a transitive rather than an intransitive verb, has the sanction of some of the best of the old writers. See quotations from Shakespeare, Dryden, Bacon, Clarendon, and others, who use it actively as equivalent to 'withdraw,' in Johnson's *Dictionary*.

Any devotion that is not to the greater advantage of him that uses it than anything that he can do in the room of it ; any devotion that does not procure an infinitely greater good than can be got by neglecting it, is freely yielded up ; here is no demand of it.

But if people will live in so much ignorance as never to put these questions to themselves, but push on a blind life at all chances, in quest of they know not what, nor why, without ever considering the worth or value or tendency of their actions, without considering what God, reason, eternity, and their own happiness require of them ; it is for the honour of devotion that none can neglect it but those who are thus inconsiderate, who dare not inquire after that which is the best and most worthy of their choice.

It is true, CLAUDIUS, you are a man of figure and estate, and are to act the part of such a station in human life; you are not called, as Elijah was, to be a Prophet, or as St. Paul, to be an Apostle.

But will you, therefore, not love yourself? Will you not seek and study your own happiness because you are not called to preach up the same things to other people?

You would think it very absurd for a man not to value his own health because he was not a physician, or the preservation of his limbs because he was not a bone-setter. Yet it is more absurd for you, Claudius, to neglect the improvement of your soul in piety because you are not an Apostle or a Bishop.

Consider this text of Scripture, "If ye live after the flesh, ye shall die ; but if through the Spirit ye do mortify the deeds of the body, ye shall live. For as many as are led by the Spirit of God, they are the sons of God" (Rom. viii. 13, 14). Do you think that this Scripture does not equally relate to all mankind? Can you find any exception here for men of figure and estates? Is not a spiritual and devout life here made the common condition on which all men are to become sons of God? Will you leave hours of prayer and rules of devotion to particular states of life when nothing but the same spirit of devotion can save you or any man from eternal death?

Consider again this text, "For we must all appear before the judgment seat of Christ; that every one may receive the things done in his body, according to that he hath done, whether it be good or bad" (2 Cor. v. 10). Now if your estate would excuse you from appearing before this judgment seat; if your figure could protect you from receiving according to your works, there would be some pretence for your leaving devotion to other people. But if you who are now thus distinguished must then appear naked amongst common souls, without any other distinction from others but such as your virtues or sins give you, does it not as much concern you as any Prophet or Apostle to make the best provision for the best rewards at that great day?

Again, consider this great doctrine of the Apostle, "For none of us," that is, of us Christians, "liveth to himself, and no man dieth to himself. For whether we live, we live unto the Lord; and whether we die, we die unto the Lord. For to this end Christ both died, and rose, and revived, that He might be Lord both of the dead and the living" (Rom. xiv. 7-9).

Now are you, Claudius, excepted out of the doctrine of this text? Will you, because of your condition, leave it to any particular sort of people to live and die unto Christ? If so, you must leave it to them to be redeemed by the death and resurrection of Christ. For it is the express doctrine of the text that for this end Christ died and rose again, that none of us should live to himself. It is not that priests, or apostles, or monks, or hermits should live no longer to themselves, but that none of us, that is, no Christian of what state soever, should live unto himself.

If, therefore, there be any instances of piety, any rules of devotion, which you can neglect, and yet live as truly unto Christ as if you observed them, this text calls you to no such devotion. But if you forsake such devotion as you yourself know is expected from some particular sorts of people, such devotion as you know becomes people that live wholly unto Christ, that aspire after great piety; if you neglect such devotion for any worldly consideration, that you may live more to your own temper and taste, more to the fashions and ways of the world, you forsake the terms on which all Christians are to receive the benefit of Christ's death and resurrection.

Observe further, how the same doctrine is taught by St. Peter: "As He which hath called you is holy, so be ye holy in all manner of conversation" (1 Pet. i. 15).

If, therefore, Claudius, you are one of those that are here called, you see what it is you are called to. It is not to have so much religion as suits with your temper, your business, or your pleasures; it is not to a particular sort of piety that may be sufficient for gentlemen of figure and estates, but it is first, to be "holy as He which hath called you is holy"; secondly, it is to be thus holy in all manner of conversation, that is, to carry this spirit and

CH. XX. degree of holiness into every part, and through the whole form of your life.

And the reason the Apostle immediately gives why this spirit of holiness must be the common spirit of Christians, as such, is very affecting, and such as equally calls upon all sorts of Christians. "Forasmuch as ye know," says he, "that ye were not redeemed with corruptible things, as silver and gold, from your vain conversation,—but with the precious blood of Christ," etc.

As if he had said, Forasmuch as ye know ye were made capable of this state of holiness, entered into a society with Christ, and made heirs of His glory, not by any human means, but by such a mysterious instance of love as infinitely exceeds everything that can be thought of in this world; since God has redeemed you to Himself, and your own happiness, at so great a price; how base and shameful must it be, if you do not henceforth devote yourselves wholly to the glory of God, and become holy as He Who hath called you is holy!

If, therefore, Claudius, you consider your figure and estate; or if, in the words of the text, you consider your gold and silver and the corruptible things of this life as any reason why you may live to your own humour and fancy, why you may neglect a life of strict piety and great devotion; if you think anything in the world can be an excuse for you not imitating the holiness of Christ in the whole course and form of your life, you make yourself as guilty as if you should neglect the holiness of Christianity for the sake of picking straws.

For the greatness of this new state of life to which we are called in Christ Jesus to be for ever as the angels of God in heaven, and the greatness of the price by which we are made capable of this state of glory, has turned everything that is worldly, temporal, and corruptible into an equal littleness, and made it as great baseness and folly, as great a contempt of the blood of Christ, to neglect any degrees of holiness because you are a man of some estate and quality, as it would be to neglect it because you had a fancy to pick straws.

Again, the same Apostle saith, "Know ye not that your body is the temple of the Holy Ghost which is in you, and ye are not your own? For ye are bought with a price; therefore glorify God in your body, and in your spirit, which are God's" (1 Cor. vi. 19, 20).

How poorly, therefore, Claudius, have you read the Scripture;

how little do you know of Christianity, if you can yet talk of your estate and condition as a pretence for a freer kind of life!

Are you any more your own than he that has no estate or dignity in the world? Must mean and little people preserve their bodies as temples of the Holy Ghost by watching, fasting, and prayer; but may you indulge yours in idleness, in lusts, and sensuality because you have so much rent or such a title of distinction? How poor and ignorant are such thoughts as these! And yet you must either think thus, or else acknowledge that the holiness of saints, Prophets, and Apostles is the holiness that you are to labour after with all the diligence and care that you can.

And if you leave it to others to live in such piety and devotion, in such self-denial, humility, and temperance as may render them able to glorify God in their body and in their spirit, you must leave it to them also to have the benefit of the blood of Christ.

Again, the Apostle saith, "You know how we exhorted, comforted, and charged every one of you, that you would walk worthy of God, Who hath called you to His kingdom and glory" (1 Thess. ii. 11, 12).

You, perhaps, Claudius, have often heard these words without ever thinking how much they required of you. And yet you cannot consider them without perceiving to what an eminent state of holiness they call you.

For how can the holiness of the Christian life be set before you in higher terms than when it is represented to you as walking worthy of God? Can you think of any abatements of virtue, any neglects of devotion, that are well consistent with a life that is to be made worthy of God? Can you suppose that any man walks in this manner but he that watches over all his steps, and considers how everything he does may be done in the spirit of holiness? And yet, as high as these expressions carry this holiness, it is here plainly made the necessary holiness of all Christians. For the Apostle does not here exhort his fellow Apostles and saints to this holiness, but he commands all Christians to endeavour after it: "We charged," says he, "every one of you, that you would walk worthy of God, Who hath called you to His kingdom and glory."

Again, St. Peter saith, "If any man speak, let him speak as the oracles of God; if any man minister, let him do it as of the ability that God giveth: that God in all things may be glorified in Christ Jesus" (1 St. Pet. iv. 11).

Do you not here, Claudius, plainly perceive your high calling? Is he that speaketh to have such regard to his words that he appear to speak as by the direction of God? Is he that giveth to take care that he so giveth that what he disposeth of may appear to be a gift that he hath of God? And is all this to be done that God may be glorified in all things?

Must it not then be said, Has any man nobility, dignity of state, or figure in the world? Let him so use his nobility or figure of life that it may appear he uses these as the gifts of God, for the greater setting forth of His glory. Is there now, Claudius, anything forced or far-fetched in this conclusion? Is it not the plain sense of the words, that everything in life is to be made a matter of holiness unto God? If so, then your estate and dignity is so far from excusing you from great piety and holiness of life, that it lays you under a greater necessity of living more to the glory of God, because you have more of His gifts that may be made serviceable to it.

For people, therefore, of figure, or business, or dignity in the world to leave great piety and eminent devotion to any particular orders of men, or such as they think have little else to do in the world, is to leave the kingdom of God to them. For it is the very end of Christianity to redeem all orders of men into one holy society, that rich and poor, high and low, masters and servants, may in one and the same spirit of piety become a "chosen generation, a royal priesthood, an holy nation, a peculiar people, that are to show forth the praises of Him Who hath called them out of darkness into His marvellous light" (1 St. Peter ii. 9).

Thus much being said to show that great devotion and holiness is not to be left to any particular sort of people, but to be the common spirit of all that desire to live up to the terms of common Christianity; I now proceed to consider the nature and necessity of universal love, which is here recommended to be the subject of your devotion at this hour. You are here also called to intercession, as the most proper exercise to raise and preserve that love. By intercession is meant a praying to God, and interceding with Him for our fellow-creatures.

Our blessed Lord hath recommended His love to us as the pattern and example of our love to one another. As, therefore, He is continually making intercession for us all, so ought we to intercede and pray for one another.

"A new commandment," saith He, "I give unto you, that ye

love one another, as I have loved you.  By this shall all men CH. XX.
know that ye are My disciples, if ye love one another."

The newness of this precept did not consist in this, that men
were commanded to love one another; for this was an old precept,
both of the law of Moses and of nature.  But it was new in this
respect, that it was to imitate a new and, till then, unheard of
example of love; it was to love one another as Christ had
loved us.

And if men are to know that we are disciples of Christ by thus
loving one another according to His new example of love, then it
is certain that if we are void of this love we make it as plainly
known unto men that we are none of His disciples.

There is no principle of the heart that is more acceptable to
God than a universal fervent love to all mankind, wishing and
praying for their happiness, because there is no principle of the
heart that makes us more like God, Who is love and goodness
itself, and created all beings for their enjoyment of happiness.

The greatest idea that we can frame of God is when we conceive Him to be a Being of infinite love and goodness, using
an infinite wisdom and power for the common good and happiness of all His creatures.

The highest notion, therefore, that we can form of man is when
we conceive him as like to God in this respect as he can be, using
all his finite faculties, whether of wisdom, power, or prayers, for
the common good of all his fellow-creatures, heartily desiring they
may have all the happiness they are capable of, and as many
benefits and assistances from him as his state and condition in the
world will permit him to give them.

And on the other hand, what a baseness and iniquity is there in
all instances of hatred, envy, spite, and ill-will, if we consider that
every instance of them is so far acting in opposition to God, and
intending mischief and harm to those creatures which God favours,
and protects, and preserves, in order to their happiness!  An ill-
natured man amongst God's creatures is the most perverse creature
in the world, acting contrary to that love by which himself subsists, and which alone gives subsistence to all that variety of beings
that enjoy life in any part of the creation.  "Whatsoever ye would
that men should do unto you, even so do unto them."

Now though this is a doctrine of strict justice, yet it is only a
universal love that can comply with it.  For as love is the measure
of our acting towards ourselves, so we can never act in the same

CH. XX. manner towards other people till we look upon them with that love with which we look upon ourselves.

As we have no degrees of spite, or envy, or ill-will to ourselves, so we cannot be disposed towards others as we are towards ourselves till we universally renounce all instances of spite, and envy, and ill-will even in the smallest degrees.

If we had any imperfection in our eyes that made us see any one thing wrong, for the same reason they would show us a hundred things wrong.

So if we have any temper of our hearts that makes us envious, or spiteful, or ill-natured towards any one man, the same temper will make us envious, and spiteful, and ill-natured towards a great many more.

If, therefore, we desire this divine virtue of love, we must exercise and practise our hearts in the love of all, because it is not Christian love till it is the love of all.

If a man could keep this whole law of love, and yet offend in one point, he would be guilty of all. For as one allowed instance of injustice destroys the justice of all our other actions, so one allowed instance of envy, spite, and ill-will renders all our other acts of benevolence and affection nothing worth.

Acts of love that proceed not from a principle of universal love are but like acts of justice that proceed from a heart not disposed to universal justice.

A love which is not universal may indeed have tenderness and affection, but it hath nothing of righteousness or piety in it ; it is but humour, and temper, or interest, or such a love as publicans and heathens practise.

All particular envies and spite are as plain departures from the spirit of Christianity as any particular acts of injustice. For it is as much a law of Christ to treat everybody as your neighbour, and to love your neighbour as yourself, as it is a law of Christianity to abstain from theft.

Now the noblest motive to this universal tenderness and affection is founded in this doctrine, "God is love, and he that dwelleth in love dwelleth in God."

Who, therefore, whose heart has any tendency towards God, would not aspire after this divine temper which so changes and exalts our nature into a union with Him ?

How should we rejoice in the exercise and practice of this love which, so often as we feel it, is so often an assurance to us that God is in us, that we act according to His spirit, and is love itself? But we must observe that love has then only this mighty power of uniting us to God when it is so pure and universal as to imitate that love which God beareth to all His creatures.

God willeth the happiness of all beings, though it is no happiness to Himself. Therefore we must desire the happiness of all beings, though no happiness cometh to us from it.

God equally delighteth in the perfections of all His creatures; therefore we should rejoice in those perfections wherever we see them, and be as glad to have other people perfect as ourselves.

As God forgiveth all, and giveth grace to all, so we should forgive all those injuries and affronts which we receive from others, and do all the good that we can to them.

God Almighty, besides His own great example of love, which ought to draw all His creatures after it, has so provided for us, and made our happiness so common to us all, that we have no occasion to envy or hate one another.

For we cannot stand in one another's way, or by enjoying any particular good, keep another from his full share of it. As we cannot be happy but in the enjoyment of God, so we cannot rival or rob one another of this happiness.

And as to other things, the enjoyments and prosperities of this life, they are so little in themselves, so foreign to our happiness, and, generally speaking, so contrary to that which they appear to be, that they are no foundation for envy or spite or hatred.

How silly would it be to envy a man that was drinking poison out of a golden cup! And yet, who can say that he is acting wiser than thus, when he is envying any instance of worldly greatness?

How many saints has adversity sent to heaven? And how many poor sinners has prosperity plunged into everlasting misery? A man seems then to be in the most glorious state when he has conquered, disgraced, and humbled his enemy, though it may be that same conquest has saved his adversary and undone himself.

This man had perhaps never been debauched but for his fortune and advancement; that had never been pious but through his poverty and disgrace.

She that is envied for her beauty may perchance owe all her misery to it, and another may be for ever happy for having had no admirers of her person.

CH. XX.    One man succeeds in everything, and so loses all. Another meets with nothing but crosses and disappointments, and thereby gains more than all the world is worth.

This clergyman may be undone by his being made a bishop; and that may both save himself and others by being fixed to his first poor vicarage.

How envied was Alexander when, conquering the world, he built towns, set up his statues, and left marks of his glory in so many kingdoms! And how despised was the poor preacher St. Paul when he was beaten with rods! And yet how strangely was the world mistaken in their judgment! How much to be envied was St. Paul! How much to be pitied was Alexander!

These few reflections sufficiently show us that the different conditions of this life have nothing in them to excite our uneasy passions, nothing that can reasonably interrupt our love and affection to one another.

To proceed now to another motive to this universal love.

Our power of doing external acts of love and goodness is often very narrow and restrained. There are, it may be, but few people to whom we can contribute any worldly relief.

But though our outward means of doing good are often thus limited, yet if our hearts are but full of love and goodness, we get, as it were, an infinite power, because God will attribute to us those good works, those acts of love and tender charities which we sincerely desired, and would gladly have performed, had it been in our power.

You cannot heal all the sick, relieve all the poor ; you cannot comfort all in distress, nor be a father to all the fatherless. You cannot, it may be, deliver many from their misfortunes, or teach them to find comfort in God.

But if there is a love and tenderness in your heart, that delight in these good works, and excites you to do all that you can ; if your love has no bounds, but continually wishes and prays for the relief and happiness of all that are in distress, you will be received by God as a benefactor to those who have had nothing from you but your goodwill and tender affections.

You cannot build hospitals for the incurable ; you cannot erect monasteries for the education of persons in holy solitude, continual prayer, and mortification ;[3] but if you join in your heart with those

---

[3] Another instance of the differences between Law and the popular theo- logy, whether 'evangelical' or 'ortho- dox,' of the eighteenth century. He

that do, and thank God for their pious designs; if you are a friend CH. XX.
to these great friends to mankind, and rejoice in their eminent
virtues, you will be received by God as a sharer of such good works
as, though they had none of your hands, yet had all your heart.

This consideration surely is sufficient to make us look to, and
watch over our hearts with all diligence, to study the improvement
of our inward tempers, and aspire after every height and perfection
of a loving, charitable, and benevolent mind.

And on the other hand, we may hence learn the great evil and
mischief of all wrong turns of mind, of envy, spite, hatred, and ill-
will. For if the goodness of our hearts will entitle us to the reward
of good actions which we never performed, it is certain that the
badness of our hearts, our envy, ill-nature, and hatred, will bring
us under the guilt of actions that we have never committed.

As he that lusteth after a woman shall be reckoned an adulterer,
though he has only committed the crime in his heart, so the mali-
cious, spiteful, ill-natured man, that only secretly rejoices at evil,
shall be reckoned a murderer, though he has shed no blood.

Since, therefore, our hearts, which are always naked and open
to the eyes of God, give such an exceeding extent and increase
either to our virtues or vices, it is our best and greatest business to
govern the motions of our hearts, to watch, correct, and improve
the inward state and temper of our souls.

Now there is nothing that so much exalts our souls as this
heavenly love; it cleanses and purifies like a holy fire, and all ill-
tempers fall away before it. It makes room for all virtues, and
carries them to their greatest height. Everything that is good and
holy grows out of it, and it becomes a continual source of all holy
desires and pious practices. By love, I do not mean any natural
tenderness which is more or less in people according to their
constitutions, but I mean a larger principle of the soul, founded
in reason and piety, which makes us tender, kind, and benevolent
to all our fellow-creatures, as creatures of God, and for His sake.[4]

made no secret of his regret for the
loss of the monastic system; he admired, instead of condemning as
superstitious, 'the holy solitude of the
hermit'; he thought the virgin state
a higher state than that of matrimony
in all classes and both sexes, and he
regarded celibacy as all but binding
on the clergy.

[4] Law never shirks a difficulty. His
injunction to 'universal love' lay open
to the objection that, if all men were
to be loved alike, the distinction between the way in which we should
regard a good and a bad man would
be done away; but he fairly meets it
by distinguishing between the love
engendered by universal benevolence,
and by personal esteem. The latter
is not the outcome of Christian charity
at all; the former is.

It is this love that loves all things in God, as His creatures, as the images of His power, as the creatures of His goodness, as parts of His family, as members of His society, that becomes a holy principle of all great and good actions.

The love, therefore, of our neighbour is only a branch of our love to God. For when we love God with all our hearts, and with all our souls, and with all our strength, we shall necessarily love those beings that are so nearly related to God, that have everything from Him, and are created by Him to be objects of His own eternal love. If I hate or despise any one man in the world, I hate something that God cannot hate, and despise that which He loves.

And can I think that I love God with all my heart whilst I hate that which belongs only to God, which has no other master but Him, which bears His image, is part of His family, and exists only by the continuance of His love towards it? It was the impossibility of this that made St. John say, "That if any man saith, he loveth God, and hateth his brother, he is a liar."

These reasons sufficiently show us that no love is holy or religious till it becomes universal.

For if religion requires me to love all persons, as God's creatures, that belong to Him, that bear His image, enjoy His protection, and make parts of His family and household; if these are the great and necessary reasons why I should live in love and friendship with any one man in the world, they are the same great and necessary reasons why I should live in love and friendship with every man in the world; and consequently I offend against all these reasons, and break through all these ties and obligations, whenever I want love towards any one man. The sin, therefore, of hating or despising any one man is like the sin of hating all God's creation, and the necessity of loving any one man is the same necessity of loving every man in the world. And though many people may appear to us ever so sinful, odious, or extravagant in their conduct, we must never look upon that as the least motive for any contempt or disregard of them, but look upon them with the greater compassion as being in the most pitiable condition that can be.

As it was the sins of the world that made the Son of God become a compassionate suffering Advocate for all mankind, so none is of the spirit of Christ but he that has the utmost compassion for sinners. Nor is there any greater sign of your own

CH. XX.

perfection than when you find yourself all love and compassion towards them that are very weak and defective. And on the other hand, you have never less reason to be pleased with yourself than when you find yourself most angry and offended at the behaviour of others. All sin is certainly to be hated and abhorred wherever it is; but then we must set ourselves against sin, as we do against sickness and diseases, by showing ourselves tender and compassionate to the sick and diseased.[5]

All other hatred of sin, which does not fill the heart with the softest, tenderest affections towards persons miserable in it, is the servant of sin, at the same time that it seems to be hating it.

And there is no temper which even good men ought more carefully to watch and guard against than this. For it is a temper that lurks and hides itself under the cover of many virtues, and, by being unsuspected, does the more mischief.

A man naturally fancies that it is his own exceeding love of virtue that makes him not able to bear with those that want it. And when he abhors one man, despises another, and cannot bear the name of a third, he supposes it all to be a proof of his own high sense of virtue and just hatred of sin.

And yet one would think that a man needed no other cure for this temper than this one reflection:

That if this had been the spirit of the Son of God, if He had hated sin in this manner, there had been no redemption of the world; that if God had hated sinners in this manner day and night, the world itself had ceased long ago.

This, therefore, we may take for a certain rule, that the more we partake of the divine nature, the more improved we are ourselves; and the higher our sense of virtue is, the more we shall pity and compassionate those that want it. The sight of such people will then, instead of raising in us a haughty contempt or peevish indignation towards them, fill us with such bowels of compassion as when we see the miseries of a hospital.

That the follies, therefore, crimes, and ill-behaviour of our fellow-creatures may not lessen that love and tenderness which we are to have for all mankind, we should often consider the reasons on which this duty of love is founded.

[5] The illustration of the point referred to in the last note, taken from a man's feeling towards himself, is very apposite. He may detest many of his own past actions, and lament his own past folly, but need not, therefore, cease to love himself. So he may detest the sin in a bad man, but never cease to love him.

Now we are to love our neighbour, that is, all mankind, not because they are wise, holy, virtuous, or well-behaved; for all mankind neither ever was nor ever will be so. Therefore it is certain that the reason of our being obliged to love them cannot be founded in their virtue.

Again, if their virtue or goodness were the reason of our being obliged to love people, we should have no rule to proceed by; because though some people's virtues or vices are very notorious, yet, generally speaking, we are but very ill judges of the virtue and merit of other people.

Thirdly, We are sure that the virtue or merit of persons is not the reason of our being obliged to love them, because we are commanded to pay the highest instances of love to our worst enemies; we are to love, and bless, and pray for those that most injuriously treat us. This, therefore, is demonstration that the merit of persons is not the reason on which our obligation to love them is founded.

Let us farther consider what that love is which we owe to our neighbour. It is to love him as ourselves, that is, to have all those sentiments towards him which we have towards ourselves; to wish him everything that we may lawfully wish to ourselves; to be glad of every good, and sorry for every evil that happens to him; and to be ready to do him all such acts of kindness as we are always ready to do to ourselves.

This love, therefore, you see is nothing else but a love of benevolence; it requires nothing of us but such good wishes, tender affections, and such acts of kindness as we show to ourselves.

This is all the love that we owe to the best of men; and we are never to want any degree of this love to the worst or most unreasonable man in the world.

Now what is the reason why we are to love every man in this manner? It is answered that our obligation to love all men in this manner is founded upon many reasons.

First, Upon a reason of equity; for if it is just to love ourselves in this manner, it must be unjust to deny any degree of this love to others, because every man is so exactly of the same nature and in the same condition as ourselves.

If, therefore, your own crimes and follies do not lessen your obligation to seek your own good and wish well to yourself, neither do the follies and crimes of your neighbour lessen your obligation to wish and seek the good of your neighbour.

Another reason for this love is founded in the authority of God, Who has commanded us to love every man as ourself.

Thirdly, We are obliged to this love in imitation of God's goodness, that we may be children of our Father which is in heaven, Who willeth the happiness of all His creatures, and maketh His sun to rise on the evil and on the good.

Fourthly, Our redemption by Jesus Christ calleth us to the exercise of this love, Who came from heaven, and laid down His life out of love to the whole sinful world.

Fifthly, By the command of our Lord and Saviour, Who has required us to love one another as He has loved us.

These are the great, perpetual reasons on which our obligation to love all mankind as ourselves is founded.

These reasons never vary or change; they always continue in their full force, and, therefore, equally oblige at all times, and in regard to all persons.

God loves us, not because we are wise, and good, and holy, but in pity to us, because we want this happiness. He loves us in order to make us good. Our love, therefore, must take this course, not looking for or requiring the merit of our brethren, but pitying their disorders, and wishing them all the good that they want and are capable of receiving.

It appears now plainly from what has been said that the love which we owe to our brethren is only a love of benevolence. Secondly, That this duty of benevolence is founded upon such reasons as never vary or change, such as have no dependence upon the qualities of persons. Because he that denies any of this benevolence to a bad man offends against all the same reasons of love as he does that denies any benevolence to a good man. And consequently it is the same sin.

When, therefore, you let loose an ill-natured passion, either of hatred or contempt towards (as you suppose) an ill man, consider what you would think of another that was doing the same towards a good man, and be assured that you are committing the same sin.

You will perhaps say, How is it possible to love a good and a bad man in the same degree?

Just as it is possible to be as just and faithful to a good man as to an evil man. Now are you in any difficulty about performing justice and faithfulness to a bad man? Are you in any doubts whether you need to be so just and faithful to him as you need be to a good man? Now why is it that you are in no doubt about

CH. XX. it?  It is because you know that justice and faithfulness are founded upon reasons that never vary or change, that have no dependence upon the merits of men, but are founded in the nature of things, in the laws of God, and, therefore, are to be observed with an equal exactness towards good and bad men.[6]

Now do but think thus justly of charity or love to your neighbour, that it is founded upon reasons that vary not, that have no dependence upon the merits of men, and then you will find it as possible to perform the same exact charity, as the same exact justice, to all men, whether good or bad.

You will perhaps farther ask if you are not to have a particular esteem, veneration, and reverence for good men?  It is answered, Yes.  But then this high esteem and veneration is a thing very different from that love of benevolence which we owe to our neighbour.

The high esteem and veneration which you have for a man of eminent piety is no act of charity to him ; it is not out of pity and compassion that you so reverence him, but it is rather an act of charity to yourself that such esteem and veneration may excite you to follow his example.

You may and ought to love, like, and approve the life which the good man leads; but then this is only the loving of virtue, wherever we see it.  And we do not love virtue with the love of benevolence, as anything that wants our good wishes, but as something that is our proper good.

The whole of the matter is this.  The actions which you are to love, esteem, and admire are the actions of good and pious men ; but the persons to whom you are to do all the good you can, in all sorts of kindness and compassion, are all persons, whether good or bad.

This distinction betwixt love of benevolence, and esteem or veneration is very plain and obvious.  And you may perhaps still better see the plainness and necessity of it by this following instance.

No man is to have a high esteem or honour for his own accomplishments or behaviour; yet every man is to love himself, that is, to wish well to himself.  Therefore this distinction betwixt love and esteem is not only plain, but very necessary to be observed.

---

[6] Observe this ingenious argument, which cannot easily be refuted.  Love, as a Christian virtue, stands on the same footing as justice and faithfulness.  A Christian would not be acting as a Christian if he was unjust or unfaithful even to the worst of men ; therefore, neither is he, if he does not love them.

Again, if you think it hardly possible to dislike the actions of unreasonable men and yet have a true love for them, consider this with relation to yourself.

It is very possible, I hope, for you not only to dislike, but to detest and abhor a great many of your own past actions, and to accuse yourself of great folly for them. But do you then lose any of those tender sentiments towards yourself which you used to have? Do you then cease to wish well to yourself? Is not the love of yourself as strong then as at any other time?[7]

Now what is thus possible with relation to ourselves is in the same manner possible with relation to others. We may have the highest good wishes towards them, desiring for them every good that we desire for ourselves, and yet at the same time dislike their way of life.

To proceed: all that love which we may justly have for ourselves we are in strict justice obliged to exercise towards all other men; and we offend against the great law of our nature and the greatest laws of God when our tempers towards others are different from those which we have towards ourselves.

Now that self-love which is just and reasonable, keeps us constantly tender, compassionate, and well affected towards ourselves. If, therefore, you do not feel these kind dispositions towards all other people, you may be assured that you are not in that state of charity which is the very life and soul of Christian piety.

You know how it hurts you to be made the jest and ridicule of other people, how it grieves you to be robbed of your reputation, and deprived of the favourable opinion of your neighbours. If, therefore, you expose others to scorn and contempt in any degree, if it pleases you to see or hear of their frailties or infirmities, or if you are only loath to conceal their faults, you are so far from loving such people as yourself, that you may be justly supposed to have as much hatred for them as you have love for yourself. For such tempers are as truly the proper fruits of hatred as the contrary tempers are the proper fruits of love.

And as it is a certain sign that you love yourself, because you are tender of everything that concerns you; so it is as certain a sign that you hate your neighbour when you are pleased with anything that hurts him.

[7] Bishop Butler's admirable sermon on 'Self-Love' (Sermon XI. in his *Fifteen Sermons preached at the Chapel of the Rolls Court*) is a good comment upon this sentiment.

But now, if the want of a true and exact charity be so great a want that, as St. Paul saith, it renders our greatest virtues but empty sounds and tinkling cymbals, how highly does it concern us to study every art and practise every method of raising our souls to this state of charity? It is for this reason that you are here desired not to let this hour of prayer pass without a full and solemn supplication to God for all the instances of a universal love and benevolence to all mankind.

Such daily, constant devotion being the only likely means of preserving you in such a state of love as is necessary to prove you to be a true follower of Jesus Christ.

# CHAPTER XXI.

*Of the necessity and benefit of intercession considered as an exercise of universal love. How all orders of men are to pray and intercede with God for one another. How naturally such intercession amends and reforms the hearts of those that use it.*

THAT intercession is a great and necessary part of Christian devotion is very evident from Scripture.

The first followers of Christ seem to support all their love, and to maintain all their intercourse and correspondence, by mutual prayers for one another.

St. Paul, whether he writes to churches or particular persons, shows his intercession to be perpetual for them, that they are the constant subject of his prayers.

Thus to the Philippians, " I thank my God upon every remembrance of you, always in every prayer of mine for you all, making request with joy " (Phil. i. 4, 5). Here we see not only a continual intercession, but performed with so much gladness as shows that it was an exercise of love in which he highly rejoiced.

His devotion had also the same care for particular persons, as appears by the following passage : " I thank my God, Whom I serve from my forefathers with a pure conscience, that without ceasing I have remembrance of thee in my prayers night and day " (2 St. Tim. i. 3). How holy an acquaintance and friendship was this, how worthy of persons that were raised above the world, and related to one another as new members of a kingdom of heaven !

Apostles and great saints did not only thus benefit and bless particular churches and private persons, but they themselves also received graces from God by the prayers of others. Thus saith St. Paul to the Corinthians, " You also helping together by prayer

CH. XXI. for us, that, for the gift bestowed upon us by the means of many persons, thanks may be given by many on our behalf" (2 Cor. i. 11).

This was the ancient friendship of Christians, uniting and cementing their hearts, not by worldly considerations or human passions, but by the mutual communication of spiritual blessings, by prayers and thanksgivings to God for one another.

It was this holy intercession that raised Christians to such a state of mutual love as far exceeded all that had been praised and admired in human friendship. And when the same spirit of intercession is again in the world, when Christianity has the same power over the hearts of people that it then had, this holy friendship will be again in fashion, and Christians will be again the wonder of the world for that exceeding love which they bear to one another.

For a frequent intercession with God, earnestly beseeching Him to forgive the sins of all mankind, to bless them with His providence, enlighten them with His Spirit, and bring them to everlasting happiness, is the divinest exercise that the heart of man can be engaged in.

Be daily, therefore, on your knees in a solemn, deliberate performance of this devotion, praying for others in such forms, with such length, importunity, and earnestness as you use for yourself; and you will find all little ill-natured passions die away, your heart grow great and generous, delighting in the common happiness of others as you used only to delight in your own.

For he that daily prays to God that all men may be happy in heaven takes the likeliest way to make him wish for and delight in their happiness on earth. And it is hardly possible for you to beseech and entreat God to make anyone happy in the highest enjoyments of His glory to all eternity, and yet be troubled to see him enjoy the much smaller gifts of God in this short and low state of human life.

For how strange and unnatural would it be to pray to God to grant health and a longer life to a sick man, and at the same time to envy him the poor pleasures of agreeable medicines?

Yet this would be no more strange or unnatural than to pray to God that your neighbour may enjoy the highest degrees of His mercy and favour, and yet at the same time envy him the little credit and figure he hath amongst his fellow-creatures.

When, therefore, you have once habituated your heart to a CH. XXI. serious performance of this holy intercession, you have done a great deal to render it incapable of spite and envy, and to make it naturally delight in the happiness of all mankind.

This is the natural effect of a general intercession for all mankind. But the greatest benefits of it are then received when it descends to such particular instances as our state and condition in life more particularly require of us.

Though we are to treat all mankind as neighbours and brethren, as any occasion offers, yet as we can only live in the actual society of a few, and are by our state and condition more particularly related to some than others, so when our intercession is made an exercise of love and care for those amongst whom our lot is fallen, or who belong to us in a nearer relation, it then becomes the greatest benefit to ourselves, and produces its best effects in our own hearts.

If, therefore, you should always change and alter your intercessions, according as the needs and necessities of your neighbours or acquaintance seem to require, beseeching God to deliver them from such or such particular evils, or to grant them this or that particular gift or blessing, such intercessions, besides the great charity of them, would have a mighty effect upon your own heart, as disposing you to every other good office, and to the exercise of every other virtue towards such persons as have so often a place in your prayers.

This would make it pleasant to you to be courteous, civil, and condescending to all about you, and make you unable to say or do a rude or hard thing to those for whom you had used yourself to be so kind and compassionate in your prayers.

For there is nothing that makes us love a man so much as praying for him; and when you can once do this sincerely for any man, you have fitted your soul for the performance of everything that is kind and civil towards him. This will fill your heart with a generosity and tenderness that will give you a better and sweeter behaviour than anything that is called fine breeding and good manners.

By considering yourself as an advocate with God for your neighbours and acquaintance, you would never find it hard to be at peace with them yourself. It would be easy to you to bear with, and forgive those, for whom you particularly implored the divine mercy and forgiveness.

Such prayers as these, amongst neighbours and acquaintance, would unite them to one another in the strongest bonds of love and tenderness. It would exalt and ennoble their souls, and teach them to consider one another in a higher state, as members of a spiritual society, that are created for the enjoyment of the common blessings of God, and fellow-heirs of the same future glory.

And by being thus desirous that every one should have their full share of the favours of God, they would not only be content but glad, to see one another happy in the little enjoyments of this transitory life.

These would be the natural effects of such an intercession amongst people of the same town or neighbourhood, or that were acquainted with one another's state and condition.

OURANIUS [1] is a holy priest, full of the spirit of the Gospel, watching, labouring, and praying for a poor country village. Every soul in it is as dear to him as himself, and he loves them all as he loves himself, because he prays for them all as often as he prays for himself.

If his whole life is one continual exercise of great zeal and labour, hardly ever satisfied with any degrees of care and watchfulness, it is because he has learned the great value of souls by so often appearing before God as an intercessor for them.

He never thinks he can love or do enough for his flock, because he never considers them in any other view than as so many persons that, by receiving the gifts and graces of God, are to become his hope, his joy, and his crown of rejoicing.

---

[1] Although the circumstances of William Law differed in some repects from those of Ouranius, he evidently drew the character from his own experience. As a nonjuror he never had the charge of 'a poor country village,' nor, except in his first brief curacy (about which there is much obscurity), any parochial charge at all. But the personal character of Ouranius is just what Law, who never wrote what he did not try to practise, strove to make his own. Like Ouranius, he seems to have had naturally 'a haughtiness in his temper,' and the *Serious Call* itself is sufficient to show that, if he had given way to it, he would have had 'a great contempt and disregard for all foolish and unreasonable people'—and he had a painfully keen eye for what was foolish and unreasonable; but, like Ouranius, 'he prayed away this spirit.' Like Ouranius, he was a scholar, and gave 'a close application to his studies,' which interested him quite as much as if he had 'writ notes upon Homer and Plautus'; but he made it a rule at King's Cliffe, when an applicant for relief (and their name was Legion) appeared, to attend to him immediately, no matter how busily he was engaged. Like Ouranius, 'he erected,' at King's Cliffe, 'a charitable retirement for ancient poor people'; and, like Ouranius, he certainly was 'exceeding studious of Christian perfection,' and strove to 'live according to the strictest rules of temperance, meekness, and humility.'

He goes about his parish and visits everybody in it, but visits in the same spirit of piety that he preaches to them. He visits them to encourage their virtues, to assist them with his advice and counsel, to discover their manner of life, and to know the state of their souls, that he may intercede with God for them, according to their particular necessities.

When Ouranius first entered into holy orders, he had a haughtiness in his temper, a great contempt and disregard for all foolish and unreasonable people; but he has prayed away this spirit, and has now the greatest tenderness for the most obstinate sinners, because he is always hoping that God will sooner or later hear those prayers that he makes for their repentance.

The rudeness, ill-nature, or perverse behaviour of any of his flock used at first to betray him into impatience, but now it raises no other passion in him than a desire of being upon his knees in prayer to God for them.

Thus have his prayers for others altered and amended the state of his own heart.

It would strangely delight you to see with what spirit he converses, with what tenderness he reproves, with what affection he exhorts, and with what vigour he preaches; and it is all owing to this, because he reproves, exhorts, and preaches to those for whom he first prays to God.

This devotion softens his heart, enlightens his mind, sweetens his temper, and makes everything that comes from him instructive, amiable, and affecting.

At his first coming to his little village it was as disagreeable to him as a prison, and every day seemed too tedious to be endured in so retired a place. He thought his parish was too full of poor and mean people, that were none of them fit for the conversation of a gentleman.

This put him upon a close application to his studies. He kept much at home, writ notes upon Homer and Plautus, and sometimes thought it hard to be called to pray by any poor body when he was just in the midst of one of Homer's battles.

This was his polite, or I may rather say poor, ignorant turn of mind before devotion had got the government of his heart.

But now his days are so far from being tedious, or his parish too great a retirement, that he now only wants more time to do that variety of good which his soul thirsts after. The solitude of his little parish is become matter of great comfort to him,

CH. XXI. because he hopes that God has placed him and his flock there to make it their way to heaven.

He can now not only converse with, but gladly attend and wait upon the poorest kind of people. He is now daily watching over the weak and infirm, humbling himself to perverse, rude, ignorant people wherever he can find them; and is so far from desiring to be considered as a gentleman, that he desires to be used as the servant of all, and in the spirit of his Lord and Master girds himself, and is glad to kneel down and wash any of their feet.

He now thinks the poorest creature in his parish good enough and great enough to deserve the humblest attendances, the kindest friendships, the tenderest offices he can possibly show them.

He is so far now from wanting agreeable company that he thinks there is no better conversation in the world than to be talking with poor and mean people about the kingdom of heaven.

All these noble thoughts and divine sentiments are the effects of his great devotion; he presents every one so often before God in his prayers that he never thinks he can esteem, reverence, or serve those enough for whom he implores so many mercies from God.

Ouranius is mightily affected with this passage of holy Scripture: "The effectual fervent prayer of a righteous man availeth much" (St. James v. 16).

This makes him practise all the arts of holy living, and aspire after every instance of piety and righteousness, that his prayers for his flock may have their full force, and avail much with God.

For this reason he has sold a small estate that he had, and has erected a charitable retirement for ancient poor people to live in prayer and piety, that his prayers, being assisted by such good works, may pierce the clouds, and bring down blessings upon those souls committed to his care.

Ouranius reads how God Himself said unto Abimelech concerning Abraham, "He is a prophet; he shall pray for thee, and thou shalt live" (Gen. xx. 7).

And again, how He said of Job, "And my servant Job shall pray for you; for him will I accept" (Job xlii. 8).

From these passages Ouranius justly concludes that the prayers of men eminent for holiness of life have an extraordinary power with God; that He grants to other people such pardons, reliefs, and blessings through their prayers as would not be granted to

men of less piety and perfection. This makes Ouranius exceeding CH. XXI.
studious of Christian perfection, searching after every grace and
holy temper, purifying his heart all manner of ways, fearful of every
error and defect in his life, lest his prayers for his flock should be
less availing with God through his own defects in holiness.

This makes him careful of every temper of his heart, give alms
of all that he hath, watch, and fast, and mortify, and live according
to the strictest rules of temperance, meekness, and humility, that
he may be in some degree like an Abraham or a Job in his parish,
and make such prayers for them as God will hear and accept.

These are the happy effects which a devout intercession hath
produced in the life of Ouranius.

And if other people in their several stations were to imitate
this example in such a manner as suited their particular state
of life, they would certainly find the same happy effects from it.

If masters, for instance, were thus to remember their servants in
their prayers, beseeching God to bless them, and suiting their
petitions to the particular wants and necessities of their servants,
letting no day pass without a full performance of this part of
devotion, the benefit would be as great to themselves as to their
servants.

No way so likely as this, to inspire them with a true sense of
that power which they have in their hands, to make them delight
in doing good, and becoming exemplary in all the parts of a wise
and good master.

The presenting their servants so often before God, as equally
related to God, and entitled to the same expectations of heaven
as themselves, would naturally incline them to treat them, not
only with such humanity as became fellow-creatures, but with
such tenderness, care, and generosity as became fellow-heirs of
the same glory. This devotion would make masters inclined to
everything that was good towards their servants, be watchful of
their behaviour, and as ready to require of them an exact observance of the duties of Christianity as of the duties of their
service.

This would teach them to consider their servants as God's
servants, to desire their perfection, to do nothing before them
that might corrupt their minds, to impose no business upon
them that should lessen their sense of religion, or hinder them
from their full share of devotion, both public and private. This
praying for them would make them as glad to see their servants

CH. XXI. eminent in piety as themselves, and contrive that they should have all the opportunities and encouragements, both to know and perform all the duties of the Christian life.

How natural would it be for such a master to perform every part of family devotion, to have constant prayers, to excuse no one's absence from them, to have the Scriptures and books of piety often read amongst his servants, to take all opportunities of instructing them, of raising their minds to God, and teaching them to do all their business as a service to God, and upon the hopes and expectations of another life?

How natural would it be for such a one to pity their weakness and ignorance, to bear with the dulness of their understandings, or the perverseness of their tempers, to reprove them with tenderness, exhort them with affection, as hoping that God would hear his prayers for them?

How impossible would it be for a master that thus interceded with God for his servants to use any unkind threatenings towards them, to damn and curse them as dogs and scoundrels, and treat them only as the dregs of the creation?

This devotion would give them another spirit, and make them consider how to make proper returns of care, kindness, and protection to those who had spent their strength and time in service and attendance upon them.

Now if gentlemen think it too low an employment for their state and dignity to exercise such a devotion as this for their servants, let them consider how far they are from the spirit of Christ, Who made Himself not only an intercessor but a sacrifice for the whole race of sinful mankind.

Let them consider how miserable their greatness would be if the Son of God should think it as much below Him to pray for them as they do to pray for their fellow-creatures.

Let them consider how far they are from that spirit, which prays for its most unjust enemies, if they have not kindness enough to pray for those by whose labours and service they live in ease themselves.

Again, if parents should thus make themselves advocates and intercessors with God for their children, constantly applying to heaven in behalf of them, nothing would be more likely, not only to bless their children, but also to form and dispose their own minds to the performance of everything that was excellent and praiseworthy.

I do not suppose but that the generality of parents remember CH. XXI. their children in their prayers, and call upon God to bless them. But the thing here intended is not a general remembrance of them, but a regular method of recommending all their particular needs and necessities unto God, and of praying for every such particular grace and virtue for them, as their state and condition of life shall seem to require.

The state of parents is a holy state, in some degrees like that of the priesthood, and calls upon them to bless their children with their prayers and sacrifices to God. Thus it was that holy Job watched over and blessed his children; he "sanctified them, he rose up early in the morning and offered burnt-offerings, according to the number of them all" (Job i. 5).

If parents, therefore, considering themselves in this light, should be daily calling upon God in a solemn, deliberate manner, altering and extending their intercessions as the state and growth of their children required, such devotion would have a mighty influence upon the rest of their lives; it would make them very circumspect in the government of themselves, prudent and careful of everything they said or did, lest their example should hinder that which they so constantly desired in their prayers.

If a father was daily making particular prayers to God that He would please to inspire his children with true piety, great humility, and strict temperance, what could be more likely to make the father himself become exemplary in these virtues? How naturally would he grow ashamed of wanting such virtues as he thought necessary for his children? So that his prayers for their piety would be a certain means of exalting his own to its greatest height.

If a father thus considered himself as an intercessor with God for his children, to bless them with his prayers, what more likely means to make him aspire after every degree of holiness, that he might thereby be fitter to obtain blessings from heaven for them? How would such thoughts make him avoid everything that was sinful and displeasing to God, lest when he prayed for his children God should reject his prayers?

How tenderly, how religiously would such a father converse with his children, whom he considered as his little spiritual flock, whose virtues he was to form by his example, encourage by his authority, nourish by his counsel, and prosper by his prayers to God for them.

How fearful would he be of all greedy and unjust ways of raising their fortune, of bringing them up in pride and indulgence, or of making them too fond of the world, lest he should thereby render them incapable of those graces which he was so often beseeching God to grant them?

These being the plain, natural, happy effects of this intercession, all parents, I hope, who have the real welfare of their children at heart, who desire to be their true friends and benefactors, and to live amongst them in the spirit of wisdom and piety, will not neglect so great a means, both of raising their own virtue and doing an eternal good to those who are so near and dear to them by the strongest ties of nature.

Lastly, if all people when they feel the first approaches of resentment, envy, or contempt towards others, or if in all little disagreements and misunderstandings whatever, they should, instead of indulging their minds with little low reflections, have recourse at such times to a more particular and extraordinary intercession with God for such persons as had raised their envy, resentment, or discontent; this would be a certain way to prevent the growth of all uncharitable tempers.

If you were also to form your prayer or intercession at that time to the greatest degree of contrariety to that temper which you were then in, it would be an excellent means of raising your heart to the greatest state of perfection.

As for instance, when at any time you find in your heart motions of envy towards any person, whether on account of his riches, power, reputation, learning, or advancement, if you should immediately betake yourself at that time to your prayers and pray to God to bless and prosper him in that very thing which raised your envy, if you should express and repeat your petitions in the strongest terms, beseeching God to grant him all the happiness from the enjoyment of it that can possibly be received, you would soon find it to be the best antidote in the world to expel the venom of that poisonous passion.

This would be such a triumph over yourself, would so humble and reduce your heart into obedience and order, that the devil would even be afraid of tempting you again in the same manner when he saw the temptation turned into so great a means of amending and reforming the state of your heart.

Again, if in any little difference or misunderstandings that you happen to have at any time with a relation, a neighbour, or anyone else, you should pray for them in a more extraordinary manner than you ever did before, beseeching God to give them every grace, and blessing, and happiness you can think of, you would have taken the speediest method that can be of reconciling all differences and clearing up all misunderstandings. You would then think nothing too great to be forgiven, stay for no condescensions, need no mediation of a third person, but be glad to testify your love and goodwill to him who had so high a place in your secret prayers.

This would be the mighty power of such Christian devotion; it would remove all peevish passions, soften your heart into the most tender condescensions, and be the best arbitrator of all differences that happened betwixt you and any of your acquaintance.

The greatest resentments amongst friends and neighbours most often arise from poor punctilios and little mistakes in conduct. A certain sign that their friendship is merely human, not founded upon religious considerations, or supported by such a course of mutual prayer for one another as the first Christians used.

For such devotion must necessarily either destroy such tempers or be itself destroyed by them.

You cannot possibly have any ill-temper or show any unkind behaviour to a man for whose welfare you are so much concerned as to be his advocate with God in private.

Hence we may learn the odious nature and exceeding guilt of spite, hatred, contempt, and angry passions. They are not to be considered as defects in good nature and sweetness of temper, not as failings in civility of manners or good breeding, but as such base tempers as are entirely inconsistent with the charity of intercession.

You think it a small matter to be peevish or ill-natured to such or such a man, but you should consider whether it be a small matter to do that which you could not do if you had but so much charity as to be able to recommend him to God in your prayers.

You think it a small matter to ridicule one man and despise another, but you should consider whether it be a small matter to want that charity towards these people which Christians are not allowed to want towards their most inveterate enemies.

For be but as charitable to these men, do but bless and pray for them, as you are obliged to bless and pray for your enemies, and then you will find that you have charity enough to make

CH. XXI. it impossible for you to treat them with any degree of scorn or contempt.

For you cannot possibly despise and ridicule that man whom your private prayers recommend to the love and favour of God.

When you despise and ridicule a man, it is with no other end but to make him ridiculous and contemptible in the eyes of other men, and in order to prevent their esteem of him. How, therefore, can it be possible for you sincerely to beseech God to bless that man with the honour of His love and favour whom you desire men to treat as worthy of their contempt?

Could you out of love to a neighbour desire your Prince to honour him with every mark of esteem and favour, and yet at the same time expose him to the scorn and derision of your own servants?

Yet this is as possible as to expose that man to the scorn and contempt of your fellow-creatures, whom you recommend to the favour of God in your secret prayers.

From these considerations we may plainly discover the reasonableness and justice of this doctrine of the Gospel, "Whosoever shall say unto his brother, Raca, shall be in danger of the council; but whosoever shall say, Thou fool, shall be in danger of hell fire" (St. Matt. v. 22).

We are not, I suppose, to believe that every hasty word or unreasonable expression that slips from us by chance or surprise, and is contrary to our intention and tempers, is the great sin here signified. But he that says Raca, or Thou fool, must chiefly mean him that allows himself in deliberate, designed acts of scorn and contempt towards his brother, and in that temper speaks to him and of him in reproachful language.[2]

Now since it appears that these tempers are at the bottom the most rank uncharitableness, since no one can be guilty of them, but because he has not charity enough to pray to God for his brother; it cannot be thought hard or rigorous justice that such tempers should endanger the salvation of Christians. For who would think it hard that a Christian cannot obtain the favour of God for himself unless he reverence and esteem his brother Christian as one that bears the image of God, as one for whom Christ died, as a member of Christ's body, as a

---

[2] Observe especially the explanation of a somewhat difficult text (St. Matt. v. 22) which follows.

member of that holy society on earth which is in union with that triumphant church in heaven?

Yet all these considerations must be forgot, all these glorious privileges disregarded, before a man can treat him that has them as an object of scorn and contempt.

So that to scorn or despise a brother, or, as our blessed Lord says, to call him Raca or fool, must be looked upon as amongst the most odious, unjust, and guilty tempers that can be supported in the heart of a Christian, and justly excluding him from all his hopes in the salvation of Jesus Christ.

For to despise one for whom Christ died is to be as contrary to Christ as he that despises anything that Christ has said or done.

If a Christian that had lived with the holy Virgin Mary should, after the death of our Lord, have taken any occasion to treat her with contempt, you would certainly say that he had lost his piety towards our blessed Lord. For a true reverence for Christ must have forced him to treat her with respect who was so nearly related to Him.[3]

I dare appeal to any man's mind whether it does not tell him that this relation of the Virgin Mary to our blessed Lord must have obliged all those that lived and conversed with her to treat her with great respect and esteem. Might not a man have justly dreaded the vengeance of God upon him for any scorn and contempt that he had shown to her?

Now if this be plain and obvious reasoning, if a contempt offered to the Virgin Mary must have been interpreted a contempt of Christ, because of her near relation to Him, then let the same reasoning show you the great impiety of despising any brother.

You cannot despise a brother without despising him that stands in a high relation to God, to His Son Jesus Christ, and to the Holy Trinity.

You would certainly think it a mighty impiety to treat a writing with great contempt that had been written by the finger of God, and can you think it a less impiety to contemn and vilify a brother who is not only the workmanship but the image of God?

---

[3] In the extreme recoil from Mariolatry, many seemed to forget that 'all generations should call her blessed.' Richard Cecil, an unexceptionable witness, for he was a leader of the Evangelicals, complains that "some do not treat the name of the Virgin Mary with common civility." (See Cecil's *Remains*, ed. by Josiah Pratt.)

You would justly think it a great profaneness to contemn and trample upon an Altar, because it was appropriated to holy uses, and had had the body of Christ so often placed upon it;[4] and can you suppose it to be less profaneness to scorn and trample upon a brother who so belongs to God that his very body is to be considered as the "temple of the Holy Ghost"? (1 Cor. vi. 15).

Had you despised and ill-treated the Virgin Mary, you had been chargeable with the impiety of despising her of whom Christ was born. And if you scorn and despise a brother, you are chargeable with the impiety of despising him for whom Christ laid down His life.

And now if this scornful temper is founded upon a disregard of all these relations which every Christian bears to God and Christ and the Holy Trinity, can you wonder or think it hard that a Christian who thus allows himself to despise a brother should be in danger of hell fire?

Secondly, It must here be observed that though in these words, "Whosoever shall say, Thou fool," etc., the great sin there condemned is an allowed temper of despising a brother; yet we are also to believe that all hasty expressions and words of contempt, though spoken by surprise or accident, are by this text condemned as great sins and notorious breaches of Christian charity.

They proceed from great want of Christian love and meekness, and call for great repentance. They are only little sins when compared with habits and settled tempers of treating a brother despitefully, and fall as directly under the condemnation of this text as the grossest habits of uncharitableness.

And the reason why we are always to apprehend great guilt, and call ourselves to a strict repentance for these hasty expressions of anger and contempt, is this: because they seldom are what they seem to be, that is, mere starts of temper that were occasioned purely by surprise or accident, but are much more our own proper acts than we generally imagine.

A man says a great many bitter things; he presently forgives himself, because he supposes it was only the suddenness of the occasion, or something accidental, that carried him so far beyond himself.

But he should consider that perhaps the accident or surprise

---

[4] This is a very outspoken expression of Law's belief in the Real Presence, and one which is rare in eighteenth century writers.

was not the occasion of his angry expressions, but might only CH. XXI. be the occasion of his angry temper showing itself.

Now as this is, generally speaking, the case; as all haughty angry language generally proceeds from some secret habits of pride in the heart; so people that are subject to it, though only now and then as accidents happen, have great reason to repent of more than their present behaviour, to charge themselves with greater guilt than accidental passion, and to bring themselves to such penance and mortification as is proper to destroy habits of a haughty spirit.

And this may be the reason why the text looks no farther than the outward language; why it only says, "Whosoever shall say, Thou fool"; because few can proceed so far as to the accidental use of haughty, disdainful language but they whose hearts are more or less possessed with habits and settled tempers of pride and haughtiness.

But to return: Intercession is not only the best arbitrator of all differences, the best promoter of true friendship, the best cure and preservative against all unkind tempers, all angry and haughty passions, but is also of great use to discover to us the true state of our own hearts.

There are many tempers which we think lawful and innocent, which we never suspect of any harm; which, if they were to be tried by this devotion, would soon show us how we have deceived ourselves.

SUSURRUS is a pious, temperate, good man, remarkable for abundance of excellent qualities. No one more constant at the service of the church, or whose heart is more affected with it. His charity is so great that he almost starves himself to be able to give greater alms to the poor.

Yet Susurrus had a prodigious failing along with these great virtues.

He had a mighty inclination to hear and discover all the defects and infirmities of all about him. You were welcome to tell him anything of anybody, provided that you did not do it in the style of an enemy. He never disliked an evil speaker but when his language was rough and passionate. If you would but whisper anything gently, though it was ever so bad in itself, Susurrus was ready to receive it.

When he visits, you generally hear him relating how sorry he is for the defects and failings of such a neighbour. He is

CH. XXI. always letting you know how tender he is of the reputation of his neighbour, how loath to say that which he is forced to say, and how gladly he would conceal it if it could be concealed.

Susurrus had such a tender, compassionate manner of relating things the most prejudicial to his neighbour that he even seemed, both to himself and others, to be exercising a Christian charity at the same time that he was indulging a whispering, evil-speaking temper.

Susurrus once whispered to a particular friend in great secrecy something too bad to be spoken of publicly. He ended with saying how glad he was that it had not yet took wind, and that he had some hopes it might not be true, though the suspicions were strong. His friend made him this reply:

You say, Susurrus, that you are glad it has not yet taken wind, and that you have some hopes it may not prove true. Go home, therefore, to your closet, and pray to God for this man in such a manner and with such earnestness as you would pray for yourself on the like occasion.

Beseech God to interpose in his favour, to save him from false accusers, and bring all those to shame who, by uncharitable whispers and secret stories, wound him like those that stab in the dark. And when you have made this prayer, then you may, if you please, go tell the same secret to some other friend that you have told to me.

Susurrus was exceedingly affected with this rebuke, and felt the force of it upon his conscience in as lively a manner as if he had seen the books opened at the day of judgment.

All other arguments might have been resisted, but it was impossible for Susurrus either to reject or to follow this advice without being equally self-condemned in the highest degree.

From that time to this he has constantly used himself to this method of intercession, and his heart is so entirely changed by it that he can now no more privately whisper anything to the prejudice of another than he can openly pray to God to do people hurt.

Whisperings and evil-speakings now hurt his ears like oaths and curses, and he has appointed one day in the week to be a day of penance as long as he lives to humble himself before God in the sorrowful confession of his former guilt.

It may well be wondered how a man of so much piety as Susurrus could be so long deceived in himself as to live in such a state of scandal and evil-speaking without suspecting CH. XXI. himself to be guilty of it. But it was the tenderness and seeming compassion with which he heard and related everything that deceived both himself and others.

This was a falseness of heart which was only to be fully discovered by the true charity of intercession.

And if people of virtue, who think little harm of themselves, as Susurrus did, were often to try their spirit by such an intercession, they would often find themselves to be such as they least of all suspected.

I have laid before you the many and great advantages of intercession. You have seen what a divine friendship it must needs beget amongst Christians, how dear it would render all relations and neighbours to one another; how it tends to make clergymen, masters, and parents exemplary and perfect in all the duties of their station; how certainly it destroys all envy, spite, and ill-natured passions; how speedily it reconciles all differences, and with what a piercing light it discovers to a man the true state of his heart.

These considerations will, I hope, persuade you to make such intercession as is proper for your state the constant, chief matter of your devotion at this hour of prayer.

# CHAPTER XXII.

*Recommending devotion at three o'clock, called in Scripture the ninth hour of the day. The subject of prayer at this hour is resignation to the divine pleasure. The nature and duty of conformity to the will of God in all our actions and designs.*

I HAVE recommended certain subjects to be made the fixed and chief matter of your devotions at all hours of prayer that have been already considered.

As thanksgiving and oblation of yourself to God at your first prayers in the morning; at nine, the great virtue of Christian humility is to be the chief part of your petition; at twelve, you are called upon to pray for all the graces of universal love, and to raise it in your heart by such general and particular intercessions as your own state and relation to other people seem more particularly to require of you.

At this hour of the afternoon you are desired to consider the necessity of resignation and conformity to the will of God, and to make this great virtue the principal matter of your prayers.

There is nothing wise, or holy, or just, but the great will of God. This is as strictly true in the most rigid sense as to say that nothing is infinite and eternal but God. No beings, therefore, whether in heaven or on earth, can be wise, or holy, or just, but so far as they conform to this will of God. It is conformity to this will that gives virtue and perfection to the highest services of angels in heaven; and it is conformity to the same will that makes the ordinary actions of men on earth become an acceptable service unto God.

The whole nature of virtue consists in conforming to, and the whole nature of vice in declining from, the will of God.[1]   All

---

[1] Law's great contemporary, Bishop Butler, asserts sweepingly that the whole of piety consists in resignation. (See Butler's *Analogy*, Pt. I.) And taking 'resignation' as synonymous with 'conformity to the will of God,' Law seems to agree with him by anticipation.

God's creatures are created to fulfil His will; the sun and CH. XXII.
moon obey His will by the necessity of their nature; angels
conform to His will by the perfection of their nature. If,
therefore, you would show yourself not to be a rebel and apostate
from the order of the creation, you must act like beings both
above and below you; it must be the great desire of your
soul that God's will may be done by you on earth as it is
done in heaven. It must be the settled purpose and intention
of your heart to will nothing, design nothing, do nothing, but
so far as you have reason to believe that it is the will of
God that you should so desire, design, and do.

'Tis as just and necessary to live in this state of heart, to
think thus of God and yourself, as to think that you have any
dependence upon Him. And it is as great a rebellion against
God to think that your will may ever differ from His as to think
that you have not received the power of willing for Him.

You are, therefore, to consider yourself as a being that has no
other business in the world but to be that which God requires you
to be; to have no tempers, no rules of your own, to seek no self-
designs or self-ends, but to fill some place and act some part in
strict conformity and thankful resignation to the divine pleasure.

To think that you are your own, or at your own disposal, is
as absurd as to think that you created and can preserve yourself.
It is as plain and necessary a first principle to believe you are
thus God's, that you thus belong to Him, and are to act and
suffer all in a thankful resignation to His pleasure, as to believe
that in Him you live, and move, and have your being.

Resignation to the divine will signifies a cheerful approbation
and thankful acceptance of everything that comes from God. It
is not enough patiently to submit, but we must thankfully receive
and fully approve of everything that by the order of God's providence happens to us.

For there is no reason why we should be patient, but what
is as good and strong a reason why we should be thankful.
If we were under the hands of a wise and good physician that
could not mistake or do anything to us but what certainly
tended to our benefit, it would not be enough to be patient
and abstain from murmuring against such a physician; but it
would be as great a breach of duty and gratitude to him not to
be pleased and thankful for what he did as it would be to murmur at him.

CH. XXII.    Now this is our true state with relation to God; we cannot
be said so much as to believe in Him unless we believe Him to
be of infinite wisdom.    Every argument, therefore, for patience
under His disposal of us is as strong an argument for approbation and thankfulness for everything that He does to us.
And there needs no more to dispose us to this gratitude towards
God than a full belief in Him that He is this Being of infinite
wisdom, love, and goodness.

Do but assent to this truth, in the same manner as you
assent to things of which you have no doubt, and then you will
cheerfully approve of everything that God has already approved
for you.

For as you cannot possibly be pleased with the behaviour of
any person towards you but because it is for your good, is
wise in itself, and the effect of his love and goodness towards
you; so when you are satisfied that God does not only do
that which is wise, and good, and kind, but that which is the
effect of an infinite wisdom and love in the care of you, it
will be as necessary, whilst you have this faith, to be thankful
and be pleased with everything which God chooses for you as
to wish your own happiness.

Whenever, therefore, you find yourself disposed to uneasiness
or murmuring at anything that is the effect of God's providence
over you, you must look upon yourself as denying either the
wisdom or goodness of God.    For every complaint necessarily
supposes this.    You would never complain of your neighbour,
but that you suppose you can show either his unwise, unjust,
or unkind behaviour towards you.

Now every murmuring, impatient reflection under the providence of God is the same accusation of God.    A complaint
always supposes ill usage.

Hence also you may see the great necessity and piety of this
thankful state of heart, because the want of it implies an accusation of God's want either of wisdom or goodness in His disposal
of us.    It is not, therefore, any high degree of perfection, founded
in any uncommon nicety of thinking or refined notions, but a
plain principle founded in this plain belief that God is a Being
of infinite wisdom and goodness.

Now this resignation to the divine will may be considered
in two respects.    First, As it signifies a thankful approbation
of God's general providence over the world; Secondly, As it

signifies a thankful acceptance of His particular providence CH. XXII.
over us.

First, Every man is by the law of his creation, by the first article
of his creed, obliged to consent to and acknowledge the wisdom
and goodness of God in His general providence over the whole
world. He is to believe that it is the effect of God's great wisdom
and goodness that the world itself was formed at such a particular
time and in such a manner; that the general order of nature, the
whole frame of things, is contrived and formed in the best manner.
He is to believe that God's providence over states and kingdoms,
times and seasons, is all for the best; that the revolutions
of state and changes of empire, the rise and fall of monarchies,
persecutions, wars, famines, and plagues are all permitted and
conducted by God's providence to the general good of man in
this state of trial.

A good man is to believe all this with the same fulness of
assent as he believes that God is in every place, though he
neither sees nor can comprehend the manner of His presence.

This is a noble magnificence of thought, a true religious
greatness of mind, to be thus affected with God's general providence, admiring and magnifying His wisdom in all things, never
murmuring at the course of the world, or the state of things, but
looking upon all around, at heaven and earth, as a pleased
spectator, and adoring that invisible hand which gives laws to
all motions and overrules all events to ends suitable to the
highest wisdom and goodness.

It is very common for people to allow themselves great liberty
in finding fault with such things as have only God for their
cause.

Everyone thinks he may justly say what a wretched, abominable climate he lives in. This man is frequently telling you what
a dismal, cursed day it is, and what intolerable seasons we have.
Another thinks he has very little to thank God for, that it is hardly
worth his while to live in a world so full of changes and revolutions. But these are tempers of great impiety, and show that
religion has not yet its seat in the heart of those that have
them.

It sounds indeed much better to murmur at the course of the
world, or the state of things, than to murmur at providence, to
complain of the seasons and weather than to complain of God;
but if these have no other cause but God and His providence, it

CH. XXII. is a poor distinction to say that you are only angry at the things, but not at the cause and director of them.[2]

How sacred the whole frame of the world is, how all things are to be considered as God's and referred to Him, is fully taught by our blessed Lord in the case of oaths : " But I say unto you, swear not at all ; neither by heaven, for it is God's throne; nor by the earth, for it is His footstool; neither by Jerusalem, for it is the city of the great king ; neither shalt thou swear by thy head, because thou canst not make one hair white or black " (St. Matt. v. 34-36) ; that is, because the whiteness or blackness of thy hair is not thine, but God's.

Here you see all things in the whole order of nature, from the highest heavens to the smallest hair, are always to be considered, not separately as they are in themselves, but as in some relation to God. And if this be good reasoning, thou shalt not swear by the earth, a city, or thy hair, because these things are God's, and in a certain manner belong to Him ; is it not exactly the same reasoning to say, Thou shalt not murmur at the seasons of the earth, the states of cities, and the change of times, because all these things are in the hands of God, have Him for their author, are directed and governed by Him to such ends as are most suitable to His wise providence ?

If you think you can murmur at the state of things without murmuring at providence, or complain of seasons without complaining of God, hear what our blessed Lord says farther upon oaths : " Whoso shall swear by the altar, sweareth by it, and by all things thereon ; and whoso shall swear by the temple, sweareth by Him that dwelleth therein : and he that shall swear by heaven, sweareth by the throne of God, and by Him that sitteth thereon " (St. Matt. xxiii. 20-22).

Now does not this Scripture plainly oblige us to reason after this manner : Whoso murmurs at the course of the world, murmurs at God that governs the course of the world. Whoso repines at seasons and weather, and speaks impatiently of times and events, repines and speaketh impatiently of God, Who is the sole Lord and Governor of times, seasons and events.

As, therefore, when we think of God Himself, we are to have no sentiments but of praise and thanksgiving ; so when we look

---

[2] It is supposed to be an Englishman's privilege to grumble at the weather, but it is hard for a Christian to find a flaw in Law's argument, that to murmur at the seasons is to murmur at Him Who orders the seasons.

at those things which are under the direction of God, and governed by His providence, we are to receive them with the same temper of praise and gratitude. And though we are not to think all things right, and just, and lawful which the providence of God permits; for then nothing could be unjust, because nothing is without His permission: yet we must adore God in the greatest public calamities, the most grievous persecutions, as things that are suffered by God, like plagues and famines, for ends suitable to His wisdom and glory in the government of the world.

There is nothing more suitable to the piety of a reasonable creature, or the spirit of a Christian, than thus to approve, admire, and glorify God in all the acts of His general providence, considering the whole world as His particular family, and all events as directed by His wisdom.

Everyone seems to consent to this as an undeniable truth, "That all things must be as God pleases"; and is not this enough to make every man pleased with them himself? And how can a man be a peevish complainer of anything that is the effect of providence but by showing that his own self-will and self-wisdom is of more weight with him than the will and wisdom of God? And what can religion be said to have done for a man whose heart is in this state?

For if he cannot thank and praise God as well in calamities and sufferings as in prosperity and happiness, he is as far from the piety of a Christian as he that only loves them that love him is from the charity of a Christian. For to thank God only for such things as you like is no more a proper act of piety than to believe only what you see is an act of faith.[3]

Resignation and thanksgiving to God are only acts of piety when they are acts of faith, trust, and confidence in divine goodness.

The faith of Abraham was an act of true piety, because it stopped at no difficulties, was not altered or lessened by any human appearances. It first of all carried him against all show of happiness from his own kindred and country into a strange land, not knowing whither he went. It afterwards made him, against all appearance of nature, when his "body was dead,

---

[3] Two strong arguments for Christian thankfulness under trouble. There is nothing essentially Christian in loving those who love you, and in believing what you see; and by parity of reasoning, there is nothing essentially Christian in being thankful for what you like.

CH. XXII. when he was about an hundred years old," depend upon the promise of God, "being fully persuaded that what God had promised, He was able to perform." It was this same faith that against so many pleas of nature, so many appearances of reason, prevailed upon him to "offer up Isaac—accounting that God was able to raise him up from the dead" (Heb. xi. 17, 19).

Now this faith is the true pattern of Christian resignation to the divine pleasure; you are to thank and praise God, not only for things agreeable to you, that have the appearance of happiness and comfort, but when you are like Abraham, called from all appearance of comfort to be a pilgrim in a strange land, to part with an only son, being as fully persuaded of the divine goodness in all things that happen to you as Abraham was of the divine promise, when there was the least appearance of its being performed.

This is true Christian resignation to God, which requires no more to the support of it than such a plain assurance of the goodness of God as Abraham had of His veracity. And if you ask yourself what greater reason Abraham had to depend upon the divine veracity than you have to depend upon the divine goodness, you will find that none can be given.

You cannot, therefore, look upon this as an unnecessary, high pitch of perfection, since the want of it implies the want, not of any high notions, but of a plain and ordinary faith in the most certain doctrines, both of natural and revealed religion.

Thus much concerning resignation to the divine will, as it signifies a thankful approbation of God's general providence. It is now to be considered, as it signifies a thankful acceptance of God's particular providence over us.

Every man is to consider himself as a particular object of God's providence; under the same care and protection of God as if the world had been made for him alone. It is not by chance that any man is born at such a time, of such parents, and in such a place and condition. It is as certain that every soul comes into the body at such a time and in such circumstances by the express designment of God, according to some purposes of His will, and for some particular ends; this is as certain as that it is by the express designment of God that some beings are angels and others are men.

It is as much by the counsel and eternal purpose of God that you should be born in your particular state, and that Isaac should be the son of Abraham, as that Gabriel should be an CH. XXII. angel and Isaac a man.

The Scriptures assure us that it was by divine appointment that our blessed Saviour was born at Bethlehem, and at such a time. Now although it was owing to the dignity of His person and the great importance of His birth that thus much of the divine counsel was declared to the world concerning the time and manner of it, yet we are as sure from the same Scriptures that the time and manner of every man's coming into the world is according to some eternal purpose and direction of divine providence, and in such time, and place, and circumstances as are directed and governed by God, for particular ends of His wisdom and goodness.

This we are as certain of from plain revelation as we can be of anything. For if we are told that not a "sparrow falleth to the ground without our heavenly Father," can anything more strongly teach us that much greater beings, such as human souls, come not into the world without the care and the direction of our heavenly Father? If it is said, "the very hairs of your head are all numbered," is it not to teach us that nothing, not the smallest things imaginable, happen to us by chance? But if the smallest things we can conceive are declared to be under the divine direction, need we, or can we be, more plainly taught that the greatest things of life, such as the manner of our coming into the world, our parents, the time, and other circumstances of our birth and condition, are all according to the eternal purposes, direction, and appointment of divine providence?

When the disciples put this question to our blessed Lord concerning the blind man, saying, "Master, who did sin, this man, or his parents, that he was born blind?" He that was the eternal wisdom of God made this answer, "Neither hath this man sinned, nor his parents; but that the works of God should be made manifest in him" (St. John ix. 3, 7); plainly declaring that the particular circumstances of every man's birth, the body that he receives, and the condition and state of life into which he is born, are appointed by a secret providence, which directs all things to their particular times, and seasons, and manner of existence, that the wisdom and works of God may be made manifest in them all.

As, therefore, it is thus certain that we are what we are, as to birth, time, and condition of entering into the world; since all that is particular in our state is the effect of God's particular providence over us, and intended for some particular ends both of His glory and our own happiness; we are, by the greatest obligations of gratitude, called upon to conform and resign our will to the will of God in all these respects, thankfully approving and accepting everything that is particular in our state; praising and glorifying His name for our birth of such parents, and in such circumstances of state and condition; being fully assured that it was for some reasons of infinite wisdom and goodness that we were so born into such particular states of life.

If the man above-mentioned was born blind, that the works of God might be manifested in him, had he not great reason to praise God for appointing him in such a particular manner to be the instrument of His glory? And if one person is born here and another there, if one falls amongst riches and another into poverty, if one receives his flesh and blood from these parents and another from those, for as particular ends as the man was born blind; have not all people the greatest reason to bless God, and to be thankful for their particular state and condition, because all that is particular in it is as directly intended for the glory of God and their own good as the particular blindness of that man who was so born, that "the works of God might be manifested in him"?

How noble an idea does this give us of the divine Omniscience presiding over the whole world, and governing such a long chain and combination of seeming accidents and chances to the common and particular advantage of all beings! So that all persons, in such a wonderful variety of causes, accidents, and events, should all fall into such particular states, as were foreseen, and foreordained to their best advantage, and so as to be most serviceable to the wise and glorious ends of God's government of all the world.

Had you been anything else than what you are, you had, all things considered, been less wisely provided for than you are now; you had wanted some circumstances and conditions that are best fitted to make you happy yourself and serviceable to the glory of God.

Could you see all that which God sees, all that happy chain of causes and motives which are to move and invite you to a right course of life, you would see something to make you like that state you are in as fitter for you than any other.

But as you cannot see this, so it is here that your Christian CH. XXII. faith and trust in God is to exercise itself, and render you as grateful and thankful for the happiness of your state as if you saw everything that contributes to it with your own eyes.

But now if this is the case of every man in the world thus blessed with some particular state that is most convenient for him, how reasonable is it for every man to will that which God has already willed for him; and by a pious faith and trust in the divine goodness thankfully adore and magnify that wise providence which he is sure has made the best choice for him of those things which he could not choose for himself.

Every uneasiness at our own state is founded upon comparing it with that of other people. Which is full as unreasonable as if a man in a dropsy should be angry at those that prescribe different things to him from those which are prescribed to people in health. For all the different states of life are like the different states of diseases; what is a remedy to one man in his state, may be poison to another.

So that to murmur because you are not as some others are is as if a man in one disease should murmur that he is not treated like him that is in another. Whereas if he were to have his will, he would be killed by that which will prove the cure of another.

It is just thus in the various conditions of life; if you give yourself up to uneasiness, or complain at anything in your state, you may, for aught you know, be so ungrateful to God as to murmur at that very thing which is to prove the cause of your salvation.

Had you it in your power to get that which you think is so grievous to want, it might perhaps be that very thing which of all others would most expose you to eternal damnation.

So that whether we consider the infinite goodness of God, that cannot choose amiss for us, or our own great ignorance of what is most advantageous to us, there can be nothing so reasonable and pious as to have no will but that of God's, and desire nothing for ourselves, in our persons, our state, and condition, but that which the good providence of God appoints us.

Farther, as the good providence of God thus introduces us into the world, into such states and conditions of life as are most convenient for us, so the same unerring wisdom orders all events and changes in the whole course of our lives, in

CH. XXII. such a manner, as to render them the fittest means to exercise and improve our virtue.

Nothing hurts us, nothing destroys us, but the ill use of that liberty with which God has entrusted us.

We are as sure that nothing happens to us by chance as that the world itself was not made by chance; we are as certain that all things happen and work together for our good as that God is goodness itself. So that a man has as much reason to will everything that happens to him because God wills it as to think that is wisest which is directed by infinite wisdom.

This is not cheating or soothing ourselves into any false content or imaginary happiness, but is a satisfaction grounded upon as great a certainty as the being and attributes of God.

For if we are right in believing God to act over us with infinite wisdom and goodness, we cannot carry our notions of conformity and resignation to the divine will too high; nor can we ever be deceived by thinking that to be best for us which God has brought upon us.

For the providence of God is not more concerned in the government of night and day and the variety of seasons than in the common course of events that seem most to depend upon the mere wills of men. So that it is as strictly right to look upon all worldly accidents and changes, all the various turns and alterations in your own life, to be as truly the effects of divine providence as the rising and setting of the sun, or the alterations of the seasons of the year. As you are, therefore, always to adore the wisdom of God in the direction of these things, so it is the same reasonable duty always to magnify God as an equal director of everything that happens to you in the course of your own life.

This holy resignation and conformity of your will to the will of God, being so much the true state of piety, I hope you will think it proper to make this hour of prayer a constant season of applying to God for so great a gift; that by thus constantly praying for it, your heart may be habitually disposed towards it, and always in a state of readiness to look at everything as God's, and to consider Him in everything; that so everything that befalls you may be received in the spirit of piety, and made a means of exercising some virtue.

There is nothing that so powerfully governs the heart, that so strongly excites us to wise and reasonable actions, as a true

sense of God's presence. But as we cannot see or apprehend CH. XXII.
the essence of God, so nothing will so constantly keep us
under a lively sense of the presence of God as this holy resignation, which attributes everything to Him and receives everything
as from Him.

Could we see a miracle from God, how would our thoughts
be affected with a holy awe and veneration of His presence!
But if we consider everything as God's doing, either by order
or permission, we shall then be affected with common things as
they would be who saw a miracle.

For as there is nothing to affect you in a miracle, but as it
is the action of God and bespeaks His presence; so when you
consider God as acting in all things and all events, then all
things will become venerable to you like miracles, and fill you
with the same awful sentiments of the divine presence.

Now you must not reserve the exercise of this pious temper
to any particular times or occasions, or fancy how resigned
you will be to God if such or such trials should happen. For
this is amusing yourself with the notion or idea of resignation,
instead of the virtue itself.

Do not, therefore, please yourself with thinking how piously
you would act and submit to God in a plague, a famine, or
persecution, but be intent upon the perfection of the present
day; and be assured that the best way of showing a true zeal
is to make little things the occasions of great piety.

Begin, therefore, in the smallest matters and most ordinary
occasions, and accustom your mind to the daily exercise of this
pious temper in the lowest occurrences of life. And when a
contempt, an affront, a little injury, loss or disappointment, or
the smallest events of every day, continually raise your mind to
God in proper acts of resignation, then you may justly hope
that you shall be numbered amongst those that are resigned and
thankful to God in the greatest trials and afflictions.

# CHAPTER XXIII.

*Of evening prayer. Of the nature and necessity of examination. How we are to be particular in the confession of all our sins. How we are to fill our minds with a just horror and dread of all sin.*

CH. XXIII. I AM now come to six o'clock in the evening, which, according to the Scripture account, is called the twelfth or last hour of the day. This is a time so proper for devotion that I suppose nothing need be said to recommend it as a season of prayer to all people that profess any regard to piety.

As the labour and action of every state of life is generally over at this hour, so this is the proper time for everyone to call himself to account, and review all his behaviour from the first action of the day.[1] The necessity of this examination is founded upon the necessity of repentance. For if it be necessary to repent of all our sins, if the guilt of unrepented sins still continue upon us, then it is necessary, not only that our sins, but the particular circumstances and aggravations of them, be known and recollected, and brought to repentance.

The Scripture saith, "If we confess our sins, He is faithful and just to forgive us our sins, and to cleanse us from all unrighteousness" (1 St. John i. 9); which is as much as to say, that then only our sins are forgiven, and we cleansed from the guilt and unrighteousness of them, when they are thus confessed and repented of.

There seems, therefore, to be the greatest necessity that all our daily actions be constantly observed, and brought to account, lest by a negligence we load ourselves with the guilt of unrepented sins.

---

[1] It must be remembered that hours were much earlier in Law's time than they are now. The dimness of artificial light, before the use of gas was known, would make evening work, during at least half the year, exceedingly inconvenient.

This examination, therefore, of ourselves every evening is not only to be considered as a commendable rule, and fit for a wise man to observe, but as something that is as necessary as a daily confession and repentance of our sins; because this daily repentance is of very little significancy, and loses all its chief benefit, unless it be a particular confession and repentance of the sins of that day. This examination is necessary to repentance in the same manner as time is necessary; you cannot repent, or express your sorrow, unless you allow some time for it; nor can you repent, but so far as you know what it is that you are repenting of. So that, when it is said that it is necessary to examine and call your actions to account, it is only saying that it is necessary to know what and how many things you are to repent of.

You, perhaps, have hitherto only used yourself to confess yourself a sinner in general, and asked forgiveness in the gross, without any particular remembrance or contrition for the particular sins of that day. And by this practice you are brought to believe that the same short, general form of confession of sin in general is a sufficient repentance for every day.

Suppose another person should hold that a confession of our sins in general once at the end of every week was sufficient; and that it was as well to confess the sins of seven days altogether as to have a particular repentance at the end of every day.

I know you sufficiently see the unreasonableness and impiety of this opinion, and that you think it is easy enough to show the danger and folly of it.

Yet you cannot bring one argument against such an opinion but what will be as good an argument against such a daily repentance as does not call the particular sins of that day to a strict account.

For as you can bring no express text of Scripture against such an opinion, but must take all your arguments from the nature of repentance and the necessity of a particular repentance for particular sins, so every argument of that kind must as fully prove the necessity of being very particular in our repentance of the sins of every day. Since nothing can be justly said against leaving the sins of the whole week to be repented for in the gross, but what may as justly be said against a daily repentance which considers the sins of that day only in the gross.

CH. XXIII.    Would you tell such a man that a daily confession was necessary to keep up an abhorrence of sin, that the mind would grow hardened and senseless of the guilt of sin without it? And is not this as good a reason for requiring that your daily repentance be very express and particular for your daily sins? For if confession is to raise an abhorrence of sin, surely that confession which considers and lays open your particular sins, that brings them to light with all their circumstances and aggravations, that requires a particular sorrowful acknowledgment of every sin, must in a much greater degree fill the mind with an abhorrence of sin than that which only, in one and the same form of words, confesses you only to be a sinner in general. For as this is nothing but what the greatest saint may justly say of himself, so the daily repeating of only such a confession has nothing in it to make you truly ashamed of your own way of life.

Again, must you not tell such a man that by leaving himself to such a weekly, general confession, he would be in great danger of forgetting a great many of his sins? But is there any sense or force in this argument, unless you suppose that our sins are all to be remembered, and brought to a particular repentance? And is it not necessary that our particular sins be not forgotten, but particularly remembered in our daily, as in a repentance at any other time?

So that every argument for a daily confession and repentance is the same argument for the confession and repentance of the particular sins of every day.

Because daily confession has no other reason or necessity but our daily sins; and, therefore, is nothing of what it should be, but so far as it is a repentance and sorrowful acknowledgment of the sins of the day.

You would, I suppose, think yourself chargeable with great impiety if you were to go to bed without confessing yourself to be a sinner and asking pardon of God; you would not think it sufficient that you did so yesterday. And yet if, without any regard to the present day, you only repeat the same form of words that you used yesterday, the sins of the present day may justly be looked upon to have had no repentance. For if the sins of the present day require a new confession, it must be such a new confession as is proper to itself. For it is the state and condition of every day that is to determine the state and manner of your repentance in the evening; otherwise the same general form of

words is rather an empty formality that has the appearance of a CH. XXIII.
duty than such a true performance of it as is necessary to make
it truly useful to you.

Let it be supposed that on a certain day you have been guilty
of these sins; that you have told a vain lie upon yourself, ascribing
something falsely to yourself through pride; that you have been
guilty of detraction, and indulged yourself in some degree of
intemperance. Let it be supposed that on the next day you
have lived in a contrary manner; that you have neglected no
duty of devotion, and been the rest of the day innocently employed in your proper business. Let it be supposed that on
the evening of both these days you only use the same confession
in general, considering it rather as a duty that is to be performed
every night, than as a repentance that is to be suited to the
particular state of the day.

Can it with any reason be said that each day has had its proper
repentance? Is it not as good sense to say there is no difference
in the guilt of these days as to say that there need be no different
repentance at the end of them? Or how can each of them have
its proper repentance, but by its having a repentance as large,
and extensive, and particular as the guilt of each day.

Again, let it be supposed that in that day when you had been
guilty of the three notorious sins above-mentioned, that in your
evening repentance you had only called one of them to mind;
is it not plain that the other two are unrepented of, and that
therefore their guilt still abides upon you? So that you are
then in the state of him who commits himself to the night
without the repentance for such a day as had betrayed him
into two such great sins.

Now these are not needless particulars, or such scrupulous
niceties as a man need not trouble himself about, but are such
plain truths as essentially concern the very life of piety. For
if repentance is necessary, it is full as necessary that it be
rightly performed, and in due manner.

And I have entered into all these particulars, only to show
you in the plainest manner that examination and a careful review
of all the actions of the day is not only to be looked upon as
a good rule, but as something as necessary as repentance itself.

If a man is to account for his expenses at night, can it be
thought a needless exactness in him to take notice of every
particular expense in the day?

CH. XXIII.  And if a man is to repent of his sins at night, can it be
thought too great a piece of scrupulosity in him to know and
call to mind what sins he is to repent of? [2]

Farther, though it should be granted that a confession in
general be a sufficient repentance for the end of such days as
have only the unavoidable frailties of our nature to lament, yet
even this fully proves the absolute necessity of this self-examination;
for without this examination, who can know that he has gone
through any day in this manner?

Again, an evening repentance, which thus brings all the actions
of the day to account, is not only necessary to wipe off the
guilt of sin, but is also the most certain way to amend and
perfect our lives.

For it is only such a repentance as this that touches the
heart, awakens the conscience, and leaves a horror and detes-
tation of sin upon the mind.

For instance, if it should happen that upon any particular
evening, all that you could charge yourself with should be this,
viz., a hasty, negligent performance of your devotions, or too
much time spent in an impertinent conversation; if the unreasonableness of these things were fully reflected upon and acknowledged; if you were then to condemn yourself before God for
them, and implore His pardon and assisting grace, what could
be so likely a means to prevent your falling into the same
faults the next day?

Or if you should fall into them again the next day; yet if
they were again brought to the same examination and condemnation in the presence of God, their happening again would
be such a proof to you of your own folly and weakness, would
cause such a pain and remorse in your mind, and fill you with
such shame and confusion at yourself, as would in all probability make you exceedingly desirous of greater perfection.

Now in the case of repeated sins, this would be the certain
benefit that we should receive from this examination and confession; the mind would thereby be made humble, full of sorrow and
deep compunction, and by degrees forced into amendment.

Whereas a formal, general confession that is only considered
as an evening duty, that overlooks the particular mistakes of the

[2] Observe this strong, common-
sense argument. You cannot make
up your daily accounts without taking
notice of every particular expense of
the day, and so you cannot make
up your accounts with God without
taking note of every particular sin of
the day.

day, and is the same whether the day be spent ill or well, has CH. XXIII. little or no effect upon the mind; a man may use such a daily confession and yet go on sinning and confessing all his life without any remorse of mind or true desire of amendment.

For if your own particular sins are left out of your confession, your confessing of sin in general has no more effect upon your mind than if you had only confessed that all men in general are sinners. And there is nothing in any confession to show that it is yours, but so far as it is a self-accusation, not of sin in general, or such as is common to all others, but of such particular sins as are your own proper shame and reproach.

No other confession, but such as thus discovers and accuses your own particular guilt, can be an act of true sorrow or real concern at your own condition. And a confession that is without this sorrow and compunction of heart has nothing in it either to atone for past sins, or to produce in us any true reformation and amendment of life.

To proceed: in order to make this examination still farther beneficial, every man should oblige himself to a certain method in it. As every man has something particular in his nature, stronger inclinations to some vices than others, some infirmities that stick closer to him, and are harder to be conquered than others; and as it is as easy for every man to know this of himself as to know whom he likes or dislikes; so it is highly necessary that these particularities of our natures and tempers should never escape a severe trial at our evening repentance: I say a severe trial, because nothing but a rigorous severity against these natural tempers is sufficient to conquer them.

They are the right eyes that are not to be spared, but to be plucked out and cast from us. For as they are the infirmities of nature, so they have the strength of nature,[3] and must be treated with great opposition, or they will soon be too strong for us.

He, therefore, who knows himself most of all subject to anger and passion, must be very exact and constant in his examination of this temper every evening. He must find out every slip that he has made of that kind, whether in thought, or word, or action; he must shame, and reproach, and accuse

[3] Observe how ingeniously Law turns the argument used by so many in excuse of their sins, that they are the infirmities of nature. If they are the infirmities of nature, they have the strength of nature, and must be resisted all the more strongly on that account.

CH. XXIII. himself before God, for everything that he has said or done in obedience to his passion. He must no more allow himself to forget the examination of this temper than to forget his whole prayers.

Again : if you find that vanity is your prevailing temper, that is always putting you upon the adornment of your person, and catching after everything that compliments or flatters your abilities, never spare or forget this temper in your evening examination, but confess to God every vanity of thought, or word, or action that you have been guilty of, and put yourself to all the shame and confusion for it that you can.

In this manner should all people act with regard to their chief frailty, to which their nature most inclines them. And though it should not immediately do all that they would wish, yet by a constant practice it would certainly in a short time produce its desired effect.

Farther : as all states and employments of life have their particular dangers and temptations, and expose people more to some sins than others, so every man that wishes his own improvement should make it a necessary part of his evening examination to consider how he has avoided or fallen into such sins as are most common to his state of life.

For as our business and condition of life has great power over us, so nothing but such watchfulness as this can secure us from those temptations to which it daily exposes us.

The poor man, from his condition of life, is always in danger of repining and uneasiness ; the rich man is most exposed to sensuality and indulgence ; the tradesman to lying and unreasonable gains ; the scholar to pride and vanity ; so that in every state of life a man should always, in his examination of himself, have a strict eye upon those faults to which his state of life most of all exposes him.

Again : as it is reasonable to suppose that every good man has entered into, or at least proposed to himself, some method of holy living, and set himself some such rules to observe as are not common to other people, and only known to himself ; so it should be a constant part of his night recollection to examine how and in what degree he has observed them, and to reproach himself before God for every neglect of them.

By rules I here mean, such rules as relate to the well-ordering of our time and the business of our common life ; such rules

as prescribe a certain order to all that we are to do, our busi- CH. XXIII.
ness, devotion, mortifications, readings, retirements, conversation,
meals, refreshments, sleep, and the like.

Now as good rules relating to all these things are certain
means of great improvement, and such as all serious Christians
must needs propose to themselves, so they will hardly ever
be observed to any purpose unless they are made the constant
subject of our evening examination.

Lastly, You are not to content yourself with a hasty general
review of the day, but you must enter upon it with deliberation;
begin with the first action of the day, and proceed step by step
through every particular matter that you have been concerned
in, and so let no time, place, or action be overlooked.

An examination thus managed will in a little time make
you as different from yourself as a wise man is different from
an idiot. It will give you such a newness of mind, such a spirit
of wisdom and desire of perfection, as you were an entire stranger
to before.

Thus much concerning the evening examination.

I proceed now to lay before you such considerations as may
fill your mind with a just dread and horror of all sin, and help
you to confess your own in the most passionate[4] contrition and
sorrow of heart.

Consider first, how odious all sin is to God, what a mighty
baseness it is, and how abominable it renders sinners in the
sight of God. That it is sin alone that makes the difference
betwixt an angel and the devil; and that every sinner is, so
far as he sins, a friend of the devil's, and carrying on his work
against God. That sin is a greater blemish and defilement of
the soul than any filth or disease is a defilement of the body.
And to be content to live in sin is a much greater baseness
than to desire to wallow in the mire, or love any bodily impurity.

Consider how you must abhor a creature that delighted in
nothing but filth and nastiness, that hated everything that was
decent and clean; and let this teach you to apprehend how
odious that soul that delights in nothing but the impurity of
sin must appear unto God.

For all sins, whether of sensuality, pride, or falseness, or any
other irregular passion, are nothing else but the filth and impure

---

[4] 'Passionate' is here used in its primary sense of 'causing or expressing
great commotion of mind' (Johnson).

CH. XXIII. diseases of the rational soul. And all righteousness is nothing else but the purity, the decency, the beauty, and perfection of that spirit which is made in the image of God.

Again, learn what horror you ought to have for the guilt of sin from the greatness of that atonement which has been made for it.

God made the world by the breath of His mouth, by a word speaking, but the redemption of the world has been a work of longer labour.[5]

How easily God can create beings, we learn from the first chapter of Genesis; but how difficult it is for infinite mercy to forgive sins, we learn from that costly atonement, those bloody sacrifices, those pains and penances, those sicknesses and deaths, which all must be undergone before the guilty sinner is fit to appear in the presence of God.

Ponder these great truths: that the Son of God was forced to become man, to be partaker of all our infirmities, to undergo a poor, painful, miserable, and contemptible life, to be persecuted, hated, and at last nailed to a cross, that by such sufferings He might render God propitious to that nature in which He suffered.

That all the bloody sacrifices and atonements of the Jewish law were to represent the necessity of this great sacrifice, and the great displeasure God bore to sinners.

That the world is still under the curse of sin, and certain marks of God's displeasure at it; such as famines, plagues, tempests, sickness, diseases and death.

Consider that all the sons of Adam are to go through a painful, sickly life, denying and mortifying their natural appetites, and crucifying the lusts of the flesh, in order to have a share in the atonement of our Saviour's death.

That all their penances and self-denials, all their tears and repentance, are only made available by that great intercession which is still making for them at the right hand of God.

Consider these great truths; that this mysterious redemption, all these sacrifices and sufferings, both of God and man, are only to remove the guilt of sin; and then let this teach you with what tears and contritions you ought to purge yourself from it.

After this general consideration of the guilt of sin which has

[5] Archbishop Trench sees in the fact that the first Paradise is represented as a garden, the second as a city, an illustration of the point on which Law here insists. A garden implies natural growth; a city, great labour and time in its construction.

done so much mischief to your nature, and exposed it to so CH. XXIII. great punishment, and made it so odious to God, that nothing less than so great an atonement of the Son of God, and so great repentance of our own, can restore us to the divine favour.

Consider next your own particular share in the guilt of sin. And if you would know with what zeal you ought to repent yourself, consider how you would exhort another sinner to repentance; and what repentance and amendment you would expect from him whom you judged to be the greatest sinner in the world.

Now this case every man may justly reckon to be his own. And you may fairly look upon yourself to be the greatest sinner that you know in the world.

For though you may know abundance of people to be guilty of some gross sins with which you cannot charge yourself, yet you may justly condemn yourself as the greatest sinner that you know. And that for these following reasons: [6]

First, Because you know more of the folly of your own heart than you do of other people's; and can charge yourself with various sins that you only know of yourself, and cannot be sure that other sinners are guilty of them. So that, as you know more of the folly, the baseness, the pride, the deceitfulness and negligence of your own heart, than you do of any one's else, so you have just reason to consider yourself as the greatest sinner that you know; because you know more of the greatness of your own sins than you do of other people's.

Secondly, The greatness of our guilt arises chiefly from the greatness of God's goodness towards us, from the particular graces and blessings, the favours, the lights, and instructions that we have received from Him.

Now as these graces and blessings, and the multitude of God's favours towards us, are the great aggravations of our sins against God, so they are only known to ourselves. And, therefore, every

---

[6] Among the incidental merits of the *Serious Call* is the way in which Law grapples with the moral difficulties which the thoughtful and earnest student of Holy Scripture has to encounter. One instance has been seen in his explanation of a passage in the Sermon on the Mount. Here is another. How could St. Paul call himself 'the chief of sinners,' when he must have known many who were obviously more glaring offenders than himself? And how can others apply his language to themselves without a certain unreality? Law, it will be seen, devotes a considerable space to grappling with this difficulty. He has done it most convincingly, and the student should make himself thoroughly master of the reasons he gives for the adoption of this language by the greatest saints.

CH. XXIII. sinner knows more of the aggravation of his own guilt than he does of other people's, and consequently may justly look upon himself to be the greatest sinner that he knows.

How good God hath been to other sinners, what light and instruction He has vouchsafed to them, what blessings and graces they have received from Him, how often He has touched their hearts with holy inspirations, you cannot tell. But all this you know of yourself; therefore you know greater aggravations of your own guilt, and are able to charge yourself with greater ingratitude than you can charge upon other people.

And this is the reason why the greatest saints have in all ages condemned themselves as the greatest sinners, because they knew some aggravations of their own sins which they could not know of other people's.

The right way, therefore, to fill your heart with true contrition, and a deep sense of your own sins, is this: You are not to consider or compare the outward form or course of your life with that of other people's, and then think yourself to be less sinful than they because the outward course of your life is less sinful than theirs.

But in order to know your own guilt, you must consider your own particular circumstances, your health, your sickness, your youth, your age, your particular calling, the happiness· of your education, the degrees of light and instruction that you have received, the good men that you have conversed with, the admonitions that you have had, the good books that you have read, the numberless multitude of divine blessings, graces, and favours that you have received, the good motions of grace that you have resisted, the resolutions of amendment that you have so often broken, and the checks of conscience that you have disregarded.

For it is from these circumstances that everyone is to state the measure and greatness of his own guilt. And as you know only these circumstances of your own sins, so you must necessarily know how to charge yourself with higher degrees of guilt than you can charge upon other people.

God Almighty knows greater sinners, it may be, than you are, because He sees and knows the circumstance of all men's sins. But your own heart, if it is faithful to you, can discover no guilt so great as your own, because it can only see in you those circumstances on which great part of the guilt of sin is founded.

You may see sins in other people that you cannot charge upon yourself; but then you know a number of circumstances of your own guilt that you cannot lay to their charge.

And perhaps that person that appears at such a distance from your virtue, and so odious in your eyes, would have been much better than you are had he been altogether in your circumstances, and received all the same favours and graces from God that you have.

This is a very humbling reflection, and very proper for those people to make who measure their virtue by comparing the outward course of their lives with that of other people's.

For look at whom you will, however different from you in his way of life, yet you can never know that he has resisted so much divine grace as you have, or that in all your circumstances he would not have been much truer to his duty than you are.

Now this is the reason why I desired you to consider how you would exhort that man to confess and bewail his sins whom you looked upon to be one of the greatest sinners.

Because if you will deal justly, you must fix the charge at home, and look no farther than yourself. For God has given no one any power of knowing the true greatness of any sins but his own; and therefore the greatest sinner that everyone knows is himself.

You may easily see how such a one in the outward course of his life breaks the laws of God; but then you can never say, that had you been exactly in all his circumstances, that [sic] you should not have broken them more than he has done.

A serious and frequent reflection upon these things will mightily tend to humble us in our own eyes, make us very apprehensive of the greatness of our own guilt, and very tender in censuring and condemning other people.

For who would dare to be severe against other people, when, for aught he can tell, the severity of God may be more due to him than to them? Who would exclaim against the guilt of others, when he considers that he knows more of the greatness of his own guilt than he does of theirs?

How often you have resisted God's Holy Spirit; how many motives to goodness you have disregarded; how many particular blessings you have sinned against; how many good resolutions you have broken; how many checks and admonitions of conscience you have stifled, you very well know. But how often

CH. XXIII. this has been the case of other sinners you know not. And, therefore, the greatest sinner that you know must be yourself.

Whenever, therefore, you are angry at sin or sinners, whenever you read or think of God's indignation and wrath at wicked men, let this teach you to be the most severe in your censure, and most humble and contrite in the acknowledgment and confession of your own sins, because you know of no sinner equal to yourself.

Lastly, To conclude this chapter: Having thus examined and confessed your sins at this hour of the evening, you must afterwards look upon yourself as still obliged to betake yourself to prayer again just before you go to bed.

The subject that is most proper for your prayers at that time is death. Let your prayers, therefore, then be wholly upon it, reckoning up all the dangers, uncertainties, and terrors of death; let them contain everything that can affect and awaken your mind into just apprehensions of it. Let your petitions be all for right sentiments of the approach and importance of death, and beg of God that your mind may be possessed with such a sense of its nearness, that you may have it always in your thoughts, do everything as in sight of it, and make every day a day for preparation for it.

Represent to your imagination that your bed is your grave; that all things are ready for your interment; that you are to have no more to do with this world; and that it will be owing to God's great mercy if you ever see the light of the sun again, or have another day to add to your works of piety.

And then commit yourself to sleep, as into the hands of God; as one that is to have no more opportunities of doing good; but is to awake amongst spirits that are separate from the body, and waiting for the judgment of the last great day.[7]

Such a solemn resignation of yourself into the hands of God every evening, and parting with all the world as if you were never to see it any more, and all this in the silence and darkness of the night, is a practice that will soon have excellent effects upon your spirit.

[7] Observe how Law makes a marked distinction between the souls of the faithful in the intermediate state and after the last judgment. Such a very proper distinction is not to be found generally in the theology of the eighteenth century, except among the nonjurors. A most clear and admirable treatise on "The Middle State" was written by Dr. Archibald Campbell, a nonjuring Scotch bishop, a copy of which, evidently much read, I found in Law's library at King's Cliffe.

For this time of the night is exceeding proper for such prayers CH. XXIII. and meditations ; and the likeness which sleep and darkness have to death[8] will contribute very much to make your thoughts about it the more deep and affecting. So that I hope you will not let a time so proper for such prayers be ever passed over without them.

[8] 'Tum consanguineus Leti Sopor' (Virg. *Æn.* vi. 278).

# CHAPTER XXIV.

*The conclusion. Of the excellency and greatness of a devout spirit.*

I HAVE now finished what I intended in this treatise. I have explained the nature of devotion, both as it signifies a life devoted to God, and as it signifies a regular method of daily prayer.[1] I have now only to add a word or two in recommendation of a life governed by this spirit of devotion.

For though it is as reasonable to suppose it the desire of all Christians to arrive at Christian perfection as to suppose that all sick men desire to be restored to perfect health, yet experience shows us that nothing wants more to be pressed, repeated, and forced upon our minds than the plainest rules of Christianity.

Voluntary poverty, virginity, and devout retirement have been here recommended as things not necessary, yet highly beneficial, to those that would make the way to perfection the most easy and certain.[2] But Christian perfection itself is tied to no particular form of life; but is to be attained, though not with the same ease, in every state of life.

This has been fully asserted in another place, where it has been shown that Christian perfection " calls no one (necessarily) to a cloister, but to the full performance of those duties which are necessary for all Christians, and common to all states of life" (*Christ. Perfect.* p. 2).

So that the whole of the matter is plainly this: Virginity, voluntary poverty, and such other restraints of lawful things, are not necessary to Christian perfection; but are much to be

---

[1] Observe Law's double use of the term devotion, as referring (1) to the life, (2) to worship. There are few works in which the distinction is brought out more clearly than in the *Serious Call.*

[2] Here is another distinction very well and clearly brought out, the distinction between the things which are essential to a devout life, and those which are not essential, but may be made very helpful towards it.

commended in those who choose them as helps and means of CH. XXIV. a more safe and speedy arrival at it.

It is only in this manner and in this sense that I would recommend any particularity of life; not as if perfection consisted in it, but because of its great tendency to produce and support the true spirit of Christian perfection.

But the thing which is here pressed upon all is a life of great and strict devotion, which, I think, has been sufficiently shown to be equally the duty and happiness of all orders of men. Neither is there anything in any particular state of life that can be justly pleaded as a reason for any abatements of a devout spirit.

But because in this polite age of ours we have so lived away the spirit of devotion, that many seem afraid even to be suspected of it, imagining great devotion to be great bigotry; that it is founded in ignorance and poorness of spirit, and that little, weak, and dejected minds are generally the greatest proficients in it:

It shall here be fully shown that great devotion is the noblest temper of the greatest and noblest souls, and that they who think it receives any advantage from ignorance and poorness of spirit are themselves not a little, but entirely ignorant of the nature of devotion, the nature of God, and the nature of themselves.

People of fine parts and learning, or of great knowledge in worldly matters, may perhaps think it hard to have their want of devotion charged upon their ignorance; but if they will be content to be tried by reason and Scripture, it may soon be made to appear that a want of devotion, wherever it is, either amongst the learned or unlearned, is founded in gross ignorance, and the greatest blindness and insensibility that can happen to a rational creature.[3]

And that devotion is so far from being the effect of a little and dejected mind, that it must and will be always highest in the most perfect natures.

And first: Who reckons it a sign of a poor, little mind for

[3] Law fights with their own weapons those who identified piety with weakness—a mischievous notion which, as has been said in the introduction, was too rife in his day. Want of devotion, he argues, arises from ignorance of the grossest sort; those who looked down upon the pious as poor, weak, ignorant creatures, should themselves be looked down upon, not with anger, but with the deepest commiseration, as victims of the direst ignorance; and he proves his point.

CH. XXIV. a man to be full of reverence and duty to his parents, to have the truest love and honour for his friend, or to excel in the highest instances of gratitude to his benefactor?

Are not these tempers in the highest degree in the most exalted and perfect minds?

And yet, what is high devotion but the highest exercise of these tempers of duty, reverence, love, honour, and gratitude to the amiable, glorious parent, friend and benefactor of all mankind?

Is it a true greatness of mind to reverence the authority of your parents, to fear the displeasure of your friend, to dread the reproaches of your benefactor? And must not this fear, and dread, and reverence, be much more just and reasonable and honourable when they are in the highest degree towards God?

Now as the higher these tempers are, the more are they esteemed amongst men, and are allowed to be so much the greater proofs of a true greatness of mind; so the higher and greater these same tempers are towards God, so much the more do they prove the nobility, excellence, and greatness of the mind.

So that so long as duty to parents, love to friends, and gratitude to benefactors are thought great and honourable tempers; devotion, which is nothing else but duty, love, and gratitude to God, must have the highest place amongst our highest virtues.

If a prince, out of his mere goodness, should send you a pardon by one of his slaves, would you think it a part of your duty to receive the slave with marks of love, esteem, and gratitude for his great kindness in bringing you so great a gift; and at the same time think it a meanness and poorness of spirit to show love, esteem, and gratitude to the prince, who of his own goodness freely sent you the pardon?

And yet this would be as reasonable as to suppose that love, esteem, honour, and gratitude are noble tempers and instances of a great soul when they are paid to our fellow-creatures; but the effects of a poor, ignorant, dejected mind when they are paid to God.

Farther: that part of devotion which expresses itself in sorrowful confessions and penitential tears of a broken and contrite heart is very far from being any sign of a little and ignorant mind.

For who does not acknowledge it an instance of an ingenuous, generous, and brave mind to acknowledge a fault and ask pardon for any offence?    And are not the finest and most improved minds the most remarkable for this excellent temper?

Is it not also allowed that the ingenuity [4] and excellence of a man's spirit is much shown, when his sorrow and indignation at himself rises in proportion to the folly of his crime, and the goodness and greatness of the person he has offended?

Now if things are thus, then the greater any man's mind is, the more he knows of God and himself, the more will he be disposed to prostrate himself before God in all the humblest acts and expressions of repentance.    And the greater the ingenuity, the generosity, judgment, and penetration of his mind is, the more will he exercise and indulge a passionate, tender sense of God's just displeasure; and the more he knows of the greatness, the goodness, and perfection of the divine nature, the fuller of shame and confusion will he be at his own sins and ingratitude.

And on the other hand, the more dull and ignorant any soul is, the more base and ungenerous it naturally is, the more senseless it is of the goodness and purity of God; so much the more averse will it be to all acts of humble confession and repentance.

Devotion, therefore, is so far from being best suited to little ignorant minds, that a true elevation of soul, a lively sense of honour, and great knowledge of God and ourselves are the greatest natural helps that our devotion hath.

And on the other hand, it shall here be made appear by variety of arguments that indevotion is founded in the most excessive ignorance.

And, first, our blessed Lord and His Apostles were eminent instances of great and frequent devotion.    Now if we will grant (as all Christians must grant) that their great devotion was founded in a true knowledge of the nature of devotion, the nature of God, and the nature of man; then it is plain that all those that are insensible of the duty of devotion are in this excessive state of ignorance; they neither know God, nor themselves, nor devotion.

For if a right knowledge in these three respects produces great devotion, as in the case of our Saviour and His Apostles, then a neglect of devotion must be chargeable upon ignorance.

Again: how comes it that most people have recourse to

[4] That is, what we should term 'ingenuousness.'

devotion when they are in sickness, distress, or fear of death? Is it not because this state shows them more of the want of God, and their own weakness, than they perceive at other times? Is it not because their infirmities, their approaching end, convince them of something which they did not half perceive before?

Now if devotion at these seasons is the effect of a better knowledge of God and ourselves, then the neglect of devotion at other times is always owing to great ignorance of God and ourselves.

Farther: as indevotion is ignorance, so it is the most shameful ignorance, and such as is to be charged with the greatest folly.

This will fully appear to anyone that considers by what rules we are to judge of the excellency of any knowledge or the shamefulness of any ignorance.

Now knowledge itself would be no excellence, nor ignorance any reproach to us, but that we are rational creatures. But if this be true, then it follows plainly that that knowledge which is most suitable to our rational nature, and which most concerns us, as such, to know, is our highest, finest knowledge; and that ignorance which relates to things that are most essential to us as rational creatures, and which we are most concerned to know, is, of all others, the most gross and shameful ignorance.

If, therefore, there be any things that concern us more than others, if there be any truths that are more to us than all others, he that has the fullest knowledge of these things, that sees these truths in the clearest, strongest light, has, of all others, as a rational creature, the clearest understanding and the strongest parts.

If, therefore, our relation to God be our greatest relation, if our advancement in His favour be our highest advancement, he that has the highest notions of the excellence of this relation, he that most strongly perceives the highest worth and great value of holiness and virtue, that judges everything little when compared with it, proves himself to be master of the best and most excellent knowledge.

If a judge had fine skill in painting, architecture, and music, but at the same time had gross and confused notions of equity, and a poor, dull apprehension of the value of justice, who would scruple to reckon him a poor ignorant judge?

If a bishop should be a man of great address and skill in the arts of preferment, and understanding how to raise and enrich his family in the world, but should have no taste or sense of the maxims and principles of the saints and fathers of the church; if he did not conceive the holy nature and great obligations of his calling, and judge it better to be crucified to the world than to live idly in pomp and splendour, who would scruple to charge such a bishop with want of understanding?

If we do not judge and pronounce after this manner, our reason and judgment are but empty sounds.

But now, if a judge is to be reckoned ignorant, if he does not feel and perceive the value and worth of justice; if a bishop is to be looked upon as void of understanding, if he is more experienced in other things than in the exalted virtues of his apostolical calling; then all common Christians are to be looked upon as more or less knowing, accordingly as they know more or less of those great things which are the common and greatest concern of all Christians.

If a gentleman should fancy that the moon is no bigger than it appears to the eye, that it shines with its own light, that all the stars are only so many spots of light; if, after reading books of astronomy, he should still continue in the same opinion, most people would think that he had but a poor apprehension.

But if the same person should think it better to provide for a short life here than to prepare for a glorious eternity hereafter, that it was better to be rich than to be eminent in piety, his ignorance and dulness would be too great to be compared to anything else.

There is no knowledge that deserves so much as the name of it, but that which we call judgment.

And that is the most clear and improved understanding, which judges best of the value and worth of things; all the rest is but the capacity of an animal, is but mere seeing and hearing.

And there is no excellence of any knowledge in us till we exercise our judgment, and judge well of the value and worth of things.

If a man had eyes that could see beyond the stars, or pierce into the heart of the earth, but could not see the things that were before him, or discern anything that was serviceable to him, we should reckon that he had but a very bad sight.

If another had ears that received sounds from the world in the moon, but could hear nothing that was said or done upon earth, we should look upon him to be as bad as deaf.

In like manner, if a man has a memory that can retain a great many things; if he has a wit that is sharp and acute in arts and sciences, or an imagination that can wander agreeably in fictions, but has a dull, poor apprehension of his duty and relation to God, of the value of piety, or the worth of moral virtue, he may very justly be reckoned to have a bad understanding. He is but like the man that can only see and hear such things as are of no benefit to him.

As certain, therefore, as piety, virtue, and eternal happiness are of the most concern to man, as certain as the immortality of our nature and relation to God are the most glorious circumstances of our nature; so certain is it that he who dwells most in contemplation of them, whose heart is most affected with them, who sees farthest into them, who best comprehends the value and excellency of them, who judges all worldly attainments to be mere bubbles and shadows in comparison of them, proves himself to have of all others the finest understanding and the strongest judgment.

And if we do not reason after this manner, or allow this method of reasoning, we have no arguments to prove that there is any such thing as a wise man or a fool.

For a man is proved to be a natural, not because he wants any of his senses, or is incapable of everything, but because he has no judgment, and is entirely ignorant of the worth and value of things. He will perhaps choose a fine coat rather than a large estate.

And as the essence of stupidity consists in the entire want of judgment, in an ignorance of the value of things, so on the other hand the essence of wisdom and knowledge must consist in the excellency of our judgment, or in the knowledge of the worth and value of things.

This, therefore, is an undeniable proof that he who knows most of the value of the best things, who judges most rightly of the things which are of most concern to him, who had rather have his soul in a state of Christian perfection than the greatest share of worldly happiness, has the highest wisdom, and is at the farthest distance from men that are naturals that any knowledge can place him.

On the other hand, he that can talk the learned languages CH. XXIV. and repeat a great deal of history, but prefers the indulgence of his body to the purity and perfection of his soul, who is more concerned to get a name or an estate here than to live in eternal glory hereafter, is in the nearest state to that natural who chooses a painted coat rather than a large estate.

He is not called a natural by men, but he must appear to God and heavenly beings as in a more excessive state of stupidity, and will sooner or later certainly appear so to himself.

But now if this be undeniably plain, that we cannot prove a man to be a fool but by showing that he has no knowledge of things that are good and evil to himself, then it is undeniably plain that we cannot prove a man to be wise but by showing that he has the fullest knowledge of things that are his greatest good and his greatest evil.

If, therefore, God be our greatest good; if there can be no good but in His favour, nor any evil but in departing from Him, then it is plain that he who judges it the best thing he can do to please God to the utmost of his power, who worships and adores Him with all his heart and soul, who had rather have a pious mind than all the dignities and honours in the world, shows himself to be in the highest state of human wisdom.

To proceed: we know how our blessed Lord acted in a human body. It was " His meat and drink to do the will of His Father which is in heaven."

And if any number of heavenly spirits were to leave their habitations in the light of God, and be for a while united to human bodies, they would certainly tend towards God in all their actions, and be as heavenly as they could in a state of flesh and blood.

They would certainly act in this manner, because they would know that God was the only good of all spirits; and that whether they were in the body or out of the body, in heaven or on earth, they must have every degree of their greatness and happiness from God alone.

All human spirits, therefore, the more exalted they are, the more they know their divine original, the nearer they come to heavenly spirits; by so much the more will they live to God in all their actions, and make their whole life a state of devotion.

Devotion, therefore, is the greatest sign of a great and noble genius, it supposes a soul in its highest state of knowledge,

CH. XXIV. and none but little and blinded minds, that are sunk into ignorance and vanity, are destitute of it.

If an human spirit should imagine some mighty prince to be greater than God, we should take it for a poor, ignorant creature; all people would acknowledge such an imagination to be the height of stupidity.

But if this same human spirit should think it better to be devoted to some mighty prince than to be devoted to God, would not this still be a greater proof of a poor, ignorant, and blinded nature?

Yet this is what all people do who think anything better, greater, or wiser than a devout life.

So that, which way soever we consider this matter, it plainly appears that devotion is an instance of great judgment of an elevated nature; and the want of devotion is a certain proof of the want of understanding.

The greatest spirits of the heathen world, such as Pythagoras, Socrates, Plato, Epictetus, Marcus Antoninus, etc., owed all their greatness to the spirit of devotion.

They were full of God; their wisdom and deep contemplations tended only to deliver men from the vanity of the world, the slavery of bodily passions, that they might act as spirits that came from God, and were soon to return to Him.[5]

Again: to see the dignity and greatness of a devout spirit, we need only compare it with other tempers that are chosen in the room of it.

St. John tells us that "all in the world" (that is, all the tempers of a worldly life) "is the lust of the flesh, the lust of the eyes, and the pride of life."

Let us, therefore, consider what wisdom or excellency of mind there is required to qualify a man for these delights.

Let us suppose a man given up to the pleasures of the body; surely this can be no sign of a fine mind or an excellent spirit; for if he has but the temper of an animal, he is great enough for these enjoyments.

[5] In no respect does Law show himself more in advance of his age than in his estimate of the virtuous heathen. Most thoughtful and enlightened people in the present day would agree with his description of the great men here named; but such an estimate was very rare among religious writers in the eighteenth century. It is very different, e.g. from the estimate which Joseph Milner takes of them in his *History of the Church of Christ* (see I. 131 and 136), when this very Antoninus Pius, to whom Law refers, is depreciated, though his apparent virtues are allowed.

Let us suppose him to be devoted to honours and splendours, CH. XXIV. to be fond of glitter and equipage; now if this temper required any great parts or fine understanding to make a man capable of it, it would prove the world to abound with great wits.

Let us suppose him to be in love with riches, and to be so eager in the pursuit of them as never to think he has enough; now this passion is so far from supposing any excellent sense or great understanding, that blindness and folly are the best supports that it hath.

Let us, lastly, suppose him in another light, not singly devoted to any of these passions, but, as it mostly happens, governed by all of them in their turns; does this show a more exalted nature than to spend his days in the service of any one of them?

For to have a taste for these things, and to be devoted to them, is so far from arguing any tolerable parts or understanding, that they are suited to the dullest, weakest minds, and require only a great deal of pride and folly to be greatly admired.

But now let libertines bring any such charge as this, if they can, against devotion. They may as well endeavour to charge light with everything that belongs to darkness.

Let them but grant that there is a God and providence, and then they have granted enough to justify the wisdom, and support the honour of devotion.

For if there is an infinitely wise and good Creator, in Whom we live, move, and have our being, Whose providence governs all things in all places, surely it must be the highest act of our understanding to conceive rightly of Him; it must be the noblest instance of judgment, the most exalted temper of our nature, to worship and adore this universal providence, to conform to its laws, to study its wisdom, and to live and act everywhere as in the presence of this infinitely good and wise Creator.

Now he that lives thus, lives in the spirit of devotion.

And what can show such great parts and so fine an understanding as to live in this temper?

For if God is wisdom, surely he must be the wisest man in the world who most conforms to the wisdom of God, who best obeys His providence, who enters farthest into His designs, and does all he can, that God's will may be done on earth as it is done in heaven.

A devout man makes a true use of his reason; he sees through the vanity of the world, discovers the corruption of his nature,

CH. XXIV. and the blindness of his passions. He lives by a law which is not visible to vulgar eyes; he enters into the world of spirits; he compares the greatest things, sets eternity against time; and chooses rather to be for ever great in the presence of God when he dies, than to have the greatest share of worldly pleasures whilst he lives.

He that is devout is full of these great thoughts; he lives upon these noble reflections, and conducts himself by rules and principles which can only be apprehended, admired, and loved by reason.

There is nothing, therefore, that shows so great a genius, nothing that so raises us above vulgar spirits, nothing that so plainly declares a heroic greatness of mind, as great devotion.

When you suppose a man to be a saint, or all devotion, you have raised him as much above all other conditions of life as a philosopher is above an animal.

Lastly, courage and bravery are words of a great sound, and seem to signify a heroic spirit; but yet humility, which seems to be the lowest, meanest part of devotion, is a more certain argument of a noble and courageous mind.

For humility contends with greater enemies, is more constantly engaged, more violently assaulted, bears more, suffers more, and requires greater courage to support itself than any instances of worldly bravery.

A man that dares to be poor and contemptible in the eyes of the world, to approve himself to God; that resists and rejects all human glory, that opposes the clamour of his passions, that meekly puts up with all injuries and wrongs, and dares stay for his reward till the invisible hand of God gives to every one their proper places, endures a much greater trial and exerts a nobler fortitude than he that is bold and daring in the fire of battle.

For the boldness of a soldier, if he is a stranger to the spirit of devotion, is rather weakness than fortitude; it is at best but mad passion and heated spirits, and has no more true valour in it than the fury of a tiger.

For as we cannot lift up a hand, or stir a foot, but by a power that is lent us from God, so bold actions that are not directed by the laws of God, as so many executions of His will, are no more true bravery than sedate malice is Christian patience.

Reason is our universal law, that obliges us in all places, and at all times; and no actions have any honour but so far as they are CH. XXIV. instances of our obedience to reason.

And it is as base and cowardly to be bold and daring against the principle of reason and justice as to be bold and daring in lying and perjury.

Would we, therefore, exercise a true fortitude, we must do all in the spirit of devotion, be valiant against the corruptions of the world, and the lusts of the flesh, and the temptations of the devil; for to be daring and courageous against these enemies is the noblest bravery that a human mind is capable of.

I have made this digression for the sake of those who think a great devotion to be bigotry and poorness of spirit; that by these considerations they may see how poor and mean all other tempers are, if compared to it; that they may see that all worldly attainments, whether greatness, wisdom, or bravery, are but empty sounds; and there is nothing wise, or great, or noble in a human spirit, but rightly to know, and heartily worship and adore, the great God that is the support and life of all spirits, whether in heaven or on earth.

# INDEX.